OUT OF THE
DARKNESS

History of Corrections Reform at the Hampden County, MA Sheriff's Department, 1661-2022

Joseph Carvalho III & Wayne E. Phaneuf, Editors

Book Design by: Michelle Johnson and Curtis Panlilio
Editors: Joseph Carvalho III & Wayne E. Phaneuf
Printed by: Yurchak Printing • Published by: Headline Studios Massachusetts, 1860 Main Street, Springfield, MA 01103

TABLE OF CONTENTS

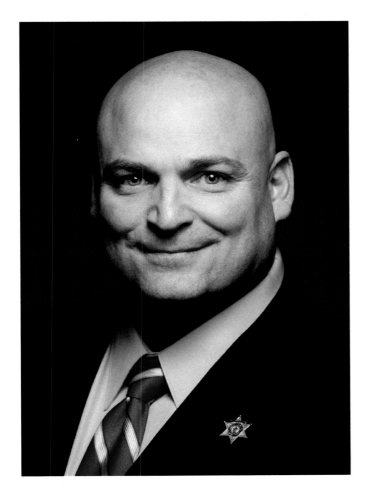

Sheriff Nick Cocchi
HAMPDEN COUNTY

When I first ran for Sheriff of Hampden County, it was not only to protect the legacy of my predecessor and friend, retired Sheriff Michael J. Ashe Jr., but also to build upon that legacy. My goal of helping to modernize this office to meet the needs and challenges of the 21st Century started on day one of my first term and continues today.

From the start, I was blessed to inherit an amazing and dedicated staff, many of whom had built careers on accepting the awesome responsibility of being a positive change agent in Western Massachusetts and beyond. And today we are lucky to have the best of the best walking through our doors, ready to lend their talents and sweat equity to making a difference in our community.

Although society's problems change with the times, a constant necessity is a public agency which stands to not only offer a hand to those in need, but to identify needs in the overall community and break the traditional paradigm of assigned roles to meet those needs.

When the opioid crisis began ravaging households in Western Massachusetts and the Northeast U.S. in particular, there were limited to no options for treatment in our half of the Commonwealth. Just as Sheriff Ashe broke the norm when he opened the Western Massachusetts Correctional Alcohol Center in Springfield to help face of the issue of alcoholism in the 1980s,

I opened the Stonybrook Stabilization & Treatment Center to provide a new treatment opportunity for families at the end of their options for helping a loved one battling a substance use disorder.

Today, that program assists around 145 families at any given time as we work to help men of all ages and walks of life work toward long-term recovery and a healthy life free of drugs and alcohol.

The role of the sheriff has evolved from a singular focus on care while in custody, to community outreach, engagement and prevention.

Our Emotional Support Division of therapy dogs have been busy in the waning days of the COVID-19 Pandemic, bringing comfort to our frontline workers in the community, as well as our staff and the people in our custody. The Freedom Pups program pairs minimum security offenders with dogs in need of household training so that they're more likely to be adopted. Since starting that program we've helped countless inmates understand that caring for somebody else and not just themselves is a great responsibility. This program has given dozens of dogs a chance at living a great life in their forever home.

In regards to giving back and assisting the aging population in Hampden County, we recently launched our TRIAD Division, which is implementing a variety of programs ranging from daily phone wellness checks to home safety inspections.

Now in its third year, our Youth Leadership Academy summer camp is providing a fantastic summer experience to 75 young people from Springfield's most economically challenged neighborhoods. In addition to the fun, our young campers are exposed to positive role models and are learning valuable life lessons over the course of six weeks at no cost to their families.

Most recently we launched our Marine Patrol Unit to keep the waterways of Western Mass. safe for all to enjoy. With three boats and 13 specially trained deputy sheriffs, this unit is a mix of proactive patrols and responding to requests for mutual aid from our law enforcement partners. From the Connecticut River to Congamond Lakes and beyond, we are on the water to help deter reckless behavior and to be a positive presence.

So while you are likely to see my staff in more and more places around Western Massachusetts, know that while we are working proactively to build good relationships between law enforcement and residents, we are still providing comprehensive rehabilitative programming inside our facilities, which helps us maintain one of the lowest recidivism rates in the entire nation.

It is an honor and privilege for me to serve as your sheriff. During my nearly 30-year journey within this department, this has certainly been one of my life's greatest blessings.

As your sheriff, I encourage you to reach out to our office if there is ever a need in the community that is not currently being addressed. We are here to provide a service to the citizens of Hampden County and we are here to be part of the solution.

Sincerely,

Sheriff Nick Cocchi

ACKNOWLEDGMENTS

First of all, we would like to thank Sheriff Nick Cocchi for initiating this project and his continuing leadership in our community.

This book couldn't have been written without the help of Sheriff Michael J. Ashe, Jr. The editors thanks Sheriff Ashe for all his information, assistance, encouragement, and inspiration. We also appreciate his careful review of the narrative and information contained in the chapters covering his long tenure as Sheriff of Hampden County.

The staff of the Hampden County Sheriff's Department has been essential in completing this project. The fact that the two primary Sheriff's Department contacts were former colleagues at the newspaper made the process one of the smoothest of any book published in our Heritage Book Series. Robert Rizzuto, Public Information Officer for the Hampden County Sheriff's Department and former journalist with The Republican newspaper, has been our indispensable liaison throughout the project. As a veteran journalist, Rob knew exactly what was needed by the editors and writers. And we also thank Sheriff's Department staff photographer, Mark M. Murray, for his excellent contemporary photography, and for his years of earlier photographic work for The Republican which we used liberally throughout this volume.

Thanks as always to our talented book program staff at the Republican: Michelle Johnson, Curtis Panlilio, and Marianna McKee. We also owe a debt of gratitude for the work of our staff photographers Don Treeger and Hoang " Leon" Nguyen.

Thanks to Richard McCarthy for reviewing drafts of the text. His intimate knowledge of the Hampden County Sheriff's Department during the late 20th and early 21st Century was invaluable to the project.

Thanks to J. John Ashe, Tom Rovelli, Kevin Warwick, and Bill Toller for their input and information about specific events and programs.

In compiling the early history of corrections in Hampden County, we drew from the work of historians past: Harry Andrew Wright, Clifton Johnson, Josiah Gilbert Holland, James E. Tower, Moses King, Mason A. Green, and our friend and colleague the late Richard "Dick" Garvey. Thanks also for the historical research by noted local historians Frances Gagnon, and the late Larry Gormally.

Once again, our colleagues at the Museum of Springfield History of the Springfield Museums, Margaret Humberston and Cliff McCarthy were essential to the compilation of this volume. Their knowledge of their archival collection and photograph collection enabled the editors/authors to efficiently and thoroughly review the historical record of the Hampden County Sheriff's Department. Years ago, Sheriff Ashe entrusted the early records of the jail to their care and we were duly impressed with the careful handling and superb condition of these valuable records when we retrieved them for research at the museum. Administrative & Collections Specialist Phyllis Jurkowski, and Assistant Registrar Stephen Sullivan once again were extremely helpful with information and images from the Museum's object collection.

Joseph Carvalho III
& Wayne E. Phaneuf, Editors

Congressman Richard E. Neal
FIRST CONGRESSIONAL DISTRICT OF MASSACHUSETTS
CHAIR, HOUSE COMMITTEE ON WAYS AND MEANS

Sheriff Ashe has spent his life embodying the fundamental principle that all who are willing to work for a second chance ought to receive one.

His signature philosophy of "strength reinforced with decency; firmness dignified in fairness" led to countless lives being changed for the better, while resulting in one of the lowest reincarceration rates in the United States.

Anyone who has gotten to know Sheriff Ashe will affirm that he had never been in the business of incarceration, rather his focus was on corrections. His doctrine on correctional supervision was guided by the simple principle that inmates should be held accountable and be positive and productive.

The Sheriff long understood that if he were to adequately rehabilitate his inmates, he would need to put together a competent coalition of staff and volunteers who could command the situation, while exemplifying the upmost professionalism.

Throughout his career, Sheriff Ashe's tireless work has made our community a safer, more just, caring place. During his tenure, Sheriff Ashe witnessed over 4,600 inmates graduate his educational programs, earning a GED or a high school equivalent diploma.

Sheriff Ashe oversaw the inmates in his facilities contribute over 1 million hours of community service to Hampden County communities.

Sheriff Nick Cocchi has continued Sheriff Ashe's legacy and policies and added new practices that have kept the Hampden County Correctional System a model for the nation. These men have made the Commonwealth proud while illustrating that the United States is indeed a nation of second chances. I am proud to call them both dear friends.

Congressman Richard E. Neal

First Congressional District of Massachusetts
Chair, House Committee on Ways and Means

CHAPTER ONE

JAILS, MARSHALLS, AND SHERIFFS OF
OLD HAMPSHIRE AND HAMPDEN COUNTY
1662-1886

JAILS, MARSHALLS, AND SHERIFFS OF OLD HAMPSHIRE AND HAMPDEN COUNTY

BY JOSEPH CARVALHO III

From the earliest days of the colonial settlement of Springfield, the community set about creating rules and regulations on how individuals should conduct themselves and their businesses in a "well-ordered" society. Local laws followed the legal precedents set by the colonial authorities of the Massachusetts Bay Colony. As Treasurer of the Colony and founder of the settlement of Springfield, William Pynchon also served as the community's magistrate to settle civil disputes and preside over criminal proceedings. For the first twenty-two years following its founding, Springfield did not require a jail for punishment of civil or criminal offenses. In the early years of the settlement, those accused of serious crimes were sent to a Boston prison run by the Massachusetts Bay government.

By the late 1650s, the colonial government finally decided that it required a jail house in Western Massachusetts as an option for punishment. On March 26, 1661, the General Court in Boston ordered Springfield's magistrate, John Pynchon, to begin building a "House of Corrections" in Springfield. The county government lagged behind in completing the expanded building and Nathanial Ely was directed on Jan. 17, 1665 to finish "said House with all possible speed to compleat it for ye service to which it is appointed." Springfield's first jail was built in the vicinity of present day Maple

Street. It was constructed of Hand-sawed hard wood planks and beams 40 feet long. It included quarters for the jail-keeper, Simon Lobdell (b. Dec. 23, 1632 in Northam, Devon, England; d. Nov. 4, 1717 in Milford, Connecticut). Lobdell served as "jail-keeper" in Springfield from 1666 to 1674.

Founded in 1636, Springfield became the county seat of Hampshire County which was formed by the Massachusetts Bay General Court on May 7, 1662. On Sept. 30, 1662, the General Court set a tax rate to raise funds for

"ye House of Corrections." The colonial government appointed a marshall for Hampshire County in 1668. The men who served in that capacity were the chief law enforcement officers of the county until 1692. The first individual recorded as having been committed to the "House of Corrections" on Maple Street was a 14-year old servant girl named Katherine Hunter who was sentenced to incarceration in 1671.

Four years later, native American allies of Metacomet aka "King Phillip" burned the jail on Maple Street in 1675 along with most of the town's other structures in one of the most dramatic attacks of English settlements during King Philip's War. After the war, the Hampshire County Court presided by Maj. John Pynchon ordered that a new jail be constructed in Springfield with an allowed construction cost of 50 to 55 pounds sterling. It was Pynchon's task to choose the proper location. He subsequently purchased adjacent lots from Thomas Merrick and Samuel Ely. No deed was executed on the property at the time as Springfield was still recovering from the devastation of the war. Ultimately a paper record of the land transfer was created in May of 1683.

The second jail was built in Springfield in 1680 at a cost of 60 pounds sterling. It was located on the western side of Main Street near the corner of Bliss Street. With exterior walls made of thick logs, it was two stories high 25 feet long and 18 feet wide with a single large room and closets on the first floor, and three rooms on the second floor. Walls and partitions were constructed of heavy oak planks set endwise. The house of the jail keeper adjoined it on the north side.

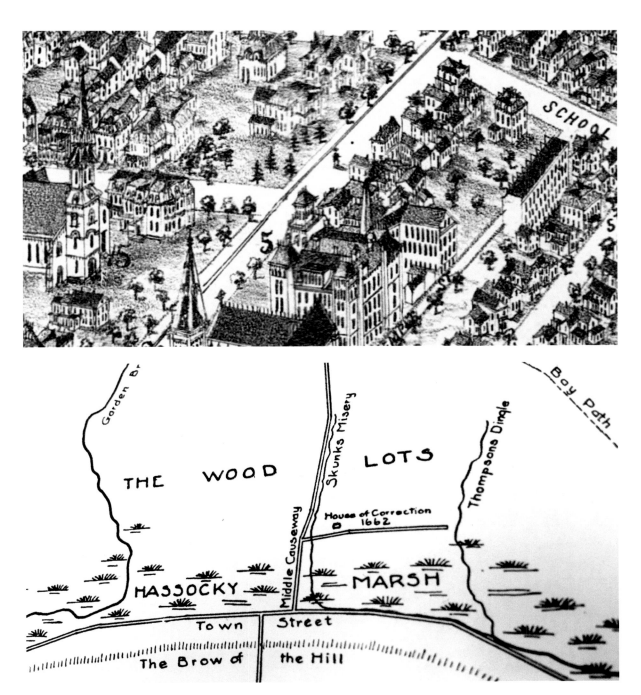

OPPOSITE PAGE: Engraving of the Hampden County House of Correction on State Street in Springfield. *King's Handbook of Springfield* (1884)

TOP LEFT: Detail of the *1875 Bird's Eye View of Springfield* showing the location of the Hampden County jail on State Street. Courtesy of the Library of Congress.

LEFT: Detail of colonial map of Springfield by Harry Andrew Wright showing the location of the first jail in old Hampshire County on what would later become Maple Street in Springfield. In Harry Andrew Wright, *The Story of Western Massachusetts*, Vol. I (1949).

ABOVE: The Hampden County House of Corrections on State Street, 1880s. Photo courtesy of the Lyman and Merrie Wood Museum of Springfield History, Springfield Museums.
OPPOSITE PAGE: The Hampden County House of Corrections on State Street, 1882. Photo courtesy of the Lyman and Merrie Wood Museum of Springfield History, Springfield Museums.

The first inmate was a fugitive slave, "Jack," from Wethersfield, Connecticut who was apprehended by the local constable and placed in the Springfield Jail in July of 1680. On Dec. 24th of that year, a fugitive indentured servant, Thomas Hancock, was apprehended and placed in the jail.

In 1692, the county created the office of "Sheriff" and appointed Samuel Porter, Jr. to that post in which he served until 1696. Early records fail to reveal every succeeding county sheriff, although we do know that Captain Ebenezer Pumry (aka Pomeroy) served as "High Sheriff" of old Hampshire County in 1722. The social turmoil during the era of the American Revolution dramatically elevated the role and prominence of the county sheriff.

In 1781, General Elisha Porter was appointed sheriff of old Hampshire County. He was the first Hampshire County Sheriff appointed under the recently enacted Massachusetts State Constitution of 1780. The following year in 1782, anti-government agitator Rev. Samuel Ely was charged, sentenced, and imprisoned in the Springfield jail for inciting a mob to prevent the court in Northampton from operating. Soon after, a mob of sympathizers forcibly released him from the jail. Called up by Sheriff Porter, the 2nd Company of the Hampshire County Militia Regiment was mustered and marched to Northampton to confront the rioters and re-arrest Ely. Shielded by the mob before they dispersed, Ely escaped to Maine. It was a precursor of Shays' Rebellion four years later.

On Jan. 25, 1787, Hampshire County Deputy Sheriff Asaph King at Wilbraham learned of Daniel Shays' plans to attack the U.S. Arsenal at Springfield. Sheriff Porter sent him to alert

the Commander of the Hampshire County militia, Revolutionary War hero, General William Shephard. The Deputy Sheriff rode just ahead of the rebels to alert General Shepard who was commanding the government forces defending the arsenal at Springfield. According to contemporary accounts, "From him, Shepard learned all the particulars which he had not before known, and ascertained that the force of Shays was on the march." Forewarned by the Sheriff and his deputy, Shephard successfully and decisively defeated the Shaysite rebels advancing against the arsenal inflicting a mortal blow to "Shays' Rebellion."

The Springfield jail was closed in 1794 and was replaced by a jail in Northampton when the central Hampshire County courthouse was established in that town that year. Its new location was selected by Hampshire County authorities, "on account of its central location [it was] the most suitable place and the most likely to give general satisfaction to the inhabitants of the county." The Springfield Jail property was subsequently sold to the former "jailkeeper" William Colton.

Ebenezer Mattoon was appointed Sheriff of old Hampshire County in 1796 and served until 1811. That year, Thomas Shephard of Northampton was appointed Sheriff of old Hampshire County and served until the

West Granville Cemetery, Granville, MA
John Phekps died 1832 Jan 1, age 61 yrs
(American Revolution) &
wife Elizabeth Dubois died 1832 Jan 21

creation of the southern district into the new Hampden County with its "seat" in Springfield in 1812 the year the War of 1812 was declared. Jonathan Smith, Jr. was appointed as the first Sheriff of the newly formed Hampden County in 1812 and served until 1814.

In 1813, Hampden County purchased a 1 ½ acre lot on State Street (on the site that would later become Classical High School) for $500. The following year, John Phelps was appointed Hampden County Sheriff by Governor Caleb Strong. Phelps, was a native of Granville, served as their town clerk, as a

Granville Selectman, and as a member of the Massachusetts Legislature for many years. He served as County Sheriff until 1831.

The County began building a new Hampden County Jail and House of Correction on the State Street site at a cost of $14,164. Of stone construction, the building was two stories high and measured 18 x 30 feet. It housed up to 150 men and 10 women. The building was completed in 1815. That year, the new jail's first inmate was David Cadwell of Wilbraham who only stayed in jail for a day after he paid his fine for assault. Jesse Wright of Springfield was the first person to break out of the jail when he escaped on Feb. 12, 1816.

As the community's population grew, so did the need for additional capacity at the county

jail. The County responded by building an addition to the jail on State Street in 1830 to accommodate more inmates. In 1831, a Massachusetts State Militia Colonel, Caleb Rice was appointed Hampden County Sheriff and served until he was elected the first Mayor of the newly incorporated City of Springfield in 1851. Rice was also the first President and first Treasurer of the Massachusetts Mutual life Insurance Company of Springfield.

Of course, Sheriff Rice's duties extended beyond his management of the Hampden County House of Corrections. On New Years day of 1848, Irish workers of the Boody & Stone Canal Co. in Ireland Parish (later to be incorporated as Holyoke), went on strike. Their employer had just dramatically reduced their daily wage. A week later 12 strike-breakers were escorted to the worksite by Constable Theodore Farnham. The strikers "armed with clubs, and other weapons of Irish warfare," attacked them. While attempting to arrest some of the leaders of the strikers, Constable Farnham was "knocked down and trampled upon until nearly senseless." The next morning Sheriff Rice arrived from Springfield "with a Catholic priest who guaranteed that there should be no trouble that day of the next night." The next morning, Sheriff Rice "returned with a posse and made three arrests." The newspapers reported that the men in his "posse" did not have flints in their guns, apparently to avoid any escalation of violence.

TOP LEFT: Headstone of Sheriff John Phelps, West Granville Cemetery, Granville, Massachusetts.

CENTER: Sheriff Caleb Rice. Republican database.

OPPOSITE PAGE: Photograph of the Hampden County jail complex on State Street on far left, High School in center, and the Church of the Unity on the far right. Photo courtesy of the Lyman and Merrie Wood Museum of Springfield History, Springfield Museums

ABOVE: Ship model of the Yankee made in 1852 by a prisoner at the Hampden County House of Corrections on State Street. It was given to the Springfield Museums (then called the Springfield City Library which was a combination library and museum association established in 1859) by Charles Lee in 1860. It remains in the Springfield Museums collections today. Photo courtesy of the Springfield Museums.

OPPOSITE PAGE
LEFT: Sheriff Frederick Bush. Courtesy of the Lyman and Merrie Wood Museum of Springfield History, Springfield Museums.

ABOVE: Detail of Atlas of Springfield, 1882 showing the location of the Hampden County jail on State Street and its abutting institutions and residences. Courtesy of the Lyman and Merrie Wood Museum of Springfield History, Springfield Museums.

Once again on June 25, 1848 Sheriff Rice and his deputies had to quell a riot that broke out between Irish and "Yankee" workmen. The riot began at nine O'clock in the evening in Springfield "near the Hibernian" described by the Republican newspaper as "a sort of rum-hole below the [railroad] depot." From 10 to 12 in the evening "the church bells were rung and an immense crowd gathered." Sheriff Rice and his deputies then arrived on the scene and dispersed the mob without further incident

Col. Justin Wilson of Blandford was appointed Hampden County Sheriff to fill the post vacated by Caleb Rice. Also an officer of the Massachusetts State Militia, Col. Wilson was the first sheriff of the county without any previous legal experience. He was succeeded by attorney Patrick Boise of Westfield who was appointed by Governor John H. Clifford in 1853. He was a nephew of John Phelps, the second sheriff of Hampden County, and practiced law in Phelp's Law Office.

In 1855, Nathaniel Cutler of Chicopee was appointed Sheriff of Hampden County by Governor Henry Gardner, and was the last of the appointed sheriffs. He had served as a Chicopee Selectman and had also served prior to his appointment as deputy sheriff of the County. He only served until 1856, and critics referred to him as "the nothing Sheriff."

In 1856, Robert G. Marsh of Holyoke became the first elected Sheriff of Hampden County. Foreman of #1 Engine Co. of the Chicopee Fire Department, Marsh was nominated by the Republican Party and was elected in 1856. He served in that post until 1859 then entered into the real estate and fire insurance business.

Marsh was succeeded by Frederick Bush of Westfield who was elected in 1859. From 1848 to 1959, Bush had served as Deputy Sheriff under Sheriffs Wilson, Boise, Cutler, and Marsh. After leaving office in 1869, he operated a railroad in Columbia, South Carolina, later returning to manage hotels in Holyoke and Hartford, Connecticut.

During Bush's term of office, the first execution carried out at the jail was that of Alexander Desmarteau who was among the first criminals convicted of the new designation

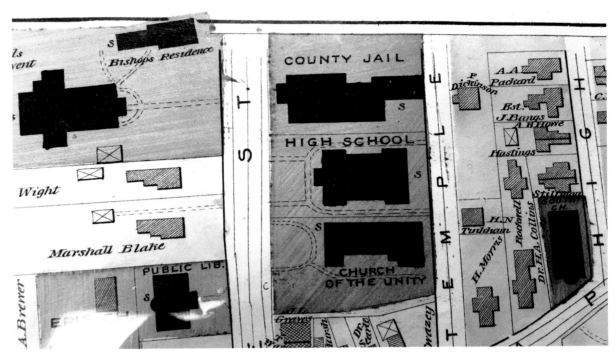

of "First degree" murder in Massachusetts. A crowd of 125 persons were allowed to witness the execution by hanging in the jail yard in 1861.

In 1869, Addison M. Bradley of Springfield was elected Sheriff of Hampden County. He had previously served as a Deputy Sheriff since 1859, and was also a Stage Driver on the Becket Mountain Route. Sheriff Bradley was faced with the growing problem of over-crowding at the county jail on State Street. In 1871, the average number of inmates at the County jail was 75. Female prisoners were sent to the jail in Springfield for "fines and costs; but were sent to Greenfield if the sentence is otherwise." It was reported that two thirds of those incarcerated was for "intoxication." L. C. Smith Co. contracted

with the jail for inmates to make "carpet slip-pers" supervised by nine Smith Co. employ-ees. Inmates made them at a rate of 400 pairs daily.

Despite Bradley's urging for expanded or new facilities to house inmates, overcrowd-ing had become the norm. By 1875, the Jail housed on average 120 inmates with only "a few" women included in that total. Many were only incarcerated for short terms, 800 were committed to the jail during that year with 650 incarcerated for "drunkenness." Inmates were kept busy making slippers for L.C. Smith Company which continued to contract with the Jail for that labor. Smith paid the jail $48 annually for each person in the House of Cor-rection and the inmates averaged 1,200 pairs of slippers daily.

That year, Sheriff Bradley did his best to try to alleviate the situation, creating a library for the inmates consisting of 500 volumes. In addition, a yard west of the jail 108 x 32 feet was created for the inmates to have a place to exercise outdoors. Unable to overcome this growing problem, he was succeeded by Hiram Q. Sanderson of Springfield who was elected Sheriff of Hampden County in 1878. The next five years witnessed the overcrowding at the jail reach a crisis point.

In January of 1880, overcrowding had be-come so bad at the State Street jail complex that Sheriff Sanderson reported to the Hamp-den County Commissioners that "in case of a riot it would be utterly impossible with the prison facilities to control the men." The state prison commssioners declared that " there is

LEFT: Photo of a page from the York Street Jail Shop Logbook for 1927 in the Hampden County House of Corrections Collection of the Lyman and Merrie Wood Museum of Springfield History.

OPPOSITE PAGE: Hampden County House of Corrections complex at York Street, Atlas of Springfield 1899.

not another jail in the state where the facilities are so poor and so limited."

Recognizing the inadequacy of the jail on State Street, Sanderson was an early advocate for the construction of a new jail. It was during this period that Sanderson and his staff had to aggressively quell a prison riot at the jail.

In a book written in 1883 and published in 1884 *(King's Handbook of Springfield)*, it was reported that overcrowding at the jail necessitated sending some prisoners to neighboring county jails. It criticized the Hampden County government, declaring that "The County is indictable for not providing better accommodations, and the time is not far distant when a new Jail must be built." The state authorities became increasingly concerned at the situation in Springfield. In 1884, the Massachusetts General Court ordered the Hampden County Commissioners to build a new "Jail and House of Correction" in Springfield, and they were given two years to do so. The Commissioners selected D.H. & A. B. Towers Company of Holyoke as the architects.

In 1885, the *Springfield Republican* exposed the conditions at the Hampden County Jail on State Street in an article, "Certain Facts About the Jail." Although the Jail only contained 116 cells for men and 28 for women, inmates numbered 175 men and 27 women at that time. Those extra 59 men were kept in various "makeshift" quarters including fifteen housed in an unventilated 250 square-foot attic space with no windows. *The Republican* also reported that the jail's hospital room had 17 inmates at that time with "healthy and sick sleeping side by side" while another

22 inmates were kept in an adjacent "poorly-ventilated" 300 square-foot room. The newspaper report went on to describe the poor sanitation at the jail:

"About 100 of the men confined in the house of correction are employed in a workroom 50 by 60 feet square, making cane-chair seats; and here also, the breathing-room is pitifully inadequate.... Every week they have to take a bath, but there are only two bath-tubs, and two men have to go through the same water and sometimes four. The prisoners march down the hall each morning to the closet with soil-buckets in hand. These are emptied into a funnel connecting directly with the sewer and though the iron doors are closed the stench is fearful; the more so as it is added to the foulness of the air that results from overcrowded sleeping apartments. A man is employed all the time in whitewashing the walls, but that is a pitifully inadequate provision for sanitation.... The law requires that jail inmates shall be given access to the open air. This is out of the question on the present premises; the men have no yard, the women have a kind of pit, only open toward the sky, and usually hung full with washing."

As Hampden County Sheriff, Hiram Sanderson was "instrumental in developing the plans for a new jail" that was to be erected on York Street. After leaving office in 1887, he continued in public service as the Chairman of the Springfield Water Commission.

In 1887, the State Street Jail was closed and was temporarily used as the 2nd Regiment of the Massachusetts Volunteer Militia's armory until a new armory on Howard Street was built in 1895. Succeeding Sheriff Sanderson, Simon Brooks of Holyoke was elected Sheriff

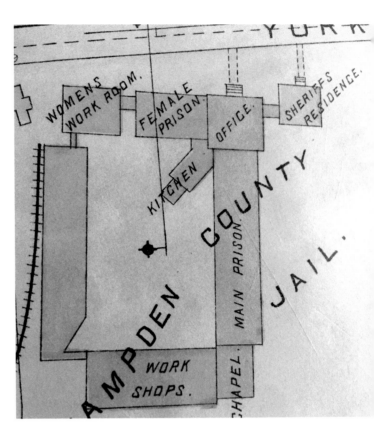

of Hampden County and presided over the opening of the new jail. Designed to hold 256 inmates, the new Jail at York Street was opened costing approximately $267,000. Brooks served until 1893 and was known as a "fine administrator" during his term of office.

SHERIFFS AND JAILS 1662 TO 1886: TIMELINE

BY JOSEPH CARVALHO III

[Hampshire County was formed by the General Court of the Colony of Massachusetts Bay on May 7, 1662. Old Hampshire County's southern district of towns became Hampden County in 1812. Its county seat was in Springfield during that period].

1658   The first jail/prison was built in the vicinity of present day Maple Street. It was constructed of hand-sawed hard-wood planks and beams.

1662   The 1658 jail/prison was also used as the county's jail.

1668   A Hampshire County Marshall was appointed. The Marshall served as the chief law enforcement officer of the county until 1692.

1671   July 29 – 14 year old servant girl, Katherine Hunter was committed to the 'House of Corrections" on Maple Street.

1675   Native American allies of "King Philip" burned the jail/prison along with most of the town's other structures in one of the most dramatic attacks during King Philip's War.

1677   The County Court led by Maj. John Pynchon ordered that a new jail be constructed in Springfield with an allowed construction cost of 50 to 55 pounds. Pynchon was directed to choose the proper location. He subsequently purchased adjacent lots from Thomas Merrick and Samuel Ely. No deed was executed on the property at the time as Springfield was still recovering from the devastation of the War. Ultimately a paper record of the land transfer was created in May of 1683.

1680   A second jail was built in Springfield at a cost of 60 pounds. It was located on the western side of Main Street near the corner of Bliss Street. With exterior walls made of thick logs, it was two stories high 25 feet long and 18 feet wide with a single large room and closets on the first floor, and three rooms on the second floor. Walls and partitions were constructed of heavy oak planks set endwise. The house of the jail keeper adjoined it on the north side. The first inmate was a Springfield native, Thomas Hancock.

1680   July- A fugitive slave, "Jack", from Wethersfield, Connecticut was apprehended by the local constable and placed in the Springfield Jail.

1680   Dec. 24 – Fugitive indentured servant, Thomas Hancock, apprehended and placed in the jail at Springfield.

1692   The office of Sheriff was created with Samuel Porter, Jr. holding the office "for a number of years" (at least until 1696).

1722   Captain Ebenezer Pumry (aka Pomeroy) served as "High Sheriff" of old Hampshire County.

1781   General Elisha Porter was appointed Sheriff of old Hampshire County. He was the first Hampshire County Sheriff appointed under the recently enacted Massachusetts State Constitution of 1780. He served until 1796. "From him, Shepard learned all the particulars which he had not before known, and ascertained that the force of Shays was on the march."

1782   Anti-government agitator Rev. Samuel Ely was charged, sentenced, and imprisoned in the Springfield for inciting a mob to prevent the court in Northampton to operate. Soon after, a mob of sympathizers forcibly released him from the jail. Called up by Sheriff Porter, the 2nd Company of the Hampshire County Militia Regiment was mustered and marched to Northampton to confront the rioters and re-arrest Ely. Shielded by the mob before they dispersed, Ely escaped to Maine. It was a precursor of Shays' Rebellion four years later.

1787   On Jan. 25th Hampshire County Deputy Sheriff Asaph King at Wilbraham learned of Daniel Shays' plans to attack the U.S. Arsenal at Springfield and rode just ahead of the rebels to alert General William Shepard who commanded the government forces defending the facility.

1794   The Springfield jail was closed; replaced by a jail in Northampton when the central Hampshire County courthouse was established in Northampton that year "on account of it's central location [it was] the most suitable place and the most likely to give general satisfaction to the inhabitants of the county." The Jail property was subsequently sold to the former "jailkeeper" William Colton.

1796   Ebenezer Mattoon was appointed Sheriff of old Hampshire County in 1796 and served until 1811.

1811   Thomas Shephard of Northampton was appointed Sheriff of old Hampshire County and served until the creation of the southern district into the new Hampden County in 1812.

1812   The southern district of old Hampshire County was re-organized as the new Hampden County with its seat in Springfield. Johnathan Smith, Jr. was appointed as the first Sheriff of Hampden County.

1813   The county purchased a 1 ½ acre lot on State Street (on the site that would later become Classical High School) for $500.

1814   John Phelps of Granville was appointed Hampden County Sheriff. The County began building a new Hampden County Jail and House of Correction on the State Street site at a cost of $14,164. Of stone construction, the building was two stories high and measured 18 x 30 feet. It housed up to 150 men and 10 women. The building was completed in 1815.

1815   The first inmate was David Cadwell of Wilbraham who only stayed in jail for a day after he paid his fine for assault.

1816 Jesse Wright of Springfield was the first person to break out of the jail when he escaped on Feb. 12, 1816.

1830 Additional jail building added at the State Street site.

1831 Col. Caleb Rice was appointed Hampden County Sheriff and served until he was elected Mayor of Springfield in 1851.

1851 Col. Justin Wilson of Blandford was appointed Hampden County Sheriff and was the first sheriff of the county without any previous legal experience.

1853 Patrick Boise of Westfield was appointed Sheriff of Hampden County.

1855 Nathaniel Cutler of Chicopee was appointed Sheriff of Hampden County and was the last of the appointed sheriffs.

1856 Robert G. Marsh of Holyoke was the first elected Sheriff of Hampden County.

1859 Frederick Bush of Westfield was elected Sheriff of Hampden County.

1861 The first execution carried out at the jail was that of Alexander Desmarteau who was among the first criminals convicted of the new designation of "First degree" murder in Massachusetts. A crowd of 125 persons were allowed to witness the execution by hanging in the jail yard.

1869 Addison M. Bradley of Springfield was elected Sheriff of Hampden County.

1870S By the 1870s, continued over-crowding led to serious consideration of building a larger facility.

1871 The average number of inmates at the County jail was 75. Female prisoners were sent to the jail for

"fines and costs; but were sent to Greenfield if the sentence is otherwise." It was reported that two thirds of those incarcerated was for "intoxication." L. C. Smith Co. contracted with the jail for inmates to make "carpet slippers" supervised by nine Smith Co. employees. Inmates made them at a rate of 400 pairs daily.

1875 The Jail housed on average 120 inmates with only "a few" women included in that total. Many were only incarcerated for short terms, 800 were committed to the jail during that year with 650 incarcerated for "drunkenness." Inmates were kept busy making slippers for L.C. Smith Company which contracted with the Jail for that labor. Smith paid the jail S48 annually for each person in the House of Correction and the inmates averaged 1,200 pairs of slippers daily. A Library for the inmates was added that year and consisted of 500 volumes. In addition, a yard west of the jail 108 x 32 feet was created for the inmates to have a place to exercise outdoors.

1878 Hiram Q. Sanderson of Springfield was elected as Sheriff of Hampden County.

1880 Sheriff Sanderson warned Hampden County Commissioners that overcrowding of the State Street jail might lead to prison unrest or a riot.

1883 In a book written in 1883 and published in 1884 (King's Handbook of Springfield), it was reported that overcrowding at the jail necessitated sending some prisoners to neighboring county jails. It criticized the Hampden County government , declaring that "The County is indictable for not providing better accommodations, and the time is not far distant when a new Jail must be built."

1884 The Massachusetts General Court ordered the Hampden County Commissioners to build a new Jail and House of Correction in Springfield, and they were given two years to do so. The Commissioners selected D.H. & A. B. Towers Company of Holyoke as the architects.

1885 The Springfield Republican exposed the conditions at the Hampden County Jail on State Street in an article, "Certain Facts About the Jail." Although the Jail only contained 116 cells for men and 28 for women, inmates numbered 175 men and 27 women at that time. Those extra 59 men were kept in various "makeshift" quarters including fifteen housed in an unventilated 250 square-foot attic space with no windows. The Republican also reported that the jail's hospital room had 17 inmates at that time with "healthy and sick sleeping side by side" while another 22 inmates were kept in an adjacent "poorly-ventilated" 300 square-foot room. The newspaper report went on to describe the poor sanitation at the jail:

"About 100 of the men confined in the house of correction are employed in a work-room 50 by 60 feet square, making cane-chair seats; and here also, the breathing-room is pitifully inadequate. . . . Every week they have to take a bath, but there are only two bath-tubs, and two men have to go through the same water and sometimes four. The prisoners march down the hall each morning to the closet with soil-buckets in hand. These are emptied into a funnel connecting directly with the sewer and though the iron doors are closed the stench is fearful; the more so as it is added to the foulness of the air that results from overcrowded sleeping apartments. A man is employed all the time in whitewashing the walls, but that is a pitifully inadequate provision for sanitation. . . . The law requires that jail inmates shall be given access to the open air. This is out of the question on the present premises; the men have no yard, the women have a kind of pit, only open toward the sky, and usually hung full with washing."

1886 Sheriff Sanderson and his deputies had to quell a prior riot at the State Street jail.

SHERIFFS OF HAMPDEN COUNTY

BY JOSEPH CARVALHO III

1ST HAMPDEN COUNTY SHERIFF (1812-1814):
JONATHAN SMITH, JR.

(b. July 31, 1757 in West Springfield, Mass.; d. Feb. 5, 1820 in Boston, Mass.) was appointed by Governor Elbridge Gerry as the first Sheriff of the newly formed Hampden County in 1812 and served until 1814. He was a prominent politician from West Springfield who served in a variety of key positions including: Town Moderator (1794, 1798-1819), Representative in the State Legislature (1794-1796, 1798-1811, and 1814-1819), Selectman of the town of West Springfield (1807-1813), Justice of the Peace (1811), and as a presidential elector (1804).

2ND HAMPDEN COUNTY SHERIFF (1814-1831):
ATTORNEY JOHN PHELPS

(b. 1767 in Granville, Mass.; d. Jan. 1, 1832 in Granville, Mass.) was appointed Sheriff of Hampden County by Governor Caleb Strong in 1814. Phelps was a native of Granville was their town clerk for 12 years, a Granville Selectman, and a member of the Massachusetts Legislature for many years. Sheriff Phelps helped plan a new county courthouse at Court Square in Springfield that was built in 1821 on Elm Street. Phelps served as County Sheriff until 1831.

3RD HAMPDEN COUNTY SHERIFF (1831-1851):
ATTORNEY CALEB RICE

(b. April 4, 1792 in Conway, Mass.; d. Mar. 1, 1873 in Springfield, Mass.) served as a Colonel in the Massachusetts State Militia and was appointed as Hampden County Sheriff in 1831.

Rice had been a practicing attorney for 14 years prior to his election as Sheriff. He served as Hampden County Sheriff until 1851 when he was elected as the first mayor of the recently incorporated City of Springfield that year. He was also the first President and first Treasurer of the Massachusetts Mutual life Insurance Company of Springfield.

4TH HAMPDEN COUNTY SHERIFF (1851-1853):
COL. JUSTIN WILSON

(b. ca. 1794 in Blandford, Mass.; d. Nov. 8, 1864 in Rockford, Ill.), a farmer from Blandford, was an officer in the Massachusetts State Militia. Appointed Sheriff of Hampden County in 1851, Wilson was the first sheriff of Hampden County without any previous law experience. Serving until 1853, he later served in the House of Representatives.

5TH HAMPDEN COUNTY SHERIFF (1853-1855):
ATTORNEY PATRICK BOISE

(b. Feb. 21, 1787 in Blandford, Mass.; d. Dec. 19, 1859 in Westfield, Mass.) practicing law in Westfield was appointed Sheriff of Hampden County in 1853 by Governor John H. Clifford. He was a nephew of John Phelps, the second sheriff of Hampden County, and practiced law in Phelp's Law Office. Boise served as Sheriff until 1855. He later served terms as a governor's councilor and in both houses of the Massachusetts General Court.

6TH HAMPDEN COUNTY SHERIFF (1855-1856):
NATHANIEL CUTLER

(b. Nov. 27, 1803 in Burlington, Mass.; d. May 10, 1887 in Chicopee, Mass.) was living in Chicopee when he was appointed Sheriff of Hampden County in 1855 by Governor Henry Gardner and was the last of the appointed sheriffs. He had served as a Chicopee Selectman

and had also served prior to his appointment as deputy sheriff of the County. He only served until 1856, and critics referred to him as "the nothing Sheriff."

7TH HAMPDEN COUNTY SHERIFF (1856-1859):
ROBERT G. MARSH

(b. 1808 in Vermont; d. Jun. 8, 1865 in Holyoke, Mass.) was living in Holyoke when he became the first elected Sheriff of Hampden County. Foreman of #1 Engine Co. of the Chicopee Fire Department, Marsh was nominated by the Republican Party and was elected in 1856. He served in that post until 1859 then entered into the real estate and fire insurance business.

8TH HAMPDEN COUNTY SHERIFF (1859-1869):
MAJ. FREDERICK BUSH

(b. Oct.1, 1820 in Westfield, Mass.; d. Jun. 23, 1909 in Westfield, Mass.) of Westfield was elected Sheriff of Hampden County in 1859. From 1848 to 1859, Bush had served as Deputy Sheriff under Sheriffs Wilson, Boise, Cutler, and Marsh. He presided over the hanging of the convicted murdered, Alexander Desmarteau on April 26, 1861. It was the first execution held at a Hampden County Jail. During the Civil War, the Governor of Massachusetts issued a proclamation that any prisoners in the jails in Massachusetts not serving terms for felonies would be pardoned if they enlisted. Under Sheriff Bush's tenure, 50 prisoners were recruited from the Hampden County jail. After leaving office in 1869, Bush operated the Columbia & Greenville railroad in Columbia, South Carolina, rebuilding it and selling the South Carolina Railroad. The 200 mile long rail line had been largely torn up during the Civil War. He later returned to New England to manage the Hotel Holyoke (aka The Hamilton) in Holyoke and the City Hotel in Hartford, Connecticut, retiring from business in 1893.

9TH HAMPDEN COUNTY SHERIFF (1869-1878):
ADDISON M. BRADLEY

Springfield Native (b. Mar. 24, 1825 in Russell, Mass.; d. Feb. 27, 1901 in Springfield, Mass.) who had previously served as a Deputy Sheriff since 1859, and was also a Stage Driver on the Becket Mountain Route, was elected Sheriff of Hampden County in 1869. Sheriff Bradley presided over the second execution at a Hampden County Jail when convicted murderer Albert H. Smith was hanged on June 27, 1873. Bradley served as Sheriff until 1878. He was to also serve in the Massachusetts State Legislature.

10TH HAMPDEN COUNTY SHERIFF (1878-1887):
HIRAM QUINCY SANDERSON

(b. Oct. 20, 1824 in Middletown, Connecticut; d. May 1, 1892 in Springfield, Mass.) came to Springfield in 1841 and worked as a grocery store clerk buying the store a year later. He sold the grocery store in 1848 and became the corporation clerk for the American Machine Works which made cotton gins and presses. In 1852, Sanderson "went west" as paymaster and bookkeeper for the firm of Phelps, Mattoon & Barnes who were constructing the Terre Haute, Alton & St. Louis Railroad. After its construction, Sanderson became General Freight and Passenger Agent of that railroad with its headquarters in St. Louis.

On the eve of the Civil War, Sanderson was sent to New York City as the railroad's "Eastern Agent." While stationed in New York City, Sanderson and another investor purchased "sleeping-cars" and soon had them running from New York to Chicago, St. Louis, and Louisville. "Their undertaking marked an epoch in railroad progress." They sold their business to George M. Pullman who further developed the use of "sleeping cars."

Returning to Springfield in 1857, Sanderson

was elected to the House of Representatives. He had previously served as a member of the first City Council for the newly incorporated City of Springfield. In 1875, he was appointed City Marshall of Springfield by Mayor Emerson Wight serving in that post until 1878.

Sanderson was elected for three 3-year terms of office as Sheriff of Hampden County beginning in 1878 – first as a Democrat and twice as a Republican. In 1881 he was also elected Chairman of the Springfield Water Board.

Recognizing the inadequacy of the jail on State Street, Sanderson was an early advocate for the construction of a new jail. It was during this period that Sanderson and his staff had to aggressively quell a prison riot at the jail. Having dealt with the consequences of poor conditions at the State Street jail, Sanderson was instrumental in developing the plans for a new jail that was to be erected on York Street. After leaving office in 1887, he continued in public service as the Chairman of the Springfield Water Commission until his death in 1892. It was the opinion of contemporary observers that "it was through his efforts that the city of Springfield has such a pure and abundant supply of water."

CENTER: Sheriff Addison M. Bradley. Courtesy of the Lyman and Merrie Wood Museum of Springfield History, Springfield Museums.

RIGHT: Sheriff Hiram Quincy Sanderson. Courtesy of the Lyman and Merrie Wood Museum of Springfield History, Springfield Museums.

THE ONLY SHERIFF EVER TO ARREST AN ENTIRE BRASS BAND

BY JOSEPH CARVALHO III

The incident occurred in May of 1860 during a court session in which Judge Otis P. Lord of Salem was presiding. Outside the Hampden County courthouse on Court Square, "firemen from all over the district were parading during their annual muster." The music from their several bands disturbed the court." Judge Lord declared that he "couldn't hear himself think." So, the Judge ordered Hampden County Sheriff Frederick Bush to go out and "quiet the band." It was reported that, "No sooner had Bush returned to the courtroom after completing his errand, than another band paraded past. Bush was also sent to quiet this one. Minutes later there was a third brass band "of course, perfectly innocent of any knowledge that it was disturbing the court," proved too much for the judge's patience. Judge Lord again ordered the sheriff out- this time with orders to arrest the band."

Bush caught the offending musicians on State Street opposite St. Michael's Cathedral and adjacent to the County Jail. The sheriff explained the judge's orders to the band leader and told him that he "would arrest the whole band if he had to call out the militia to do it." A reporter described the confrontation: "The burly firemen were at first reluctant to go with the sheriff and a fight threatened. Muster officials, however, turned the entire parade around and marched back to the courthouse, all three bands playing merrily on the way. The offenders were taken before the judge, followed by about 500 other firemen paraders, who filled the court. After city officials interceded on behalf of the marchers, Judge Lord let them off with a lecture. The jurist became so unpopular because of the incident that it was a long time before he was reassigned here."

THE DAY THEY HANGED WILLIAM SHAW

The Rev. John Ballantine of Westfield wrote in his diary on Sept. 18, 1770, "Edward East was murdered in Springfield Goal."

Murder was not the common occurrence it appears to be today back in the early days of Springfield. In fact, the murder of Edward East in the county jail would lead to Springfield's first execution, some 134 years after founding of the settlement.

The murder suspect was a shoemaker named William Shaw who had been confined to the Springfield jail for debt. The Palmer man supposedly got into an argument with East and struck him on the head with a hammer.

By Oct. 2 Shaw was found guilty of murdering Edward East and he was sentenced to be hanged.

On Dec. 12, 1770, the day before the execution was due to be carried out, Shaw tried to escape from the jail by dressing up in his wife's clothes, but he was captured before making it out the door.

OPPOSITE PAGE: Hampden County House of Corrections on State Street. ca. 1880s. Courtesy of the Lyman and Merrie Wood Museum of Springfield History, Springfield Museums.

RIGHT: 1991 Republican file photo of the location of the last hanging at the York Street jail.

On the morning of Dec. 13, Shaw was taken from his prison cell in the old jail, near the present site of Main and Bliss Streets, and brought to a spot on the hill, where seven years later the Armory would be located.

The Rev. Moses Baldwin of Palmer preached a discourse for the mercy of Shaw's soul, using as a text the First Psalm, fifth verse "Therefore the ungodly shall not stand in judgment."

A phrase I'm sure was directed at the hundreds of spectators that jammed the site where the gallows had been erected.

Early account reported the gallows was so high that the body of the executed man could be seen from Main Street.

There were only two hangings at York Street Jail in 1887 and 1894, both for robbery and murder. Beginning in 1901 the state of Massachusetts used the electric chair for death sentences. There were six executions of prisoners who were sent to Boston's Charlestown Jail. The last York Street jail convict was put to death in 1935 in Boston.

- Wayne E. Phaneuf

CHAPTER TWO

THE YORK STREET JAIL
1887-1974

THE YORK STREET JAIL: 1887 TO 1974

Designed to meet the requirements of the day, the Hampden County House of Corrections at York Street could hold 256 inmates. It was a great improvement over the previous facilities at State Street and it was well-managed for many years into the early 20th Century.

Sheriff Simon Brooks presided over the opening of the new jail and was known as "a free administrator" during his term of office.

In 1893, Col. Embury P. Clark of Holyoke was elected Sheriff of Hampden County and served for the next 35 years, one of the longest–serving sheriffs of the county. A Holyoke native, Clark was a veteran of the Civil War and remained in the Massachusetts militia until his retirement after World War I when he was promoted to the rank of brigadier general. While serving as Sheriff, Clark adopted "military standards" at the York Street Jail. He had a reputation as "a fair and just man." In 1912, Massachusetts House Committee on Legal Affairs inspected the women's facilities at the York Street jail and "expressed satisfaction at the conditions" for the 10 women housed at the jail at that time. By state regulations in 1914, the County Commissioners were required to inspect the County jail and "other reformatory institutions in the county" twice annually and must be made by at least two County Commissioners." The York Street Jail continued to receive positive reviews under Clark's leadership. He served as Sheriff until he died in his sleep on July 12, 1928 at the age of 83.

On January 11, 1916, Deputy Sheriff Richard

F. Lawton was shot and killed in Russell by Edwin D. Carter as Lawton was arresting the man on a warrant sworn by Carter's wife. Carter was sentenced to life in prison. Deputy Sheriff Lawton was the only Sheriff or Deputy Sheriff of Hampden County to be killed in the line of service.

Edward J. Leyden was appointed in 1928 as Sheriff of Hampden County to complete Clark's unexpired term of office. He had previously served as one of Clark's Deputy Sheriffs for thirty years and was also a U.S. Marshall for twenty years. Leyden was also a veteran of the 2nd Massachusetts Volunteer Militia Regiment and served in Cuba during the Spanish American War. He died suddenly on August 9, 1929 at the age of 54.

Appointed Sheriff of Hampden County after the death of Sheriff Leyden in 1929 to complete Leyden's term of office, Col. Edmund J. Slate had been Marshall of the Holyoke Police Department since 1925. Previously, he had served in the 2nd Massachusetts Volunteer Militia in Cuba during the Spanish American War, served in Gen. Pershing's Expeditionary force into Mexico in 1916, and in France during World War I.

David J. Manning was elected Sheriff of Hampden County in 1930 and was re-elected many times, serving in that post for 32 years until 1962. As an early reformer, he took a different approach to Corrections than his military-trained predecessors. During his first term, Manning up-graded the York Street Jail's sanitary facilities, installed running water, and toilets in each jail cell. Manning was cited in 1936 for the fourth consecutive year for the lowest operating costs of any jail in Massachusetts. That year, he arranged for the purchase of a 50-acre farm in Agawam in order to produce fresh vegetables for the inmates at the Jail. Over his long tenure as Sheriff, Manning received many awards and commendations including the prestigious Pynchon Medal in 1945. Two incidents in his career are remembered. In 1934, he was wounded in the leg by gunfire when he "courageously helped prevent the escape of Alexander Kaminski in the midst of his trial for murder at the Hampden County Superior Courtroom. Manning intervened when Kaminski's brother John "invaded the courtroom armed with a gun and bombs in a desperate scheme" to free his brother. In 1956, Manning played a major role in persuading one of the men who participated in the notorious Brink's robbery in Boston to turn state's evidence, "thus helping to solve one of the most puzzling cases in Massachusetts' history."

In 1960, three acres of land was taken from the York Street jail for the construction of Interstate 91. The land taken resulted in the loss of a house used by the master of the jail, a visitor's parking spaces, the jail garden, a garage, tool sheds, a vegetable storehouse, and a "turkey run." The Hampden County Commission eventually received $212,619 for the land taken for the construction of Rte 91. Historian Larry Gormally wrote that "Time proved that this was an irreparable loss to the jail, bringing the highway within a few feet of the jail property, and eliminating space for expansion, as well as adding noise and air pollution problems." Sheriff Manning was succeeded in the next election by John G. Curley.

Prior to his election as Sheriff of Hampden County in 1962, Springfield native John G. Curley had served as Deputy Chief of the Springfield District Court. He had also previously served for three terms in the Massachusetts State Legislature. Continuing the modest reform efforts begun under Manning, Curley upgraded much of the Jail's facilities including building a cafeteria and initiating a Jail Commissary. In an effort to counter recidivism, Curly installed a classroom in the Jail chapel where inmates could take classes that would improve their opportunities for employment upon their eventual release.

On July 17, 1963, the Hampden County Commissioners announced a study of the potential use of inmate labor from the county jail. Sheriff Curley and the Commissioners did not get along in those early years of his tenure. Curley charged that the Hampden County Commissioners were "trying to take over the Sheriff's Department." The dispute was over jail food costs. Under the law, the county commission could procure all the supplies for the jail. After

OPPOSITE PAGE CENTER: Sheriff Embury P. Clark.

ABOVE: Hampden County House of Correction at York Street in Springfield. Photo courtesy of the Lyman and Merrie Wood Museum of Springfield History, Springfield Museums.

food costs at the jail increased under Sheriff Curley, the commissioners invoked their power under this law mid-way through 1963. Previously, the buying of provisions at the jail was left to the Sheriff.

Curley made attempts to modernize things at the York Street jail. In 1964, Sheriff Curley had an improved AM/FM radio unit for earphones installed so that inmates could use radios in their off-time. The Commissioners continued to struggle with the increased costs of operating the jail. As reported in February of 1965, York Street jail costs topped $400,000 for the first time in history, an increase of almost $55,000 from the previous year's budget. As a way to fund part of the jail's budget in 1966, the Springfield Police Department was allowed to place prisoners in the West Block at York Street Jail while their new Police station and lock-up was being built on Pearl Street.

Another modest reform under Curley, was a collaboration with the Springfield Library & Museums Association. Curley received a federal Title 1 grant which paid for the stocking (600 books) and operation of a branch library staffed by SLMA librarians, eight hours a day at the jail. However, the main operations, rules and regulations, programs, and services at the Jail were essentially the same as those since the 1930s. Curley served until 1974 when he was defeated in that year's Democratic Primary by Michael J. Ashe, Jr. who was to usher in a new era of Corrections reform that would attract national attention.

- Joseph Carvalho III

TIMELINE OF THE SHERIFFS AND HOUSE OF CORRECTIONS OF HAMPDEN COUNTY (YORK STREET JAIL), 1887-1974

BY JOSEPH CARVALHO III

1887   Simon Brooks of Holyoke was elected Sheriff of Hampden County. The State Street Jail was closed and was temporarily used as the 2nd Regiment of the Massachusetts Volunteer Militia's armory until a new armory on Howard Street was built in 1895.

1887   The new Jail at York Street was opened costing approximately $267,000. It was designed to hold 256 inmates.

1893   Col. Embury P. Clark of Holyoke was elected Sheriff of Hampden County and served for 35 years.

1912   Massachusetts House Committee on Legal Affairs inspected the women's facilities at the York Street jail "expressed satisfaction at the conditions" for the 10 women housed at the jail at that time.

1914   County Commissioners were required to inspect the County jail and "other reformatory institutions in the county" twice annually and must be made by at least two County Commissioners.

1928   Edward J. Leyden was selected to complete Sheriff's Clark's unexpired term of office as Sheriff of Hampden County. He died on August 9, 1929 before his term expired.

1929   Col. Edmund J. Slate was selected to complete Sheriff Leyden's term as Sheriff of Hampden County.

1930   David J. Manning was elected Sheriff of Hampden County and served for 32 years.

1931-1933   Sheriff Manning upgraded the York Street Jail's sanitary facilities and had running water and toilets installed in each jail cell.

1936   Sheriff Manning arranged for the purchase of a 50 acre farm land in Agawam in order to produce fresh vegetables for the inmates at the jail.

1960   Three acres of land was taken from the York Street jail for the construction of Interstate 91. The land taking resulted in the loss of a house used by the master of the jail, a visitor's parking spaces, the jail garden, a garage, tool sheds, a vegetable storehouse, and a "turkey run." Historian Larry Gormally wrote that "Time proved that this was an irreparable loss to the jail, bringing the highway within a few feet of the jail property, and eliminating space for expansion, as well as adding noise and air pollution problems."

1962   John G. Curley of Springfield was elected Sheriff of Hampden County and served until 1974. A jail cafeteria was built during his tenure and a jail commissary was initiated. Curley also installed a classroom in the Jail Chapel where inmates could take classes.

1963   July 17 – Hampden County Commissioners announced a study of the potential use of inmate labor from the county jail.

1963   Nov. 24 -Sheriff Curley charged that the Hampden County Commissioners were "trying to take over the Sheriff's Department." The dispute was over jail food costs. Under the law, the county commission could procure all the supplies for the jail. After food costs at the jail increased under Sheriff Curley, the commissioners invoked their power under this law mid-way through 1963. Previously, the buying of provisions at the jail was left to the Sheriff.

1964   Sheriff Curley had an improved AM/FM radio unit for earphones installed so that inmates could use radios on their off-time.

1964 Mar. 11- Hampden County Commission received $212,619 for land from the York Street Jail grounds taken for the construction of Interstate Rte. 91.

1965 Feb. 16- Jail costs topped $400,000 for the first time in history, an increase of almost $55,000 from the previous year's budget.

1966 Feb. – Springfield Police Department was allowed to place prisoners in the West Block at York Street Jail while their new Police station and lock-up was being built on Pearl Street.

1972 A Federal Title 1 grant paid for the stocking (600 books) and operation of a branch library staffed by Springfield Library and Museums Association librarians eight hours a day at the jail.

TOP LEFT: Sheriff Simon Brooks. Republican file photo
TOP RIGHT: Sheriff David J. Manning. Photo courtesy of the Lyman and Merrie Wood Museum of Springfield History, Springfield Museums.
BOTTOM RIGHTT: Lobby of the York Street jail, Jan. 13, 1961. Republican file photo.

Graphic Publishing Company
93 Worthington Street.

Price, 5 Cents.

SPRINGFIELD, MASS., SATURDAY, JANUARY 7, 1893.

Number 145-
Volume VI.

HOSEA C. LOMBARD
Deputy Sheriff.

WALTER S. MILLER
Deputy Sheriff.

EMBURY P. CLARK
Sheriff of Hampden County.

HENRY McDONALD
Deputy Sheriff.

SIMON BROOKS
Deputy Sheriff.

THE SHERIFF AND HIS SPRINGFIELD DEPUTIES
Men you like to see go by your door.

SHERIFF BIOGRAPHIES
BY JOSEPH CARVALHO III

11TH HAMPDEN COUNTY SHERIFF (1887-1893):
SIMON BROOKS

(b. Mar. 28, 1834 in West Springfield, Mass.; d. Sept. 29, 1898 in West Springfield, Mass.) began his career as a post office clerk at the age of 21. He moved to Holyoke in 1877 was working as a book keeper for the Whiting paper Company of that city when he was elected Sheriff of Hampden County in 1887. Sheriff Brooks presided over the opening of the York Street Jail in that year. He was known as a "fine administrator" during his term of office which lasted until 1893. After his term of office, he entered the coal and wood business.

12TH HAMPDEN COUNTY SHERIFF (1893-1928):
COL. EMBURY PHILIP CLARK

Elected Sheriff of Hampden County in 1893 (b. Mar. 31, 1845 in Buckland, Mass.; d. July 12, 1928 in Springfield, Mass.) held the position of Sheriff for 35 years. As a long-time resident of Holyoke, he worked as a druggist, a bookkeeper, and then as registrar for the Holyoke Water Works. He also served as a member of the Holyoke School Board for 15 years. Clark was a veteran of the Civil War and the Spanish-American War and remained in the Massachusetts militia until his retirement after World War I when he was promoted to the rank of brigadier general. During the Civil War , he served as a corporal in Company B of the 46th Massachusetts Volunteer Infantry

LEFT: Cover of the Springfield Graphic magazine, January 7, 1893. Sheriff Embury P. Clark and his deputies including former Sheriff of Hampden County Simon Brooks. From the collection of the Lyman and Merrie Wood Museum of Springfield History, Springfield Museums.

OPPOSITE PAGE CENTER: Sheriff Edmund J. Slate. Republican file photo.

Regiment. He was the Colonel of the 2nd Massachusetts Regiment during the Spanish American War. After the War, he was elected Commander-in-Chief of the Naval and Military Order of the Spanish American War. Clark moved to Springfield at the time he ran for the position of County Sheriff and remained a resident there for the rest of his life. While serving as Sheriff, Clark adopted "military standards" at the York Street Jail. He had a reputation as "a fair and just man." He served as Sheriff until he died in his sleep on July 12, 1928 at the age of 83.

13TH HAMPDEN COUNTY SHERIFF (1928-1929):
EDWARD J. LEYDEN

(b. 1875 in Springfield, Mass.; d. Aug. 9, 1929 in Springfield, Mass.) was appointed in 1928 as Sheriff of Hampden County to complete Clark's unexpired term of office. He had previously served as one of Clark's Deputy Sheriffs for thirty years and was also a U.S. Marshall for twenty years. Leyden was also a veteran of the 2nd Massachusetts Volunteer Militia Regiment and served in Cuba during the Spanish American War. His tenure as sheriff was very brief, Leyden died suddenly at the age of 54.

14TH HAMPDEN COUNTY SHERIFF (1929-1930):
COL. EDMUND JUSTIN SLATE

Appointed Sheriff of Hampden County after the death of Sheriff Leyden in 1929 to complete Leyden's term of office. Col. Edmund Justin Slate (b. Nov. 6, 1875 in Hatfield, Mass.; d. Oct. 21, 1948 in Holyoke, Mass.) had been Marshall of the Holyoke Police department since 1925. Previously, he served in the 2nd Massachusetts Volunteer Militia in Cuba during the Spanish American War, served in Gen. Pershing's Expeditionary force into Mexico in 1916, and in France during World War I.

GEN. EDMUND J. SLATE AND STAFF
Grand Marshal of the Parade Gen. Edmund J. Slate with his corps of aids. "It's a mighty fine parade," general said, as he reviewed marchers.

15TH HAMPDEN COUNTY SHERIFF (1930-1962):
DAVID J MANNING, JR.

(b. Jun. 11, 1889 in Springfield, Mass.; d. May 16, 1965 in Springfield, Mass.) was elected Sheriff of Hampden County in 1930 and was re-elected many times, serving in that post for 32 years until 1962. Manning began his work in the engineering department of the Boston & Albany Railroad working in a variety of capacities from 1909 to 1912. He began his career in law enforcement in 1912 when he became a policeman in the Springfield Police Department. In 1916, he joined the Massachusetts State Police eventually being promoted to detective lieutenant. Manning earned his LL.D. (law) degree from Northeastern University in 1929. During his first term, Manning up-graded the York Street Jail's sanitary

facilities, installed running water, and toilets in each jail cell. Cited in 1936 for the fourth consecutive year for the lowest operating costs of any jail in Massachusetts, he arranged for Farm land to be acquired in Agawam in order to produce fresh vegetables for the inmates at the Jail. Over his long tenure as Sheriff, Manning received many awards and commendations including the prestigious Pynchon Medal in 1945.

The Republican newspaper recognized his service upon his passing in 1965 stating that Manning "was responsible for programs rehabilitating prisoners which are in wide use today. During his stewardship, the Hampden County Jail became nationally recognized as among the best-managed and most efficient in the country." Two incidents in his career are

ABOVE: Sheriff Edmund Slate and staff posing in the rotunda of the York Street jail in 1929. Photo courtesy of the late Larry Gormally.

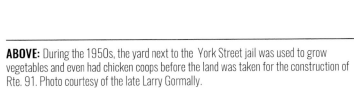

ABOVE: During the 1950s, the yard next to the York Street jail was used to grow vegetables and even had chicken coops before the land was taken for the construction of Rte. 91. Photo courtesy of the late Larry Gormally.

RIGHT : Sheriff John G. Curley (L) and library director Francis P. Keough (R) inspecting area planned for a Springfield City Library branch at the York Street jail, 1973. Republican file photo.

remembered. In 1934, he was wounded in the leg by gunfire when he "courageously helped prevent the escape of Alexander Kaminski in the midst of his trial for murder at the Hampden County Superior Courtroom. Manning intervened when Kaminski's brother John "invaded the courtroom armed with a gun and bombs in a desperate scheme" to free his brother. In 1956, Manning played a major role in persuading one of the men who participated in the notorious Brink's robbery in Boston to turn state's evidence, "thus helping to solve one of the most puzzling cases in Massachusetts' history." Manning's son David J. Manning (1915-1968) served as a deputy Sheriff in Hampden County for thirteen years.

16TH HAMPDEN COUNTY SHERIFF (1962-1974):
JOHN GEORGE CURLEY

Prior to his election as Sheriff of Hampden County in 1962, Springfield native John George Curley (b. July 15, 1916 in Springfield, Mass. ; d. Nov. 21, 1978 in Springfield, Mass.) had served as Deputy Chief of the Springfield District Court. He had also previously served for three terms in the Massachusetts State Legislature. A veteran of WWII, Curley was a master sergeant in the U.S. Army. Continuing the effort begun under Manning, Sheriff Curley upgraded much of the Jails facilities including building a Cafeteria and initiating a Jail Commissary. In an effort to counter recidivism, Curly installed a classroom in the Jail chapel where inmates could take classes that would improve their opportunities for employment upon their eventual release. Curley served until 1974.

LEFT: Sheriff John G. Curley and corrections officer Leo Milette operating the newly installed AM/FM radio unit for earphones so that inmates could use radios in their off-time, 1964. Republican file Photo.

TOP RIGHT: Sheriff John G. Curley. Photo courtesy of the Lyman and Merrie Wood Museum of Springfield History, Springfield Museums.

RIGHT: York Street Jail riot Feb. 15, 1971. Republican file photo by Steve Van Meter.

CHAPTER THREE
SHERIFF ASHE AND REFORM

SHERIFF MICHAEL J. ASHE AND THE NEW ERA OF CORRECTIONS SYSTEM REFORM

BY JOSEPH CARVALHO III

1974 was a watershed year for the corrections system in Hampden County. The campaign for sheriff of Hampden County pitted a newcomer with radically new ideas of corrections in a six-man race which included incumbent Sheriff James G. Curley, and former Massachusetts State Police officer William D. Garvey of the "old guard" and its traditional hard-line policies and procedures. Ashe bested Garvey and Curley in the Democratic primary and faced his Republican challenger Daniel J. O'Brien in the general election. The runner-up in the Democratic primary, William Garvey even endorsed Ashe, saying that he was "satisfied with [Ashe's] assurance that the safety of the public will be uppermost in his mind." Winning the election, Michael J. Ashe, Jr. became the first sheriff in the country to hold a Master's degree in Social Work, a stark departure from the long line of sheriffs with either military or law enforcement credentials.

Whereas his predecessors managed the Hampden County jail with military-style discipline, Sheriff Ashe's motto of correctional supervision was "Strength reinforced with decency; firmness dignified with fairness." From the beginning, his approach was to institute policies and treatment of inmates to dramatically reduce the revolving door of recidivism. Ashe sought to add opportunities

LEFT: Daily News front page announcing election of Michael J. Ashe, Jr. as the new Sheriff of Hampden County. Republican library file.

for redemption to the traditional "Crime and Punishment" approach of the past. In those early years, he met resistance every step of the way.

A graduate of St. Anselm's College, Michael Ashe earned his Master's degree from Boston College. Ashe's work as the head of the Battered Child Syndrome Unit in Western Massachusetts became the subject of his master's thesis. Upon graduation in 1968, Ashe and his wife Barbara served as the first house parents at Downey Side Homes for young people. They served as house parents to eight boys from 1968 to 1974 and Ashe said he "was proud of all of them." Ashe became the Assistant Director of the institution serving until 1974.

It was ingrained in Ashe's persona to help those less privileged. Humanitarian in nature, he made it his life's goal to become a positive force in people's lives. In an interview many years later, Ashe pointed out that, "there were many similarities between the troubled teenagers he dealt with at the Downey Side program and the young men in their late teens and early twenties who serve time at the Hampden County House of Corrections." He felt that traditional approaches needed to be re-evaluated, and informed by new ideas emanating from the social work scholarship of the early 1970s. It would set him on a path to becoming the state's preeminent corrections reformer.

Sheriff Ashe remembered his first experience entering York Street jail after his election flanked by a skeptical and disapproving staff. "What did this social worker know about running a jail?" was the general consensus of the guard staff. Ashe knew he had to either replace the entire staff or win them over to

his style of managing the correctional system. He boldly and confidently chose the latter. By effectively communicating to his staff why and how procedures and policies would be changed, he gradually won over the majority of the staff.

From those earliest days, Ashe began the process of professionalizing the staff through training and performance expectations. It took several years to fully implement his approach, nevertheless, Ashe ultimately succeeded. The evolution of "prison guards/ jailers" to professional correctional officers enabled the sheriff to usher a new era of humane but firm treatment of inmates at York Street.

However, one of the biggest impediments to Ashe's full program was the building itself. He was attempting to implement late 20th Century reforms in a building designed for the late 19th Century. This limited him in many ways just as the early County Jail on State Street reached its crisis point due to overcrowding. The failure of the State Street facility to meet the growing need of the county led to the design and construction of the York Street jail which was very much a reform effort at the time. By the 1970s, York Street had outlived its utility and became a dangerous barrier to reform and modern management of corrections in Hampden County. Sheriff Ashe recognized this from the outset and became an early advocate for finding a solution to the ominous overcrowding at York Street.

From the very first days of his tenure, Sheriff Ashe saw the need for additional space for inmates and programs he wanted to institute.

RIGHT: Newly elected Sheriff Michael J. Ashe, Jr. Republican file photo.

Whereas previous Sheriff's and their families lived in the "Sheriff's House" at York Street, Ashe decided to not use that building for his personal use and instead converted the building into office space freeing up space within the jail facilities for other services and inmate space. It later was converted into the County's first pre-release center in 1976. The Pre-release Center was established to provide "an alternate living environment for selected inmates who are within four months of release." These efforts helped but couldn't solve the larger problem of overcrowding at the jail. By the early 1980s, the York Street jail designed in the 1880s to house approximately 300 inmates now had over 700 inmates in the same space. Sheriff Ashe appealed to the County Commissioners, state officials, the media and anyone who would listen that a new facility was urgently needed.

Undeterred by roadblocks to progress, Ashe ran for a second term in 1980. He ran on his record of achievement. His efforts had reduced recidivism in Hampden County to 13.8% compared to the national average approaching 80% at that time. His campaign emphasized his theme of corrections management as "humanizing the county jail and eliminating the 'warehouse' school of thought in criminal justice." He touted his reform programs as designed to "reduce recidivism and help discharged inmates become taxpaying citizens and contributing members of society." Popular and running unopposed, Ashe was elected to a second six-year term.

LEFT: Signed photo of Sheriff Ashe and wife Barbara with U.S. Congressman Edward P. Boland of Springfield, taken at Boland's office in Washington, D.C., 1978. Courtesy of Michael J. Ashe, Jr.

ABOVE: Democratic office holders celebrating Democratic Party victories in the 1976 national elections: Left to right: State Rep. Anthony "Tony" M. Scibelli, U.S. Congressman Edward P. Boland, Springfield Mayor William C. Sullivan, and Hampden County Sheriff Michael J. Ashe, Jr. with campaign staff [Congressman Boland's wife Mary is on far right], Nov. 3, 1976. Republican file photo.

During his first term of office, Ashe had successfully "won over" the majority of his corrections staff to his way of thinking. More importantly, he had finally put in place "his team" in all of the key positions in the Sheriff's Department. These corrections professionals were devoted to Ashe's philosophy and were key in helping him to implement dramatic reforms in the system over the next few years.

In December of 1980, Ashe asked for an addition of 60 beds for the jail. In early 1981, Robert Tessier of Tessier Associates, an architect appointed by the Massachusetts Bureau of Building and Construction was tasked with drawing up a plan for a three-story addition to the York Street jail. This was in response to Governor Ed King's anti-crime program which Sheriff Ashe projected would raise the jail's population by up to 100 inmates. Despite all the planning and lobbying for funding, the expansion was never approved by the state. Undaunted, Sheriff Ashe continued to seek ways to improve conditions at York Street opening a new health clinic in November of 1981 which received accreditation by the American Medical Association.

In early 1982, the sheriff "with the blessings of the Hampden County Commissioners" explored using the vacant Northampton State Hospital to house 50 inmates from York Street. On March 18th, the Northampton City Council voted unanimously to reject the plan and the neighboring Smith College threatened legal action to stop the plan. The State legislature even got into the act by passing a bill to stop the planned use of the

LEFT: Sheriff Ashe touring officials from the South End Business Association through York Street jail, September 21, 1980. Republican file photo.

state hospital. Ashe was deeply disappointed stating, "The Northampton site would have been such a great asset for us....[now] we are going to have to look within the county for alternatives. We may not have much of a choice." *Republican* newspaper's chief political columnist, Glenn Briere, sympathized with Sheriff's Ashe's Northampton plan but knew that it was doomed despite Governor Ed King's initial support in his column entitled "Future of Prison Reform Bleak in Massachusetts." Governor King had sought $47.3 million for prison expansion in November of 1981 but was denied by the legislature. State politics was stymying progress.

In May of that year, Sheriff Ashe began to formulate a new plan for approval by the Hampden County Commission. The *Springfield Republican* newspaper took up the sheriff's cause publishing a series of articles highlighting the sheriff's dilemma in trying to find solutions for the overcrowding at York Street. One major expose in the *Republican* widened its scope by sharing the plight of all of the regional jails, in an article entitled "WMass County Jails: Ancient, Crowded, Unsafe." It was reported that "prisoners are being stuffed two at a time in cells that are considered too small for one person." Sheriff Ashe noted the public's antipathy to those in jail and told the reporter, people will say: 'Stuff 'em five to a cell, they deserve it." But he pointed out that on any given day one-forth of the jail inmates had not been convicted of any crime but were awaiting trial because they could not make bail. More than 400 prisoners were "jammed into the York Street facility" that was designed for 279. It was reported that inmates "are sleeping in the kitchen, in the halls, and anywhere else that will hold a cot."

ABOVE: Sheriff Ashe with Presidential candidate Jimmy Carter during his visit to Springfield, 1976. Photo Courtesy Michael J. Ashe, Jr.

Ashe was completely aware of the unfairness of the situation and he re-doubled his lobbying to find ways to improve the conditions. As a temporary stop-gap, Ashe had three trailers located outside the facility to help ease the overcrowding. He also arranged for the female inmates to be taken in by the state at Framingham State Prison in an effort to help. Without state assistance, one editorialist opined, "Sheriff Michael J. Ashe, Jr. can do no more than shake his head in frustra-

tion," as the state legislature continued to pass mandatory sentencing laws while underfunded facilities needed to house the resultant increased rate of incarceration. On top of that the tax-limiting Proposition 2 ½ made state funding of county priorities even less likely. The commissioners from all four western counties of Massachusetts "agreed with the projection that within five years the counties would go broke trying to keep jails open with limited funds and increasing inmate

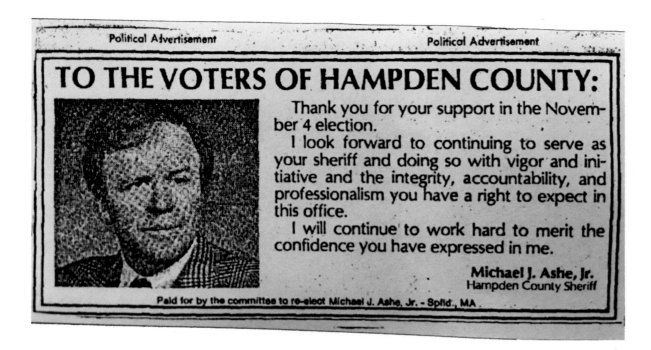

TO THE VOTERS OF HAMPDEN COUNTY:

Thank you for your support in the November 4 election.

I look forward to continuing to serve as your sheriff and doing so with vigor and initiative and the integrity, accountability, and professionalism you have a right to expect in this office.

I will continue to work hard to merit the confidence you have expressed in me.

Michael J. Ashe, Jr.
Hampden County Sheriff

Paid for by the committee to re-elect Michael J. Ashe, Jr. - Spfld., MA.

ABOVE: Newspaper notice by Sheriff Ashe thanking voters for their support in the 1980 election. Republican newspaper database.

populations." They argued that state funding needed to support the tougher sentencing laws recently passed by the state legislature.

A new jail was still far in the future. Nevertheless, while he fought for more space for inmates, Ashe was undeterred in introducing new programs to serve the needs of the community and region of Western Massachusetts. One of his early efforts was the "Decisional Training program" coordinated by Thomas Rovelli. The premise of the program was that an individual given the basic tools with which to carefully review his past mistakes and clarify his future goals would be more prepared to return to the community. As Rovelli described the program which began in August of 1981, "we are trying to change the attitude of the men we deal with...we try to make them realize that they have something to offer the world."

In May of that year, Sheriff Ashe's Pre-release Center with Joseph Nicholson as its director became the first in the state to be nationally accredited by the American Correctional Association. At the accreditation ceremony, Sheriff Ashe said, "This is a tribute to the hard work of the Pre-release Center staff, and it recognizes our vital and necessary relationships with the Hampden County Community." The aim of thwarting recidivism was clear in this and many other programs and policies instituted by the Sheriff.

Deputy Administrator of Human Services at the Hampden County House of Corrections, John "Jay" Ashe articulated the approach in a guest editorial published in the *Springfield Republican* in 1981: "Rehabilitation at the Hampden County House of Corrections starts with the realization that merely providing custodial care for inmates is a dis-service to the Hampden County community. " He added that "we function with the philosophy that it is better to release an inmate equipped with educational and vocational skills than to release an individual who believes that making it as a criminal is his only alternative."

In 1985, Massachusetts began to "crack down" on drunk driving in the state after several high-profile cases of fatalities caused by intoxicated drivers. This caused another spike in incarcerations of individuals Driving Under the Influence (D.U.I) in county jails. Sheriff Ashe reached out to the three other county sheriffs in Western Massachusetts and garnered their support for a regional center to be established in Springfield.

Ashe reached out to J. Michael Wallace of C & W Realty which owned the former Y.W.C.A. building on Howard Street and proposed that building as the site of the new regional D.U.I. alcohol treatment center. C & W Realty readily agreed and proceeded to prepare their building for its future use by the Sheriff. The building had to be "gutted" according to Wallace and the rehab took about 4 months to complete. On Nov. 22, 1985, Governor Dukakis announced that the state would allocate $1 million for the creation of a 125-bed Western Massachusetts Correctional Alcohol Center. The facility opened with Governor Dukakis attending on Dec. 15 of that year for inmates who were three-time driving under the influence offenders. Due to stricter enforcement and harsher sentencing, these individuals had to serve their sentences in a county jail. Ultimately, this facility was used for the treatment of any inmate with substance abuse problems.

With Governor Michael Dukakis' political and state funding support for the idea, Ashe proceeded to build support from Springfield's political leadership for this location in the South End neighborhood of the city. Mayor Richard E. Neal and his Director of Planning David Moriarity were the first to join the coalition of support. Ashe soon received the support of State Representative from the South End, "Tony" Scibelli – the "Dean of the House," and State Senator Linda J. Melconian who would later become the first woman to serve as Majority Leader of the Massachusetts Senate. He also appointed to his site review committee the respected local defense attorney, Victor Gagnon - the husband of noted local historian Frances Gagnon – the city's chairwoman of the Historical Commission which would later have to review the site use. But perhaps just as importantly, the sheriff received the approval and support of the neighborhood's beloved elementary school principal Alfred Zanetti of the elementary school adjacent to the property. That sealed the deal.

In December of 1985, Sheriff Ashe opened the Western Massachusetts Correctional Alcohol Center which was one of the nation's first correctional facilities dedicated to substance abuse treatment. Hampden County House of Corrections Human Services Director, J. John Ashe was tapped to oversee the program. It represented a new paradigm in correctional medicine and was selected Correctional Medical Program of the Year by the National Commission on Correctional Health Care and

ABOVE: Sheriff Ashe (Left) touring the York Street jail complex with (left to right)Massachusetts Governor Ed King, State Rep. Anthony "Tony" Scibelli, and Springfield Mayor Theodore "Ted" Dimauro, Oct. 22, 1981. Republican file photo.

won an innovations in American Government award from the Ford Foundation and the Kennedy School of Government.

Ashe's humane treatment of inmates was codified in his 1985 handbook of Inmate Rules and Regulations. The handbook which was distributed to each inmate described each program, behavioral expectations, grievance procedures, recreation opportunities, religious services, educational opportunities and training. The introduction to the handbook stated: "Besides informing you of the services, rules, and regulations of this facility and providing you with an understanding of this facility so you may make the necessary adjustment. This handbook will explain the variety of educational work training, and other human services

ABOVE: Hampden County Sheriff's Department corrections staff assembled outside of the Hampden County Hall of Justice. Republican file photo.

programs which are offered. These various programs are designed to assist you and to provide opportunities for you; you are encouraged to participate in them."

Much political energy in 1985 was taken up with a year-long debate and battle in the Massachusetts legislature and county governments about the state taking over county jails. Bills were proposed and various versions made their way through the legislature while county government fought to maintain local control. In late October, the Hampden County Commissioners were still hesitating to go forward with any plans for the jail until the State "takeover" issue was resolved. Even the Massachusetts Senate Ways and Means Committee held their prison expansion package in abeyance while the "Takeover" debate continued further frustrating Sheriff Ashe and his colleagues in counties throughout the state. It finally was passed by the Senate on Nov. 20, 1985 but the House was still haggling on details in late December. After all the legislative wrangling, the "takeover" bill died at the end of the legislative session for 1985. All this left county government planning in a state of limbo until all the political fog had cleared.

Undeterred, Sheriff Ashe continued his efforts to transform the post-incarceration lives of inmates aimed at reducing the social problem of recidivism. In 1986, Ashe instituted the nation's first Day Reporting Center which closely supervised and supported community re-entry efforts of inmates living at home at the end of their sentence. He also instituted the nation's first correctional After Incarceration Support Systems Program to assist inmates during the crucial first months after their release into the community.

ABOVE: Hampden County sheriff's deputies Michael Kolendo, Lt. Charles Camerlin and Salvador Montalvo Jr. get ready to make their next move as they track down persons wanted on warrants for failure to pay child and spouse support. Photo by Mark M. Murray/ The Republican.

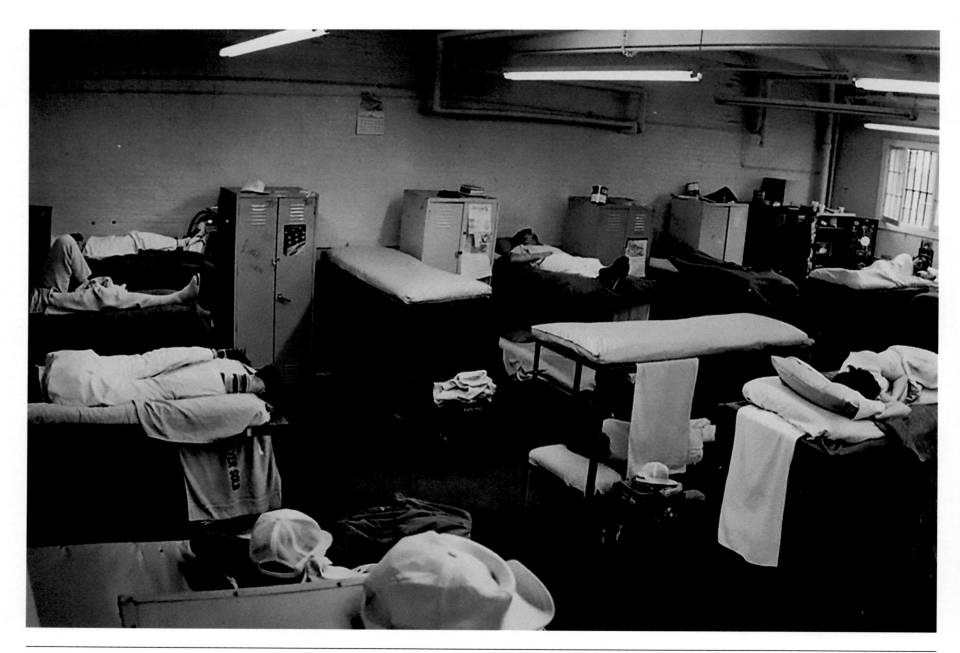

ABOVE: Photo of overcrowded conditions at York Street Jail during the 1980s. Photo by Vincent D. Addario/Union News.

By this time, Ashe and some of his talented staff were being recruited for significant positions in government at the State level and began receiving employment offers from other parts of the country. However, Ashe and his devoted staff were committed to the program they had begun in Hampden County and he was determined to run for a third term of office to complete his goals of corrections reform. County Commissioners Leonard J. Collamore and Richard Thomas, Springfield Mayor Richard E. Neal and Chicopee Mayor Richard S. Lak, Hampden County District Attorney Matthew J. Ryan, Jr., and several state senators, representatives and city councilors attended Sheriff's Ashe's re-election announcement on April 22, 1986. Thanking those in attendance, Sheriff Ashe said, "My pledge is to continue to serve the citizens of Hampden County in an honest, committed, and dignified manner," and "as Sheriff of Hampden County my duty is to maintain a clean, humane, and safe facility for those in our custody. To this end, I feel that we have been successful."

Throughout his campaign for a third term, Ashe did not shy away from the negative local politics of choosing a new jail site. Exploring possibilities in Agawam, Westfield, and West Springfield could have cost him the election. Nevertheless, Ashe and County Commissioner Collamore were both easily re-elected. Clearly, the public did not blame the sheriff for the prison crisis.

All the while, overcrowding at the jail continue to loom as a "powder-keg," and Ashe re-doubled his lobbying for solutions, and in particular, for a new jail specifically designed for modern approaches to corrections. Meanwhile, the Sheriff had to approach the State's Parole Board for approval for the early release of 20 inmates. In November of 1986, "extreme crowding" was blamed for forcing early releases of some prisoners. In December, Ashe pioneered the use of "electronic bracelets" in Massachusetts along with the early releases of inmates, and his day reporting system supervised by Kevin Warwick to combat prison overcrowding. The inmates eligible for the program were those considered "low risk" to the community.

The Sheriff began his third term in January of 1987 with ominous news with headline in the *Springfield Daily News* on January 8th: "Ashe: Jail Goes Broke This Month." In February, Ashe began meeting with District Attorney Matthew Ryan and Hampden County Court judges about the crowding issue, stating that Ryan "certainly doesn't want federal judge Frank Freedman and the federal government running the Hampden County Jail." He was referring to the federal consent decree between Hampden County and its prisoners over changes in the jail to alleviate overcrowding.

Soon after, the *Valley Advocate* wrote about the jail overcrowding with the incendiary headline, "Powder keg on York Street, Has its Luck About to Run Out?" An editorial in the *Springfield Daily News* entitled "A Perilous Situation" described the crisis: "Inmates are sleeping in hallways, in the boiler room, the mezzanine, in a recent addition that was meant to be a gymnasium, and in short, in every nook and cranny of the century-old structure." The editorial pointed out that "one of the problems has been the heavy influx of people jailed while awaiting trial." At that time, the jail handled about 5,000 individuals in that category of incarceration each year and that at the time of this editorial there were 244 inmates at the jail awaiting trial. All the while, Sheriff Ashe was doing everything he could to forestall the crisis.

On August 24, 1988, Sheriff Ashe requested $290,000 in additional money for about 200 jail employees who were not included in a pay-raise allocation for the jail guards' union in the 1989 state budget. The sheriff stated that the jails needed an additional $27 million from the state to meet all of their obligations and that Hampden County's share of the $80.5 million was "just a maintenance budget." The rate of incarcerations had brought the crisis to a head and Ashe was forced to put his foot down.

Overcrowding reached its boiling point on September 21 when 150 inmates of a total of 696 prisoners at York Street protested and for an hour refused to return to their cells from the enclosed recreation yard. The Springfield Police Department sent over 40 uniformed and plain clothes police officers to the scene to support the Correctional officers on duty at the time. In the end, the entire situation was handled by the jail staff. Sheriff Ashe was attending a Hampden County Commission meeting to discuss overcrowding at the jail when he was alerted by his staff. He immediately returned to the jail to reason with the protesting inmates. Ashe bravely strode into the yard and communicated with the inmates that they should peacefully return to their cells with the promise that he would meet with three inmates representing the group to discuss issues such as contact visiting, crowded conditions, and changes of clothes for prisoners on the following day. The inmates then relented and agreed to return to their cells. Ashe told reporters, "Overcrowding is the key issue, here."

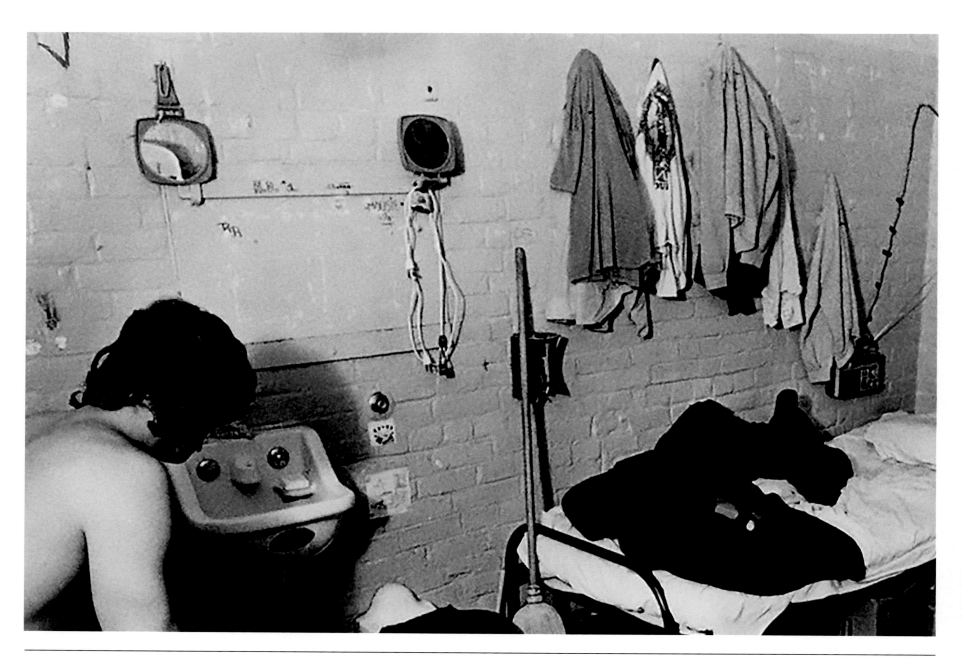

ABOVE: A cell in maximum security area in York Street Jail. Three living in cell built for at most two illustrates the problem of overcrowding. Photo by Kevin Twombly/Union News.

Elizabeth L. Curtin, Director of Community Corrections for the Crime and Justice Foundation, a non-profit group that studied the prison system and operated day programs for inmates was impressed with Sheriff Ashe's response to the inmate's one-hour "strike." Curtin said that compared to most prison systems, the York Street jail "is run in an extremely humane manner." She felt that was the reason why "he was able to walk into the yard, talk with them, and ask them to go inside, which they did." She noted that "You could put the same conditions somewhere else and have a lot of trouble." One newspaper article that reported the incident was headlined, "Sheriff's Style Kept Lid on Trouble." Indeed, Sheriff Ashe had calmed things down for the moment but even he knew that the peace would not last forever if conditions didn't change for the better.

The sheriff awarded a letter of commendation to his entire staff for "actions consistent with the highest standards of criminal justice professionals" by "continuing to maintain a safe, secure, orderly facility despite record heat and overcrowding this summer." He particularly appreciated their restraint during the recent inmate protest calling it "a heroic accomplishment" in avoiding a prison riot that summer. Ashe was gratified that his staff had adopted his non-violent approach and put it into practice that day.

On October 18, 1988, Ashe boldly announced that he refused to accept additional inmates at the York Street Jail. Two days later, the Hampden County District Court officially "froze" jail inmate admissions. On Nov. 2, the Sheriff made it clear that a new jail site was the only viable solution to this perennial problem. Supporting Ashe's position

ABOVE: Portable housing unit at the York Street Jail. Photo by Mark M. Murray/The Republican.

regarding the need for a new jail, the Hampden County Commissioners and the state approved architects announced their opposition to the renovation of the York Street jail which was deemed impractical. As almost a slap in the face, the State legislature rejected extra funding for jails on Feb. 14, 1989. The media throughout the state began publishing a stream of editorials, letters to the editor, front-page articles, television reporting and opinion pieces disapproving of the legislature's action.

U.S. District Court Magistrate, Michael A. Ponsor ordered the earliest Hampden County prisoner release to date with prisoners being set free after serving only one-third of their sentences. Earlier court orders provided for the release of prisoners after serving at least 50% of their sentence. As jail overcrowding continued throughout the year, Ponsor "ripped jail crowding" in the press in November, declaring that he "cannot order a new jail built sooner, but he can apply pressure to speed up the process by cracking down on inmate overcrowding."

In April of that year, state officials had changed their view and recommended Agawam as the site for a new Hampden County jail. Agawam town leaders immediately vowed to fight that proposal. The same response was met with site plans for a Westfield, and a West Springfield site. Neither community

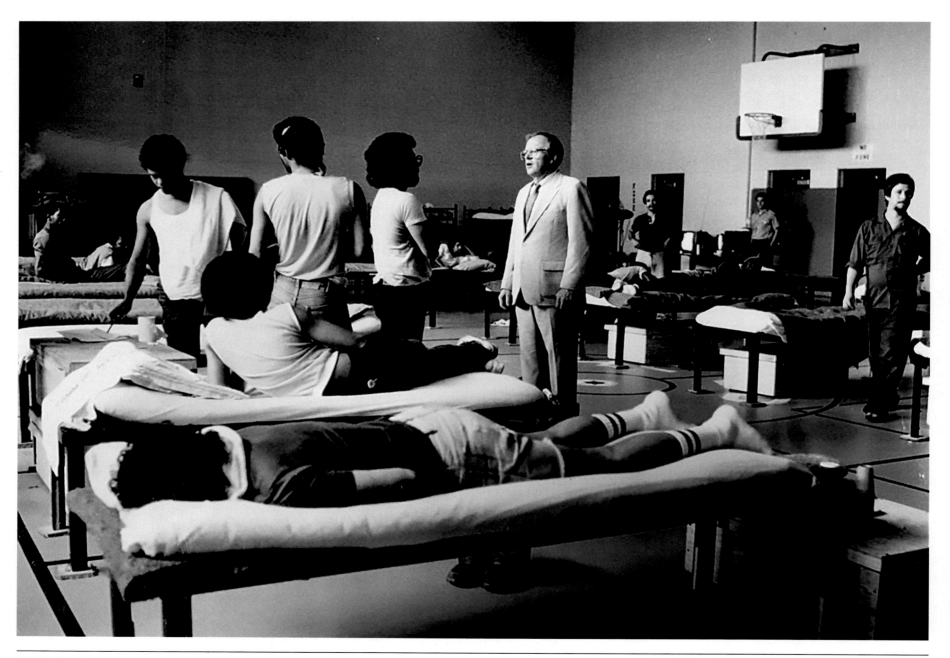

ABOVE: Sheriff Michael Ashe talking with inmates at the York St. jail gymnasium during a tour of the building, June 9, 1987. Due to overcrowding, the gym was being used to house inmates. Republican file photo.

wanted it in their "back yard." Taylor Street in Springfield was another location hotly debated by local politicians and residents, eventually being rejected. Despite the Sheriff's considerable skill at diplomacy, lobbying, and public relations, he could not change the public attitude towards his jail plans in any of those three communities. At a "Jail Summit" in April, the Agawam site was finally rejected and a new idea for a jail in Ludlow was proposed.

After much debate and negotiations, the bill to acquire the land for the Ludlow site advanced through the legislature and on Dec. 28 the Massachusetts House passed the bill with the Senate following suit the next day sending the bill to the governor for his final signature. But the pace was too slow to forestall the looming crisis of overcrowding. The federal court order capped the number of inmates allowed at York Street at 500 and as a result in the past year over 1,200 prisoners had to be released before serving their full sentences. It was looking like there would be a repeat of this number if not more in 1990.

After a decade of lobbying for a new facility to alleviate overcrowding at the jail, Sheriff Ashe felt that time had come to act boldly. On Feb. 16, 1990, Ashe dramatically commandeered the National Guard armory on Roosevelt Avenue in Springfield in order to house prisoners. Finding legal standing for his actions, Sheriff Ashe invoked the 17th Century Massachusetts law that empowered county sheriffs to do so when there was an "imminent danger of a breach of the peace." Sheriff Ashe argued that the severe overcrowding posed an "imminent danger." The National Guard was stunned by the action, and the news quickly went around the United States as one of the top news stories of the day. It remained to be seen whether this action would lead to the creation of a new jail, or legal action against the Sheriff.

ABOVE: Court yard view of interior of the York Street jail complex. Republican file photo.

ABOVE: York Street Hampden County Jail in Springfield, Sep. 4, 1989. Photo by Michelle Segall/Republican file photo.

ABOVE: Clippings of newspaper headlines regarding overcrowding at the York Street jail. Republican archives.

ABOVE: Sheriff Michael J. Ashe stands in front of the Hampden County House of Correction on Oct. 19, 1988 announcing that he will not accept new inmates at the jail due to overcrowding. Dave Roback/Republican file photo.

OPPOSITE PAGE: Springfield police gather outside the York Street Hampden County Jail as they await further orders on their participation in the inmate disturbance at the jail Sep. 21, 1988. Republican file photo by Mark M. Murray.

RIGHT: Hampden County Sheriff Michael Ashe walks by a jail guard holding a shotgun as he walks out of the jail to brief press on the events surrounding an inmate disturbance Sept. 21, 1988. Photo by Mark M. Murray/Republican.

Late City

Jail Sites In Agawam Considered

By BRAD SMITH

More than 300 acres of county-owned land on four parcels in Agawam are among the...

Governor seeks to expedite construction

By GLENN A. BRIERE
Statehouse bureau chief

BOSTON — Gov. Michael S. Dukakis asked the Legislature yesterday to give his administration sweeping powers to fast-track prison jail construction...

Hazardous waste cited as Taylor Street site hurdle

BOSTON — A proposal to shift temporary Hampden County Jail unit from Westfield to downtown Springfield could be considered until hazardous waste on the Taylor Street site is cleaned up, state Inspector General Joseph R. Barresi said yesterday.

Senator: New jail state's only option

The Morning Union

SPRINGFIELD, MASSACHUSETTS, WEDNESDAY, FEBRUARY 18, 1987

...eliminated as jail si...

SPELD. UNION Thurs. 1-1-87
Lak rules out sites
Chicopee for jail

SPELD. DAILY NEWS Tues. Dec. 30, 1986
'It Deters From the Property-Tax Base'

Opposition Grows to Jail Site

By MARIE P. GRADY

WEST SPRINGFIELD — Selectmen have firmed their resolve against locating a new $51-million county jail here...

Budd: Public must accept jails

By BRAD SMITH

Acting U.S. Attorney Wayne Budd called yesterday for an end to jail overcrowding...

BUDD WITH BOLAND — Acting U.S. Attorney Wayne Budd, left, walks with retired Congressman Edward Boland of Springfield outside Hampden County Jail on York Street yesterday.

West Side Firms Opposition To Proposed County Jail Site

THE MORNING UNION, WEDNESDAY,

10 MS THE MORNING UNION, THURSDAY, JANUARY 22, 1987

Bipartisan campaign fights jail site at Bondi's

By LESLIE PHENNER

WEST SPRINGFIELD — The Democratic and Republican town committees hope to collect "thousands" of sig...

Ashe critical of House vote concerning jail

...ringfield for jail

West Side board will deny temporary jail

Union-News

25 CENTS

Springfield Union-News

WEDNESDAY, SEPTEMBER 16, 1987

...for jail siting

...eal proposes Taylor St. s...

By BRAD SMITH

...MONDAY, OCTOBER 3, 1989

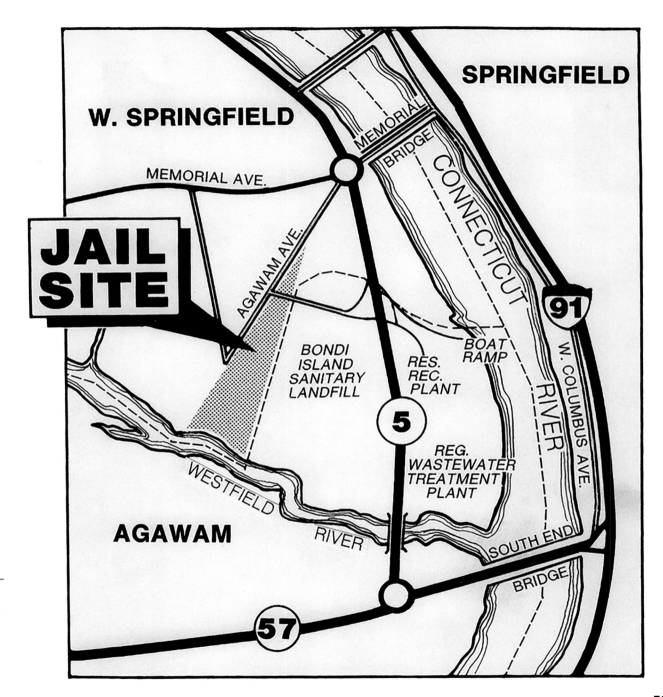

JAIL SITE

W. SPRINGFIELD

SPRINGFIELD

MEMORIAL AVE.

MEMORIAL BRIDGE

CONNECTICUT RIVER

91

AGAWAM AVE.

BONDI ISLAND SANITARY LANDFILL

RES. REC. PLANT

BOAT RAMP

W. COLUMBUS AVE.

5

REG. WASTEWATER TREATMENT PLANT

WESTFIELD RIVER

AGAWAM

SOUTH END BRIDGE

57

OPPOSITE PAGE: Clippings of newspaper headlines regarding proposed sites for a new Hampden County jail. Republican archives.

RIGHT: Proposed Bondi's Island site in West Springfield. Courtesy Hampden County Sheriff's Department.

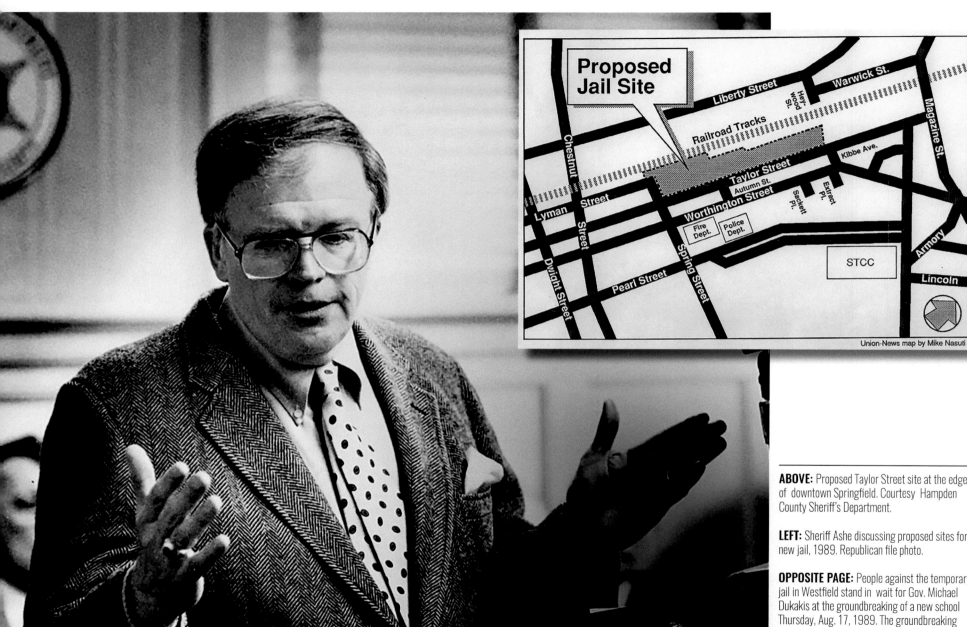

Proposed Jail Site

Liberty Street
Warwick St.
Hey'wood St.
Railroad Tracks
Chestnut Street
Kibbe Ave.
Taylor Street
Magazine St.
Autumn St.
Lyman Street
Worthington Street
Extract Pl.
Sackett Pl.
Dwight Street
Fire Dept.
Police Dept.
Spring Street
Pearl Street
STCC
Armory
Lincoln

Union-News map by Mike Nasuti

ABOVE: Proposed Taylor Street site at the edge of downtown Springfield. Courtesy Hampden County Sheriff's Department.

LEFT: Sheriff Ashe discussing proposed sites for new jail, 1989. Republican file photo.

OPPOSITE PAGE: People against the temporary jail in Westfield stand in wait for Gov. Michael Dukakis at the groundbreaking of a new school Thursday, Aug. 17, 1989. The groundbreaking was at the Paper Mill playground. Photo by Dave Roback/The Republican.

CHAPTER THREE B
HUMAN SERVICE PROGRAMS

A BRIEF HISTORY OF HUMAN SERVICES PROGRAMS AT THE HAMPDEN COUNTY JAIL AND HOUSE OF CORRECTION

By Bill Toller

Editors note: Oct. 25, 1976, Sheriff Michael J. Ashe, Jr., and Jay Ashe, Deputy Superintendent of Human Services hired Bill Toller as Education Coordinator, one of the first human services appointments in Jail History.

One of my first tasks was to assess the educational needs of the jail and house of correction population that numbered about 180 inmates at that time. The previous four years I had worked in a private residential special education school in Connecticut where I had learned about the new federal special education law-94-142-that required education for everyone with special needs, including those in jail, up to the age of 22, or when they completed high school. My initial surveys and those surveys conducted by staff on a special project from the Department of Education revealed that over 80% of the inmate population had not completed high school and over 50% of the population were under the age of 22.

The 1976 level of programming was two teachers, two nights a week for two hours, from the Onward with Learning or OWL program from the City of Springfield and its Adult Education Director, Ray Morrow. The first night I observed class at the jail I discovered that the teachers had no books, no paper, and

ABOVE: Sheriff Michael J. Ashe, Jr. standing on second level of the main cell block at York Street jail, September 1985. Photo by John Suchocki/ Republican file photo.

no pencils. I knew that I was needed! Our current enrollment of potential special education students at that time was five students.

As I continued to pursue the goal of finding additional resources for our program through the federal law and Massachusetts Chapter 766 (the federal law was modeled after our law), I continually called the Director of Special Education in Springfield. Since she never returned any of my calls, I showed up in West Springfield one Thursday afternoon for the Regional Special Education meeting at the Department of Education. I introduced myself to her as "the guy from the jail" and she smiled. She looked at me and said, "You look like a nice young man. We didn't want those kids when they were in our schools, and we certainly don't want them now." When I asked her about the law, she replied, "Oh, that's okay. I retire next year. Somebody else can deal with that!" I knew I had my work cut out for me! Her attitude was a common one I encountered in our first years of developing programs.

In early 1979, we learned of a class action lawsuit filed in *Greenfield-Green v. Department of Education* and the four Western Mass Sheriffs who were representing a young man with a special need who was incarcerated in the Greenfield jail. That case ultimately ended up in Judge Frank H. Freedman's federal court in Springfield. It was clear that the court was to decide the issue of who was responsible for education behind the walls-the State Department of Education or the sheriffs. We were part of several high-level meetings with the staff from the Department of Education before the court's decision. I remember vividly when Judge Freedman decided against the Department of Education- that they were re-

ABOVE: Interior of York Street jail. Republican file photo.

sponsible for funding education. The Associate Commissioner of Education looked at me and said, "Don't worry, Bill. We'll be out of this decision in a year."

Forty-one years later, full-time special education staff are still teaching at our Ludlow facility. This decision opened the doors for full-time education at the York Street Jail, funded by Adult Education and Title I grants.

In March 1987, Governor Michael Dukakis visited our program, which had been recognized as a model adult education in the state. Two weeks after that visit, he announced his run for the Democratic nomination for President. From 1976 until 1992, over 2,000 inmate students completed their GED through our program efforts. An additional 1,500 students completed their GED before my retirement in 2004.

ABOVE: Looking over the day's yield from the Hampden County Jail Farm off River Road in Agawam Aug. 12, 1987 are guard Mike Moynihan, county commissioner Len Collamore, county commissioner Richard S. Thomas, Hampden County sheriff Michael J. Ashe Jr., and farm supervisor Nate Sherwood. Republican file photo by Dave Roback.

VOCATIONAL TRAINING

When I was interviewed for the Education Coordinator position, the interview panel was Jay Ashe and Frank Gulluni, who was the Director of the Hampden District Regional Skills Center, a CETA-funded program, that was located on Main Street, two blocks from our program. Frank had helped the Sheriff's Department to begin a satellite vocational program inside the jail six months before I was hired by writing a grant for this initial effort and helping us to locate space for this program. We were able to find an old coal bin which was converted into space for a welding program and machine shop, and a garage which became the space for a Business course, electronics assembly training, and a graphic arts program. Frank provided staff who were working part-time with us and part-time at his Skills Center.

One of my first meetings with Frank after being hired was a luncheon meeting at his Skills Center on Main Street with Jay and Sheriff Ashe. Also in attendance was Ron, who provided staff supervision for Frank's staff. After lunch, Frank looked at Ron and said, "Ron, what do we have today?" Ron went through a long list of all the jail staff's errors in getting students to training on time, miscommunications among staff, lack of support, etc. Since I was new, I had no response to Ron's concerns, and it was obvious that both Jay and the sheriff were quite upset. Sheriff Ashe took me aside and said very succinctly, "Billy, your job is to make sure that we never

RIGHT: Bishop Joseph Maguire of the Catholic Diocese of Springfield passing out prayer cards to inmates after Christmas mass, Dec. 25, 1980, guard Bruce Strange looks on. Photo by Kevin Twombly/Republican file photo.

ABOVE: Corrections staff interacting with inmates in cafeteria ca. 1983. Republican file photo.

ABOVE: Sheriff Ashe with a work crew from the Pre-release Center cleaning a stretch of West Street in Ludlow, July 24, 1997. Republican file photo.

have a meeting like this again." Thankfully, we never did!

In 1978, the Sheriff's Department had the opportunity, with Frank Gulluni's help, to apply directly for a state grant to enable our program to be full-time for vocational students which now numbered thirty-five daily. I became the manager and vocational counselor for the program. Frank's staff were now our staff. In 1981, the passage of the Job Training Partnership Act (JTPA) enabled us to become fully integrated into the Hampden County Employment and Training System. We became the only county jail program funded

nationally under JTPA and became responsible for student outcomes as a result. From 1981 to 1992, we maintained a 70% job placement rate and received funding every year for achieving this goal. Our partnership with the Springfield Employment Resource Center, led by Donna Hobart, provided job training and aftercare services for our graduating students upon their release from custody. Like our program, Donna and her staff utilized the Pre-Employment training Program developed under the Model Inmate Employment Program of 1974 which helped inmates in achieving the soft skills to secure and maintain employment. This was

DEVELOPMENT OF YORK STREET INDUSTRIES

In 1985, Sheriff Ashe, Jay Ashe, and I were approached by members of the Springfield Chamber of Commerce, led by Bob Schwarz who worked for Peter Pan Bus Lines, about Chief Justice Warren Burger's idea that jails and prisons should "become factories behind fences." After two years of planning, Frank Gulluni provided space for our new program at the Massachusetts Career Development Institute on Wilbraham Avenue in Springfield. Joe Trevathan, Pretrial Services Manager, was appointed our first manager and Ralph Kudla, then a Bible Studies volunteer, became our shop supervisor. Initially, twelve trainees from York Street came daily in a van to Wilbraham Avenue. Our product line consisted of assembled secretarial chairs that were sold to state agencies. Mike Mastriani, a young correctional officer on the midnight shift, became our second shop supervisor in 1989 and program manager in 2007. This program continues today in Ludlow with a huge sewing operation, upholstery repair, cafes in the community, and other items produced in our graphic arts program and construction trades program.

- Bill Toller

end was held that February Presidents' Day weekend and twenty inmates participated in a garage across our yard area. Two years later, volunteers Ray LaFlamme and Al DiPietro worked with me to organize our second REC weekend with twenty-five inmates and twenty team members. Since that weekend in 1984, over 700 volunteer team members and 6,000 inmates have participated in the over 250 weekends that have occurred in the past thirty-six years. Nine weekends a year occur now in medium security, the women's jail and our Recovery and Wellness Center. Over thirty ex-offenders and volunteers attend community fellowship meetings every Thursday night at Trinity United Methodist Church, a program that has been offered for over twenty years. It truly is the most transformative program that the Sheriff's Department offers.

OTHER VOLUNTEER PROGRAMS

DECISIONAL TRAINING - This program was developed by Rudy Praetz and Anne Bewsee and continued under Anne's daughter, Michaelann, until the early eighties. Inmate participants were taught decision-making skills in a lecture format and then were matched with individual volunteers for follow-up. Many of these skills were later taught in our Pre-employment Training Program.

COLLEGE INTERNSHIPS - Initially coordinated through the efforts of our first volunteer coordinator, Larry Gormally, college internships are now coordinated by me for students from local colleges who are matched with our staff. These internships are for a semester or entire school year,

LEFT: Michael V. Fair (L), Massachusetts Commissioner of Corrections awarding the Certificate of Accreditation to Joseph Nicholson (Center), Director of the Hampden County Pre-release Center, and Sheriff Michael J. Ashe, Jr. Photo by Vincent S. D'Addario/Union-News.

now part of our vocational curriculum. In 1992, all of our vocational staff became full-time jail staff on the Sheriff's budget as we moved to our new facility in Ludlow.

SPIRITUAL PROGRAMS-REC

When Sheriff Ashe took office in 1975, the only spiritual programs were an English Bible Study program that met one evening a week and religious services that met on Sundays, led by Protestant Chaplain Benjamin Lockhart and Catholic Chaplain Father Michael Doyle. In 1982, Sheriff Ashe was approached by Roman Catholic Deacon Bob Morrissey about conducting a Catholic three-day retreat in the jail for twenty inmates. The first REC-Residents Encounter Christ-Week-

depending on the student's major. Hundreds of students have completed successful internships with our department during the past forty years.

BIBLE STUDIES - Bible studies have expanded to seven nights a week, in both English and Spanish, over the years. Our three chaplains- Catholic, Protestant, and Muslim, utilize volunteers to assist them in their spiritual formation offerings and religious services now in Ludlow.

OTHER PROGRAMS

SEXUAL ABUSE TREATMENT PROGRAM - This program, organized by Roy Dudley, MSW, offered intense individual counseling and group work for sex offenders. Dr. Tom Lachiusa developed a domestic violence curriculum for our offenders after our move to Ludlow.

OTHER IMPORTANT PROGRAM DATES:

1975 - The Pre-Release Program was developed in the old Sheriff's House on York Street.

1981 - Jay Ashe developed and implemented the nation's first Day Reporting Program.

1985 - Brown v. Ashe lawsuit-which led to a cap on York Street and our new jail in Ludlow.

1986 - Opening of the Western Massachusetts Correctional Alcohol Center on Howard Street in Springfield.

HISTORICAL REFLECTIONS OF THE YORK STREET YEARS

My first recollection of the York Street Jail was as a volunteer for the Decisional Training Program. Trained over a volunteer weekend in Springfield by volunteers in the program and sponsored by the Council of Churches to learn to mentor and deliver a 12 week program face-to-face to a 17 year old offender. The jail was dimly lit in the evening, and the meetings took place in the jail rotunda visiting area. It was a great experience, and it was my first step in later applying for a fulltime grant position as an aftercare counselor. The rest became my life's work in Hampden County Corrections from November 1976 to April 2012, when I retired. I wouldn't trade a minute, after having worked with Sheriff Mike Ashe and Jay Ashe, and a host of many others, who also dedicated themselves to making continuous quality improvements in the safety, security and humane conditions of operating modern day correctional facilities.

During my tenure, my work included casework counseling offenders, aftercare services, pre-employment training program, and community reintegration of model offenders to the community. These are examples of the changing role of correctional staff working within the old facility. I am proud to have been part of the team that implemented continuous improvement strategies and systems in corrections of Hampden County Sheriff's Department.

Education programs involving group work treatment, high school equivalency classes, GED attainments, special education and tutoring and vocational skill training, a skills center, were just some of the many educational offerings that were just beginning. There was a continuing presence of spiritual volunteers who also provided meaningful contributions of the community. As the Sheriff always said, the jail should not be a fortress in the woods.

We were always striving to professionalize staff training and advancing toward national accreditation worthy of recognition, even though the old jail physical plant did not make it an easy task going forward.

Managing overcrowding conditions at York Street became ever more worrisome and difficult to maintain the standards of service delivery expected nationally without the financial limitations of county government at that time. Managing scarce resources was becoming a way of doing business. At one point it became inevitable for federal lawsuits on conditions of confinement and led to the ultimate end of county government and a necessary state takeover of Sheriff's Department fiscal funding by the Commonwealth of Massachusetts.

- Tom Rovelli

ABOVE: Sheriff Michael J. Ashe, Jr. addressing a community audience regarding the Western Massachusetts Correctional Addiction Center. Republican file photo.

THE HAMPDEN COUNTY DAY REPORTING CENTER:
THE FINAL PHASE IN A CONTINUUM OF COMMUNITY REINTEGRATION OF INMATES.

By Kevin Warwick, Director, Hampden County Day Reporting Center, and Richard McCarthy, Public Information Officer, Hampden County Sheriff's Department

The Hampden County Day Reporting Center in Springfield, Massachusetts serves as the final phase in a continuum of community reintegration for inmates that Sheriff Michael J. Ashe, Jr., began to put in place when he took office in 1974.

The Hampden County Day Reporting Center supervises and counsels men and women who are within four months of their parole or sentence termination date. Thus, Day Reporting participants are still serving their sentences in the custody of the Sheriff; they are still 'incarcerated', although not in the traditional sense. Participants have earned their way to the Day Reporting program to spend the final months of their sentences living at home and participating in the community, while being monitored and supported by Day Reporting Center Staff.

HISTORY

The Hampden County Day Reporting Center began operation in October 1986 with a grant through the Massachusetts Department of Correction. At the time that the program began operation, the Hampden County Jail and House of Correction had an inmate population nearly 300% of its capacity. Traditionally, corrections has weighted its efforts toward the ends

ABOVE: Kevin Warwick at the Day Reporting Center in Springfield, Dec. 27, 1996. Photo by Christopher Evans/ The Republican.

of a continuum of possible sanctions. Either inmates were held in 24 hour security situations, or were on probation or parole with only weekly or monthly contact with probation or parole officers. A Day Reporting Program was seen as an effort to explore some new ground in between the extremes.

The Crime and Justice Foundation approached the Hampden County Sheriff's Department with the idea of establishing the first Day Reporting Center because Sheriff Ashe had a history of acting on a philosophy of institution-based programming and community corrections, and a Day Reporting Center was seen as an extension of these efforts. The Sheriff's Department subsequently rented 311 State Street from C&W Reality owned by J. Michael Wallace and Fran Cataldo who renovated the building for that purpose. Also, the Hampden County Jail and House of Correction's location and population was urban and ethnically diverse, which made it ideally suited for a prototype Day Reporting Center. The Foundation's research also indicated that part of the reason

for the British system's success lay in the use of a centralized location for community supervision. Because of its thirteen year track record of successfully supervising residents in the community, the Hampden County Pre-Release Center (separated but connected to the House of Correction's Main Institution) was a logical site for the Day Reporting Center. Staff at the Pre-Release Center applied their experience to the new program.

PARTICIPANT POPULATIONS

Residents already housed in the Pre-Release Center or Western Massachusetts Correctional Alcohol Center, who work and participate in treatment programs, are eligible for Day Reporting as they near release dates. This includes both county inmates and state inmates transferred back to Hampden County at the end of their sentenced (In Massachusetts, criminals sentences to 2 ½ years or less are sentenced to County sentences; 2 ½ years or more, State sentences). Inmates serving short term sentences at the Hampden County Jail and House of Correction can come directly from the House of Correction to the Day Reporting Center, without spending time as a Pre-Release Participant. Federal Offenders are eligible to participate through contract between the Day Reporting Center and the Federal Bureau of Prisons.

The Day Reporting Center does not serve as a diversion program. No candidates are taken into the program from the courts; before participating they must serve a portion of their sentence in a secure setting. Crowding was one impetus for the program, and accepting participants who would have been given probation or suspended sentence would just serve to "widen the net."

ELIGIBILITY CRITERIA

To be accepted into the program the client must be screened by Day Reporting Center Staff and approved through the House of Correction Classification Committee. Through the assessment process, staff evaluate the offender's possible threat to the community and willingness to participate in treatment.

ORIENTATION

Once accepted into the program, many participants are asked to participate in a three week alcohol and drug education and treatment program designed for offenders with significant substance abuse problems (Educating Recovering Addicts.) The program also provides education on AIDS, employment search, reality therapy, and men's and women's issues. If the three week program is not needed, participants access a one week program (New Directions) designed specifically for short term offenders and those with less significant substance abuse issues. Both programs involve family participation, and both involve in-house and community meetings of Alcoholics Anonymous and Narcotics Anonymous. The Educating Recovering Addicts and New Directions programs are provided as part of the grant for the Day Reporting Center are operated by the Sheriff's Department Staff. All clients completing either the three week or one week program attend Aftercare Groups once per week for twelve weeks.

In addition to participation in these substance abuse programs, orientation includes assignation of a Counselor who works with clients in developing a treatment contract. Requirements may include attendance at High School Equivalency Classes, Alcoholics Anon-

ymous or Narcotics Anonymous meetings, or Community service, depending on participant's needs. Clients may participate in either community programs or those that are offered at the Pre-Release Center.

CORRECTIONS OFFICER NATHAN G. SHERWOOD SERVED 50 YEARS

By Chris Hamel
Springfield Union-News article Sept. 2, 1997

Born in 1923, Nathan G. "Nate" Sherwood was hired in 1947. Since then, he stayed at the department in one capacity or another, becoming by its estimate the longest-serving correctional officer in county history.

Thursday, Sherwood, a native of Huntington, will mark 50 years with the department and service with three sheriffs - David J. Manning, John G. Curley and Michael J. Ashe Jr.

In a sense, it all started with Sherwood's interest in vegetables. After graduating in 1947 from the Stockbridge School of Agriculture at the University of Massachusetts, he went to work raising corn, a spinoff of his studies in growing and marketing vegetables.

But he said his initial venture flopped, and he next sought work at the sheriff's department's Agawam farm, which is no longer in operation. The farm supplied produce for the jail's kitchen and used inmates from the house of correction, then on York Street here, to do its chores.

Because the prisoners needed supervision, the farm's supervisors had to be correctional officers, known then as jail guards. Sherwood, a

World War II veteran, became a farm supervisor and one of the department's 18 guards. His training was informal and brief.

"It was one officer talking to another," he said, noting that in those days there was no instruction in handcuffing techniques, self-defense or anything else.

In 1947, the work week was 48 hours and the starting pay was only $2,770 a year. Sherwood was given a handgun and the keys to a 1941 GMC truck, which was used to haul a 15-inmate work crew to and from the farm, twice a day.

He said the corrections world was so different then, that one of the 15 inmates - the designated "pig man," who worked alone with the farm's pigs - was allowed to ride next to him in the passenger seat of the truck, within reach of the handgun.

[Editor's note; Nathan G. Sherwood was 93 when he passed away Aug. 17, 2017].

ABOVE: Nate Sherwood with tractor at Agawam farm May 10, 1988. Photo by Dave Roback/The Republican.

ABOVE: William "Bill" Toller (L), Thomas and Carleen Rovelli (center and Right), working at the raffie table during Sheriff Michael Ashe's 38th Annual Clambake at the Elks Lodge in Springfield.
Photo by Mark M. Murray/The Republican.

CHAPTER FOUR
HISTORY OF THE SHERIFF'S CLAMBAKE/COOKOUT

ABOVE: Tom Gentile of Springfield District Court, left, and Springfield City Council member Bud L. Williams, right, talk with Hampden County Sheriff Michael J. Ashe during the 18th annual clambake at Riverside Park in Agawam, August 23, 1995. Photo by Dave Roback/The Republican.

HISTORY OF THE HAMPDEN COUNTY SHERIFF'S ANNUAL COOKOUT

By Wayne E. Phaneuf & Joseph Carvalho III

Hampden County Sheriff Nick Cocchi's Re-election Kickoff & Annual Cookout/Golf Tournament drew more than 1,500 people to the Elks Lodge #61 in Springfield on August 18, 2021 for the biggest political event of the year and the kickoff of his campaign for a second term. Supporters from all walks of life attended. The event continued to attract political leaders from across the state. Massachusetts Governor Charlie Baker, Lieutenant Governor Karyn Polito, Secretary of the Commonwealth William F. Galvin and other state officials as well as a number of candidates for state-wide office attended. Mayors from local communities such as Springfield Mayor Domenic Sarno, Agawam Mayor William P. Sapelli, Westfield Mayor Donald Humason, Jr., and other mayors spent the afternoon at the event. State Senators and State Representatives as well as Springfield City Councilors mingled with the large crowd. Sheriff Cocchi enthusiastically greeted each attendee as they arrived. After a year interrupted by the pandemic, the Sheriff's annual event was re-invigorated.

Clambakes and cookouts have a long tradition in New England. They are occasions for celebration and family and organizational gatherings. Sheriff Michael J. Ashe consciously employed this tradition as a means of building community support and political consensus for his innovative approach to Hampden County's correctional system. Successful from

ABOVE: Governor William Weld, left and Senator John Kerry, Right enjoy a light moment while standing on a table at The Riverside Park Pavillion as the two ran into each other at Sheriff Ashe's Annual Clambake, Aug. 21, 1996. Photo By Mark M. Murray/The Republican.

its inception, the Sheriff's Annual Clambake exceeded his expectations. Community leaders, and politicians from both sides of the aisle soon became regular attendees. Early on, Massachusetts Governors and other key state officials made it a point to attend the Sheriff's event. Ashe took those opportunities to build consensus over Corrections issues and needs in Hampden County. It was always a tall task to get Boston-based officials to come to Western Massachusetts, and even harder to get funding for Western Massachusetts needs. Yet, Sheriff Ashe succeeded where few have. Sheriff Nicolas Cocchi has continued that tradition. The event opens lines of communication, affirms old friendships and introduces new friends and supporters to the people and mission of the Hampden County Sheriff's Department.

It all began in 1974 when newly elected Sheriff Michael J. Ashe thanked over 3,000 of his campaign workers to a picnic at Turner Park in Longmeadow. It was such a rousing success that Sheriff Ashe decided to hold an annual picnic for Hampden County court officers, jail workers, and friends and supporters. The first annual picnic was in September of 1975 and 600 people attended the event held at the Polish-American Club grounds in Feeding Hills, Agawam. In 1977, Sheriff Ashe expanded the concept and reach of the event re-naming it a "clambake" which attracted public officials from all over Western Massachusetts as well as Massachusetts state officials.

By 1984, the Sheriff's clambake was recognized by the Springfield Republican as "without a doubt the political social highlight of each summer, bringing together hundreds of Western Massachusetts public officials. That

Sheriff Michael Ashe, Jr.
cordially invites you to attend the
SHERIFF'S CLAMBAKE
Wednesday, August 26, 1981
11:00 A.M. Lunch • 6:00 P. M. Dinner
Polish Club
Route 57, Feeding Hills, Mass.
TICKETS: $20.00 RAIN OR SHINE
James Tremble, 41 Farmington Ave.; Longmeadow

TOP: Sheriff Ashe's annual clambake was held at Riverside Park in Agawam. Here acting Governor Paul Cellucci talks with Scott Harshbarger, Aug. 19, 1998. Photo by Don Fontaine/The Republican.
LEFT: Hampden County Sheriff Mike Ashe, Left, With Friend Daniel Walsh During Ashe's Clambake At Riverside Park In Agawam, Aug. 19, 1998. Photo By Don Fontaine/The Republican.
INSET: Advertisement announcing Sheriff's Ashe's Clambake, 1981. Sunday Republican, August 23, 1981,

year the number of attendees had grown to over 1,400. By 1988, the 11th Annual Clambake had grown so popular that the event was held at the expansive Riverside Park's Picnic Grove (now Six Flags) in Agawam and was held at that location for many years.

In 1994, one pundit observed that "politics was as thick as the barbeque smoke yesterday at Hampden County Sheriff Michael J. Ashe's annual clambake." The clambake was typically the sheriff's only fund-raising event each year and local and state politicians seldom missed the opportunity to attend. In 2001, over 2,000 people enjoyed the festivities and food at the clambake including "most of the candidates for local and state offices." By 2005, the Springfield Republican newspaper referred to the Sheriff's clambake as "one of the region's annual premier political events." Every Massachusetts Governor from Dukakis, King, Weld, Cellucci, Patrick, to our current Governor Charles Baker marked their political calendars to attend this all-important Western Massachusetts event each summer.

In it's 35th year, the Sheriff's popular event continued to broaden its appeal to both political parties. The Republican reported that "politicians and political hopefuls from across Massachusetts mingled with voters, colleagues and even rivals at Hampden County Sheriff Michael Ashe's 35th annual clambake. Sheriff Ashe said, "I like to believe that this is about more than politics, and we all come together because we all know the value of serving the community." People close to him knew that he meant every word.

TOP: Hampden County Sheriff Michael Ashe, right, introduces State Senate President Thomas Birmingham to attendees of the Sheriff's clambake at Picnic Grove in Agawam, Aug. 23, 2000. Photo by Gretchen Ertl/ The Republican
RIGHT: Hampden County Sheriff Michael J. Ashe Jr., right, confers over clam chowder with sheriff's department employees Kathy E. Curley, Barry L. Telfond, left, and Jay A. Moylan during Ashe's 25th annual clambake in Springfield Aug. 21, 2002. Republican file photo.

TOP: Hampden County Sheriff Michael J. Ashe Jr., center, opens some clam together with Lt. John R. Geraci of East Longmeadow, left, and Don M. Mullen Sr. of Springfield. Geraci, a control supervisor at the Hampden County Correctional Facility at Stonybrook in Ludlow and Mullen, a retired medical officer who worked at the same facility. The annual clambake was held at Six Flags New England in Agawam, Aug. 21, 2003. Republican file photo.

In 2014, one reporter gleaned from the internet the following "Tweets:"

Great to be at Sheriff Ashe's legendary clambake in Springfield. - Cong. Richard Neal

Wouldn't miss Sheriff Ashe's annual clambake for anything. - Steve Kerrigan

It was great to catch up with Senator Elizabeth Warren and Sheriff Mike Ashe at his 36th annual clambake. - Bob Jubinville

For political candidates and elected officials, Sheriff Michael Ashe's Clambake is an event not to be missed.
- Suzanne Bump

Sheriff Ashe, who started the event in an effort to build on his predecessor John G. Curley's tradition of holding Wednesday afternoon lunches with area lawyers, said the clambake — which anyone can attend — highlighted his focus on community corrections. "When I think of my work, it's been more community corrections. We know that all of the inmates return to the community, so that's sort of a theme we had in mind in terms of bringing a lot of agencies together," he said in an interview. The sheriff, who said the event typically draws about 1-2,000 people, contended that it joins together those who believe in what the Hampden County Sheriff's Department has been doing, including high-profile politicians from Beacon Hill and Washington, D.C. "It brings in people from the Boston area who also impact our budget and our policies," he said. "As we know, whether it's a U.S. senator or the governor, they always make it a point to come." 2016 was Michael Ashe's final clambake, but Sheriff Nick Cocchi continued the tradition and faithfully held the ever-popular event each year until the 2020 Covid-19 epidemic precluded events with large gatherings.

ABOVE: Sally J. Van Wright of South Hadley, left, John M. Hale of Chicopee and Adrienne C. Osborn of Springfield at the Hampden County Sheriff Michael J. Ashe's annual Clambake at Six Flags New England in Agawam, Aug. 15, 2007. Republican file photo.

ABOVE: U.S. Senate candidate Elizabeth Warren and Congressman Richard E. Neal at a press availability during Sheriff Michael Ashe's 35th annual clambake at the Springfield Elks Lodge #61 in Springfield, Aug. 15, 2012. Photo by Dave Roback/ The Republican.

ABOVE: Scenes from the Hampden County Sheriff Michael J. Ashe Jr.'s 33rd annual Sheriff's Clambake at the Six Flags Picnic Grove in Agawam. Here Congressman John W. Olver, left, met with former Springfield City Councilman Morris Jones, Aug. 18, 2010.
Photo by Dave Roback/The Republican.

RIGHT: Springfield Mayors William Sullivan, left and present Mayor Domenic J. Sarno talk during Sheriff Michael Ashe's 35th annual clambake at the Springfield Elks Lodge #61 in Springfield, Aug. 15, 2012.
Photo by Dave Roback/ The Republican.

ABOVE: Scenes from the Hampden County Sheriff Michael J. Ashe Jr.'s 33rd annual Sheriff's Clambake at the Six Flags Picnic Grove in Agawam. Here Berkshire County Sheriff Carmen C. Massimiano Jr., Gov. Deval L. Patrick and Ashe gather for a group photo, Aug. 18, 2010. Photo by Dave Roback/The Republican.

ABOVE: Scenes from the Hampden County Sheriff Michael J. Ashe Jr.'s 33rd annual Sheriff's Clambake at the Six Flags Picnic Grove in Agawam. Here Secretary of State William Galvin, left talks with Raymond H. Feyre of Holyoke, Aug. 18, 2010. Photo by Dave Roback/The Republican.

RIGHT TOP: Scenes from the Hampden County Sheriff Michael J. Ashe Jr.'s 33rd annual Sheriff's Clambake at the Six Flags Picnic Grove in Agawam. Here from left are Chicopee Mayor Michael D. Bissonnette, State Rep. Rosemary Sandlin, D-Agawam and State Rep Cheryl Coakley Rivera, D- Springfield, Aug. 18, 2010.
Photo by Dave Roback/The Republican.

RIGHT: Scenes from the Hampden County Sheriff Michael J. Ashe Jr.'s 33rd annual Sheriff's Clambake at the Six Flags Picnic Grove in Agawam. Here Raymond A. Jordan Jr. , left shares a laugh with Walter A. DeFilippi, right, Aug. 18, 2010. Photo by Dave Roback/The Republican.

LEFT: Scenes from the Hampden County Sheriff Michael J. Ashe Jr.'s 33rd annual Sheriff's Clambake at the Six Flags Picnic Grove in Agawam. Here Republican candidate for governor Charles D. Baker tours the clambake with State Rep. Donald F. Humason Jr., R-Westfield, center, and State Senator Michael R. Knapik, R-Westfield, right , Aug. 18, 2010.
Photo by Dave Roback/The Republican.

ABOVE: Hampden County Sheriff Michael Ashe held his 37th annual clambake at the Springfield Elks Lodge 61 in Springfield. Here is candidate for Hampden County Sheriff Nick Cocchi, right, with Sheriff Ashe. Photo by Dave Roback/The Republican.

ABOVE: Hampden County Sheriff Michael Ashe held his 37th annual clambake at the Springfield Elks Lodge 61 in Springfield. Photo by Dave Roback/The Republican.

ABOVE: Hampden County Sheriff Michael Ashe held his 37th annual clambake at the Springfield Elks Lodge 61 in Springfield. Here Ashe has a photo taken with Keisha Melvin-Lee.
Photo by Dave Roback/The Republican.

TOP RIGHT: Hampden County Sheriff Michael Ashe held his 37th annual clambake at the Springfield Elks Lodge #61 in Springfield. Here is United State Marshal John Gibbons. Republican file photo.

RIGHT: State Senator Donald Humason, left with Sheriff Michael Ashe at the sheriff's 37th Annual Clambake at the Springfield Elks Lodge #61. Photo by Mark M. Murray/The Republican.

ABOVE: The hard working "clam crew" at Hampden Sheriff Michael Ashe's annual clambake, including the captain of the clambake for all 38 years, Lt. John Geraci, retired from the Sheriff's Department, at center to the right of the pole. His sister, volunteer Linda Chiarizio, is to the left of him on the other side of the pole, August 19, 2015.
Photo by Michael S. Gordon / The Republican.

LEFT: Guests at Hampden Sheriff Michael Ashe's 38th clambake at Springfield Elks Lodge #61 included former Chicopee and candidate for Mayor Michael Bissonnette talking with Marjorie Hurst of Springfield, August 19, 2015.
Photo by Dave Roback / The Republican.

ABOVE: Guests at Hampden Sheriff Michael Ashe's 38th clambake at Springfield Elks Lodge #61 included Hampden County District Attorney Anthony D. Gulluni, left, and former Hampden County District Attorney William Bennett. August 19, 2015.

TOP RIGHT: Guests at Hampden Sheriff Michael Ashe's 38th clambake at Springfield Elks Lodge #61 included West Springfield Mayor Edward Sullivan with Massachusetts Lt. Gov Karyn Polito (Joan Kagan is center, with Tim Rooke on far right). August 19, 2015.

RIGHT: Guests at Hampden Sheriff Michael Ashe's 38th clambake at Springfield Elks Lodge #61 included Joan Kagan, President and CEO of Square One, left, and Candy Glazer Chairwoman of the Longmeadow Democratic Committee, August 19, 2015.
Photos by Dave Roback / The Republican.

ABOVE: Chicopee Police Chief William Jebb, left, and Nick Cocchi, deputy chief of security for the Hampden County Sheriff's Department, at Hampden Sheriff Michael Ashe's 38th clambake at Springfield Elks Lodge #61. August 19, 2015. Photo by Michael S. Gordon / The Republican.

LEFT TOP: Guests at Hampden Sheriff Michael Ashe's 38th clambake at Springfield Elks Lodge #61 included from left, Candejah Pink, Springfield mayoral candidate Michael Jones, Springfield City Council candidate Jesse Lederman and Emila Ponikiewski, August 19, 2015. Photo by Michael S. Gordon / The Republican.

LEFT: Guests at Hampden Sheriff Michael Ashe's 38th clambake at Springfield Elks Lodge #61 included former Springfield Mayor, and retired Judge Mary Hurley, August 19, 2015.
Photo of Dave Roback / The Republican.

ABOVE: People on hand at Sheriff Michael Ashes' 38th Annual Clambake at the Elks Lodge in Springfield.
Photo by Mark M. Murray / The Republican.

RIGHT TOP: Guests at Hampden Sheriff Michael Ashe's 38th Clambake at Springfield Elks Lodge #61 included from left, Edward Daly, Joe Beaulieu and Karo Schmaelzle with the Holyoke Credit Union, August 19, 2015. Photo by Michael S. Gordon / The Republican.

RIGHT: Some of the hard working "clam crew" at Hampden Sheriff Michael Ashe's annual clambake, including the captain of the clambake for all 38 years, Lt. John Geraci, left, retired from the Sheriff's Department, and other department members from left, Wayne Hughes, Angel Rivera, Jason Merced, Dino Perez and Sgt. Kevin Sloat, August 19, 2015.
Photo by Michael S. Gordon / The Republican.

ABOVE: Sheriff Michael J. Ashe holds his 39th annual clambake at the Springfield Elks Lodge #61. Here candidate for Hampden county Sheriff Nick Cocchi has a photo taken with Gov. Charlie Baker and Ashe, Aug. 17, 2016.
Photo by Dave Roback / The Republican.

ABOVE: Guests, including Collin Burnett, an estimator with Hickman and Sgroi Electric Inc, and a member of IBEW local 7, line up for steamed clams at Springfield Elks Lodge #61, August 19, 2015.
Photo of Michael S. Gordon / The Republican.

TOP RIGHT: Sheriff Michael J. Ashe holds his 39th annual clambake at the Springfield Elks Lodge #61. Here Rich Devine chats with Springfield Bishop Mitchell Rozanski, Aug. 17, 2016.
Photo by Dave Roback / The Republican.

RIGHT: Sheriff Michael J. Ashe holds his 39th annual clambake at the Springfield Elks Lodge #61, Aug. 17, 2016.
Photo by Dave Roback / The Republican.

2021 SHERIFF'S ANNUAL COOKOUT/GOLF TOURNAMENT

ABOVE: 2021 Sheriff's Cookout mailer.

RIGHT TOP: Governor Charlie Baker and Sheriff Nick Cocchi, Aug. 18, 2021. Photo by Chris Marion.

RIGHT: Sheriff Nick Cocchi and Lt. Governor Karyn Polito. Photo by Chris Marion.

98

TOP LEFT: Secretary of the Commonwealth William Galvin talks with Sheriff Cocchi at Sheriff's Cookout, Aug. 18, 2021. Photo by Chris Marion. **TOP RIGHT:** Left to Right: Agawam Mayor Bill Sapelli, Hampden County District Attorney Anthony Gulluni, and Sheriff Nick Cocchi. Photo by Chris Marion. **BOTTOM LEFT:** Left to Right: Sheriff Michael J. Ashe, jr., and his successor Hampden County Sheriff Nick Cocchi. Republican file photo.
BOTTOM RIGHT: Left to Right: State Rep. Bud L. Williams, Sheriff Nick Cocchi, Tom Ashe, and Springfield Mayor Domenic J. Sarno. Photo by Chris Marion.

TOP LEFT: Sheriff Cocchi and Westfield Mayor Donald Humason, Aug. 18, 2021. Photo by Chris Marion.

ABOVE: Left to Right: Middlesex County Sheriff Peter Koutoujian, Plymouth County Sheriff Joseph McDonald, Jr., Hampden County Sheriff Nick Cocchi, and Norfolk County Sheriff Patrick McDermott, Aug.18, 2021. Photo by Hoang "Leon" Nguyen/ The Republican.

LEFT: Hampden County Sheriff's Department Staff at the check-in table at the Annual summer cookout at the Springfield Elks Lodge #61 on Aug. 18, 2021. Photo by Hoang "Leon" Nguyen/ The Republican.

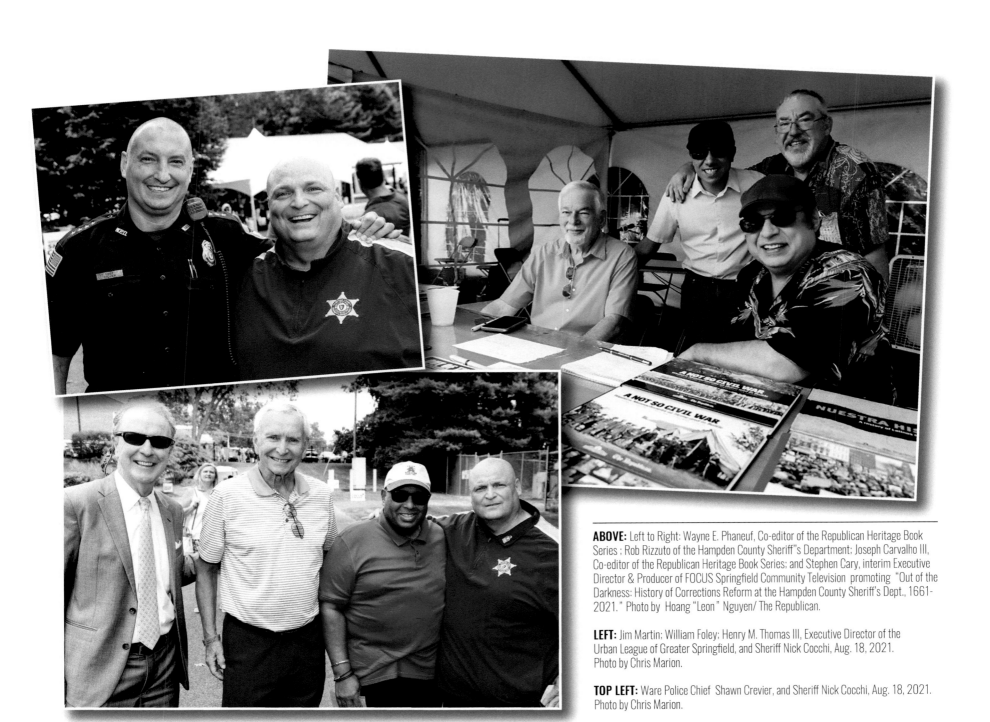

ABOVE: Left to Right: Wayne E. Phaneuf, Co-editor of the Republican Heritage Book Series ; Rob Rizzuto of the Hampden County Sheriff''s Department; Joseph Carvalho III, Co-editor of the Republican Heritage Book Series; and Stephen Cary, interim Executive Director & Producer of FOCUS Springfield Community Television promoting "Out of the Darkness: History of Corrections Reform at the Hampden County Sheriff's Dept., 1661-2021." Photo by Hoang "Leon" Nguyen/ The Republican.

LEFT: Jim Martin; William Foley; Henry M. Thomas III, Executive Director of the Urban League of Greater Springfield, and Sheriff Nick Cocchi, Aug. 18, 2021. Photo by Chris Marion.

TOP LEFT: Ware Police Chief Shawn Crevier, and Sheriff Nick Cocchi, Aug. 18, 2021. Photo by Chris Marion.

ABOVE: Heriberto Flores presenting a copy of *The Massasoit House and Paramount Theater* written by Wayne E. Phaneuf and Joseph Carvalho III to Governor Charlie Baker at the Sheriff's Cookout, Aug. 18, 2021. (Left to Right) Phaneuf, Carvalho, Flores, and Gov. Baker. Photo by Chris Manion.

RIGHT: Food booth at the 2021 Sheriff's Cookout, Aug. 18, 2021. Left to Right: Paul Chaves and Faycal Serisser of the Hampden County Sheriff's Department preparing food. Photo by Hoang "Leon" Nguyen/ The Republican.

CHAPTER FIVE
SHERIFF ASHE PAVES THE LONG ROAD TO A NEW JAIL

ABOVE: Col. William T. Whitman Jr., commander of the 3d Brigade, 26th infantry division of the National Guard, talks with Sheriff Michael Ashe Jr. outside the guard armory on Roosevelt Ave., Springfield, Feb. 1990. Republican file photo.

SHERIFF ASHE AND THE LONG ROAD TO A NEW JAIL

BY JOSEPH CARVALHO III

Sheriff Ashe sent shock waves throughout the community, state and nation with his dramatic action on Feb. 16, 1990. Political foot-dragging by state and local governments and the restrictions imposed by the federal courts left him with few options. The "takeover" of the National Guard Armory on Roosevelt Avenue in Springfield was a bold but politically risky action based upon a 1698 law enacted by the Massachusetts colonial government giving sheriffs broad powers to deal with a "breach of the peace." The sheriff felt that he was "between a rock and a hard place" and needed to act decisively. He would later explain, "I've been talking to state officials for two or three years, eventually you reach the point where you're going over the same ground, the same problems, and nothing happens, and hey, enough's enough!"

The sheriff and his staff had developed a "Confidential Action Plan" on Feb. 14 which stated as its goal: "Identify, scout, and occupy a U.S. National Guard facility through largely covert means." In its many pages of detail, two scenarios were described for moving up to 100 prisoners from York Street to the occupied space. One statement in the memo made it clear that one of the scenarios had been detailed as a "Generic Action Plan" as early as Oct. 11, 1988. The Action on Feb. 16, was carried out according to a detailed "Timetable" which read like a military operation:

1:30 p.m. Meet at Blunt Park Ice Arena

1:40 p.m. Deploy to Guard Armory

1:45 p.m. Arrive at Guard Armory; site commander situated; Sheriff Ashe arrives; food service deployed; medical service deployed

3:35 p.m. Inmates admitted

3:30 p.m. First duty watch established.

The events of Feb. 16 were set in motion when Westfield District Court Justice Philip A. Contant charged two deputy sheriffs with contempt of court and jailed them for five hours on Feb. 14 after the Sheriff's Department left a prisoner at the Westfield Court lock-up instead of transporting him to the overcrowded York Street jail. U.S. District Court Magistrate Michael Ponsor whose cap of 450 prisoners on the 102-year old jail caused the sheriff's men to refuse the inmate, called Contant's action "terribly unfair and unfortunate." Ponsor ordered the release of another inmate to make room for the prisoner from Westfield but warned that he would not "do any further ad hoc adjustments." The takeover was launched that same day.

A staffer who was present recalled that Ashe walked into the armory and before he read his formal statement of takeover, strolled up to the front desk, and said: "Hi there, I'm Sheriff Michael Ashe, Howahya?" After four hours of late afternoon meetings and telephone calls with National Guard and state officials, Ashe said he was ordered to leave the premises, but would keep 17 prisoners under guard at the armory until next week. Deputy Jail Superintendent Nicholas Fiorentino said National Guard officials limited access to most of the armory, and refused the use of showers and kitchen facilities. Fiorentino said the 17 inmates would be transported back to York Street jail once or twice a day for showers, hot meals and visiting hours. Jail guards brought in cots, mattresses and cold food for the inmates during the seizure. "I call upon the governor and the public safety commissioner to support me," Ashe said, adding that he felt compelled to secure a building to keep sentenced drug dealers and violent offenders off the streets. Ashe said chronic jail crowding and the lack of an immediate solution have been a "great source of anger and frustration." He blamed the executive and legislative branches for not coming to his assistance. "What I see is a lot of inaction," he said.

The Springfield Republican's statehouse reporter Glenn A. Briere wrote, "The legality of [Ashe's] seizure of the National Guard Armory may be in question, but the political impact is not." Well versed in Massachusetts politics, Briere observed that, "By taking a step that most politicians in this state would never dare to take, Ashe has turned the problems of his jail into, not only a state-wide story, but a national story." And indeed, he had. All the major newspapers, radio, and televisions stations carried the story and highlighted the issues that lead to the takeover. As Sheriff Ashe said on the day of the takeover, "My action today might seem extreme, but no more extreme than the danger to the public posed by convicted criminals going free for lack of jail beds."

Springfield newspapers political reporter and columnist Carol Malley praised the sheriff's action stating that, "he showed leadership and courage in treading where others feared to go." She noted that the only critics were members of the national Guard and Massachusetts Public Safety Secretary, Charles v. Barry who threatened to charge

ter instead of the Roosevelt Street armory. On Feb. 24, the sheriff's attorney Edward J. McDonough, Jr. obtained an extension from Hampden County Superior Court Judge George C. Keady, Jr. Keady's resultant order required Ashe and the Guard to "cooperate" at the Roosevelt St. Armory and allow the sheriff it's use until March 12. If a solution was not found by that date, a hearing would be scheduled on Ashe's request for an injunction that would allow him to use the armory indefinitely. State Rep. Raymond A. Jordan Jr., D-Springfield, said the seizure could set a national precedent for other armories to be used to relieve the national problem of jail crowding. "Everybody agrees we have a crisis," Jordan said.

On Jan. 16, Governor Michael S. Dukakis had signed the bill authorizing the state to purchase land owned by the Massachusetts Wholesale Electric Company in Ludlow for the construction of the new $90 million facility. Louise Pepe of the Massachusetts Division of Capital Planning and Operations, the state agency in charge of jail construction, then announced a new timetable for the new jail to be constructed in Ludlow. The plan was to move the date up by three years with completion in late 1992. But that was still two years away. Overcrowding at the jail needed an interim solution immediately.

As the March 12 deadline approached, Sheriff Ashe continued to look for alternatives. On March 5, Ashe received state support for his recommendation of using the National Guard armory on Sargeant Street in Holyoke. The idea was strongly supported by Gov. Dukakis. Once again, the local community resisted, led by Mayor Marty Dunn, who said that he was "completely and adamantly opposed to the

the sheriff with illegal trespassing and said that Ashe "should have come to him first if he had a problem." Malley remarked, "Barry's comments made one wonder where he has been for the past few years," pointing out that Barry's inaction was one of "the reasons Ashe's behavior had so much popular appeal." Ashe termed Barry's response to the takeover as a "condescending, high-handed put-down," that was also "insulting when it's been very clear in my working with the administration in a very intense way that we have gone to great

measures to document the extreme over-crowding."

To forestall legal action by Secretary Barry, the sheriff sought and won a temporary restraining order allowing him to keep 17 inmates in the armory. Meanwhile, National Guard General Chester Gorski, Commander of the 26th Yankee Division, expressed his disapproval of the sheriff's action suggesting that Ashe use the criminal justice training center in Agawam or the Springfield Civic Cen-

idea." After much political negotiations, the mayor and the sheriff ultimately came to an agreement and the site was used as a temporary site for overflow of inmates. Soon, prison crews began to help sweeping the streets and picking up litter for the Holyoke Public Library, mowing lawns and cleaning the grounds of the nearby Anne H. McHugh Early Childhood Center to the delight of the neighborhood. Chicopee's College of Our Lady of the Elms even conferred an honorary degree on Sheriff Ashe at its May commencement that year. However, when funding from the Dukakis administration ran out in December Ashe was forced to close the door of the facility in December of that year.

Nine months later in September of 1991, the new Massachusetts Governor, William F. Weld (R) announced that he was providing $800,000 in state aid to re-open the Holyoke Armory as a temporary lock-up for 70 prisoners until the Ludlow facility opened. At the September 25 announcement, Weld opened his remarks by saying to the sheriff, "Mike, you were a hero of mine in February 1990 when you took over the Springfield [Roosevelt Avenue] Armory." Ashe and his staff were to operate the facility successfully without incident, eventually transferring its operations to the new Ludlow facilities in 1992. Despite the early opposition, the Hampden County Sheriff's Department was a

OPPOSITE PAGE: Sheriff Michael J. Ashe, Jr. and Major General Chester Gorski of the Army National Guard at a hearing regarding the takeover of the National Guard armory on Roosevelt Avenue in Springfield, Feb. 1990. Republican file photo.

RIGHT: Headlines for newspaper coverage of the takeover of the Roosevelt Street National Guard Armory by the Hampden County Sheriff's Department. Republican database archives.

ABOVE: Aerial view of the York Street jail complex, Sept. 4, 1989. Republican file photo.
OPPOSITE PAGE: Newspaper headlines regarding the temporary use of the Holyoke Armory site. Republican database archives

good neighbor to the citizens of Holyoke. An appreciative Mayor William A. Hamilton utilized inmate labor to help maintain neglected areas of the city. As the temporary use of the site was coming to a close, Ashe announced that even when they moved to their permanent location in Ludlow, "As long as the mayor and the City of Holyoke has a need for us, we will respond." As Ashe has repeatedly said over the years, Holyoke has a special place in his heart.

Concurrent with his day-to-day management of the Sheriff's Department and his constant efforts to find temporary solutions for the perennial problem of jail overcrowding, the sheriff kept the plans for a new jail moving forward. When he was presented with issues regarding wetlands at the site, the sheriff worked with the state appointed architects in August of 1990 to re-design the site to avoid the wetlands problem. Ashe lobbied for and succeeded in garnering Governor Weld's support for the Ludlow site in October of 1990. Once again demonstrating Ashe's ability to bring both Democrats and Republicans to a consensus on Corrections management in Massachusetts. Throughout the year, the sheriff worked with the architects to design the facility to accommodate the correctional reforms and programs he planned to implement at the new jail. It was to be a 21st Century approach to corrections according to Ashe's 20 guiding principles of corrections management [see Chapter 7 for detailed description of these principles]. On Dec. 10, 1990, site work began on the future Hampden County Correctional Center in Ludlow.

On May 14, 1991, the first of 950 pre-cast cells began arriving to be installed at the Randall Road site in Ludlow. Over the next

ngfield **Union-News**

SATURDAY, FEBRUARY 17, 1990 ☆ 25 CENTS

Ashe seizes armory for jail

Uncertain 'jailers' on guard

By SUSANNAH PUGH

The glass display cases in the front hallway of the National Guard Armory in Springfield contained knives, sabers, firearms, uniforms, and even Nazi flags captured by fighting men in previous wars.

Yesterday, National Guardsmen heaved to and moved those cases out of the main hallway into a dining room where they could be locked up. It was a scene from another war, a turf war that was being waged in those very halls.

The weapons could have created an obvious security problem. The armory had become a temporary jail when Hampden County Sheriff Michael J. Ashe Jr. commandeered it without warning in an effort to relieve overcrowding at his Hampden County Jail and House of Correction.

* * *

Th.e cover of fog yesterday vehicles transported 17 minimum security prisoners from the York Street jail to the Roosevelt Avenue armory.

By early evening, a surprised state Secretary of Public Safety Charles V. Barry had issued a statement saying Ashe would face prosecution for criminal trespassing. But Barry's ultimatum came late yesterday and the courts were closed until Tuesday, the day after the Washington's birthday holiday. Ashe responded in essence:"See you in court."

Ashe had explained his takeover as designed to create a temporary jail.

* * *

And it seemed the building would be a temporary jail, maybe as temporary as one weekend. With the prisoners staying put for the time being, the National Guards moved the weapons out of harm's way.

National Guardsmen, dressed in camouflage uniforms, grouped in uneasy clusters in the front hall. Their counterparts, Hampden

TEMPORARY JAIL SITE — Hampden County Corrections Officer Anthony DeCasse stands yesterday at the entrance to the Springfield National Guard Armory on Roosevelt Avenue that Hampden County Sheriff Michael J. Ashe Jr. wanted to convert into a temporary jail.

Sheriff's statement

Staff photo by Michelle Segall

DRASTIC ACTION — Hampden County Sheriff Michael J. Ashe Jr. speaks at a press conference yesterday at the National Guard Armory in Springfield.

EDITORS NOTE — The following is a statement issued by Hampden County Sheriff Michael J. Ashe Jr. yesterday as he prepared to move prisoners into the National Guard Armory in Springfield:

At approximately 2 p.m. (yesterday), Hampden County Sheriff Michael J. Ashe Jr., acting for the safety of the citizens of Hampden County and to prevent the collapse of the criminal justice system in this county due to the lack of correctional facilities, read the enclosed declaration and presented the following notice to the Brigadier Commander of the Massachusetts Army National Guard Armory on Roosevelt Avenue in Springfield.

Whereas, it appears to the Sheriff of Hampden County that there is an imminent danger of a breach of the peace due to insufficient prison space in this County, and that reasonable and prudent steps must be taken in order to preserve the peace and quell such danger, and to preserve order among and between the prisoners duly remanded to the custody of the Sheriff. Now, therefore, the Sheriff of Hampden County deems it necessary that these quarters be used, temporarily, as a prison, until such time as is necessary to quell such danger, and that you provide such reasonable and necessary assistance to the Sheriff of Hampden County as he may request.

Tense takeover ensues

By BRAD SMITH and GLENN BRIERE

Tired of tending a crowded old jail, Hampden County Sheriff Michael J. Ashe Jr. seized a National Guard armory yesterday, trucked in 17 inmates and vowed to stay the weekend in defiance of surprised state officials who charged him with trespassing.

"My action today might seem extreme, but no more extreme than the danger to the public" posed by convicted criminals

More stories, photos on Pages 6 and 7.

going free for lack of jail beds, Ashe said.

State Public Safety Secretary Charles V. Barry, who controls state-owned armories, said Ashe would face criminal trespass charges Tuesday when courts reopen after the Washington's Birthday holiday.

Acknowledging that he and other state officials were caught off guard by Ashe's action, Barry said the 17 inmates could stay at the Scibelli Hall armory on Springfield's Roosevelt Avenue for the weekend.

"I told the sheriff that you just don't house prisoners in an armory when the building is not up to code," Barry said.

Gov. Michael S. Dukakis was informed of the takeover, but had no comment.

* * *

National Guard officials referred all questions to Barry.

Barry said he told Ashe: "This is no way to do business. If you would come to us to discuss the problem, we would see what we could do to accommodate you."

However, Ashe said this week's worsening crowding at Springfield's York Street jail dictated a dramatic move.

In a declaration to the commander of the National Guard

Continued on Page 6

---

several months using "fast-track construction," construction workers under the supervision of Perini Corp. of Framingham piled these 20-ton cells onto each other to form multi-story cell blocks of a "campus-style" jail that would become the largest in Massachusetts. Deputy Superintendent of the jail, J. John Ashe likened it to "Lego building blocks." Richard Askew of the Massachusetts Division of Capital Planning and Operations approved of the modular techniques being used at the site that "enabled rapid assembly at a clip three times faster than conventional methods."

The cells were arranged in two-story circular configurations around a common space that made supervision most efficient according to the sheriff. Each cell featured a steel bunk, writing desk, stool, stainless steel toilet, sink and mirror, steel bookshelf and suicide-proof clothes hangers that collapse under weight. The state's project manager at the site, Vincent Cirigliano, pointed out that instead of the traditional steel bars throughout the facility, "assault-proof" and bulletproof" glass was installed. Also, the jail design no longer made use of metal bars to keep inmates in their cells. Electronically controlled sliding glass doors to each pre-cast cell. Fifty percent of the complex was completed by August 12, 1991.

Meanwhile there was still political wrangling at the state level regarding operating funds for the new jail. Once again, Sheriff Ashe used the annual clambake as a moment for building consensus for state funding. He began garnering support from state legislators. Eventually with assistance from Rep. Anthony "Tony" Scibelli of Springfield, and Rep. Thomas Petrolati of Ludlow, Ashe succeeded in having Ways and Means Chairman Thomas M. Finneran to tour the Ludlow facility in early

ABOVE: Sheriff Michael Ashe, center, leads a press conference following the proceedings at Hampden County Superior Court. Also shown, from left to right, Lawrence Fletcher-Hill, the state asst. attorney general, Jack Bradshaw of the Massachusetts Division of Capital Planning and Operations, and Ashe's attorney Edward J. McDonough, Feb. 23, 1990. Republican file photo.
OPPOSITE PAGE: Front page of Union-News on February 17, 1990.

February of 1992. That tour went a long way to convince state legislators that they should provide the necessary funding to make the new facility to operate as planned. In March the Ways and Means Committee approved $4 million to hire and train staff for the Ludlow jail. Looking forward to implementing his corrections reform system at the new jail, Ashe announced in April his intent to run for a fourth term as sheriff, "fully confident that I have the same dogged determination, the same relish for the task, the same excitement about our future" as he had when he ran for sheriff in 1974.

In September, the new $73.5 million Hampden County Correctional Center at Stony Brook in Ludlow was completed. Over 27,000 people visited the completed facility at a public "Open House" arranged by Sheriff Ashe on Sept. 12 and 13, 1992. The dedication ceremony was held on Sept. 23 with over 400 law enforcement and political officials attending. Sheriff proudly declared, "This jail wasn't built for yesterday, but for tomorrow." Five days later on September 28, the Hampden County Correctional Center went into operation with the first contingent of inmates transferred to the facility. On Oct. 21, the first women inmates were moved to the new jail and women formerly housed at Framingham were returned to Hampden County.

LEFT: SJ. John Ashe, Deputy Jail Supervisor (L) conferring with Jack Bradshaw (r) , head of the Massachusetts Department of Capital Planning and Operations as they look over a model of the new jail in Ludlow. Sheriff Ashe was present but not in the photo. Photo by David Molnar/Republican file photo.

OPPOSITE PAGE: "Jay" Ashe touring the construction site of the new jail in Ludlow viewing one of the inmate buildings under construction, July 24, 1991. Photo by John Suchocki/The Republican.

ABOVE: Progress of the construction. Photo courtesy of the Hampden County Sheriff's Department.

RIGHT: Sheriff Ashe reviewing the progress of the construction. Photo courtesy of the Hampden County Sheriff's Department.

OPPOSITE PAGE: Progress of the construction. Photo courtesy of the Hampden County Sheriff's Department.

ABOVE AND OPPOSITE PAGE: Progress of the construction. Photos courtesy of the Hampden County Sheriff's Department.

ABOVE: Progress of the construction. Photo courtesy of the Hampden County Sheriff's Department.

INSET: Sheriff Michael J. Ashe, Jr. guiding state representatives through the new jail under construction in Ludlow. Left to Right: Sheriff Ashe, Rep. Thomas Finneran, Rep. Anthony "Tony" Scibelli, and Rep. Thomas Petrolati, Feb. 6, 1992. Photo by Frank Usin/Republican file photo

ABOVE: Progress of the construction. Photo courtesy of the Hampden County Sheriff's Department.

INSET: Aerial view of the Hampden County House of Corrections at Stony Brook, Ludlow, June 13, 2002. Photo courtesy Hampden County Sheriff's Dept.

ABOVE: Hampden County House of Corrections at Stony Brook, Ludlow. Republican file photo.

THE FATE OF THE OLD YORK STREET JAIL

BY WAYNE E. PHANEUF

When the York Street Jail was closed down in 1992 a flurry of ideas were proposed ranging from a multimillion biotech complex to an antique mall. While the buildings, some going back to the 1880s, were still standing, a huge sign announcing "Jail for Sale" hung on the wall facing Rte. 91 and West Columbus Avenue (now Hall of Fame Avenue) for years. The jail buildings stood for 16 years while every idea and offer faded like the for sale sign on the wall. The Royal Armouries of London briefly considered the site for a U.S. branch of their museum. Carlo Marchetti of Springfield Central proposed the site as a large flea market. Other ideas such as a Freshwater Aquarium, an Arts Center, a youth gymnasium, a bio-tech laboratory, and a transportation museum were also explored. None of these ideas were financially feasible at the time. In 1996, the feature film Before and After, starring Liam Neeson and Meryl Streep included scenes filmed in 1995 at the York Street jail site where Neeson and Streep's character's were visiting their "son" played by Edward Turley at York Street. The Warming Place shelter utilized the former jail's gymnasium building until 2007 for housing homeless persons.

In the end in 2008, the wrecking crew tore down the 121- year -old jail at a cost of $1.24 million. In 2019, a hotel was proposed for the site but the Covid-19 epidemic made that project problematic financially due to all of the restrictions required. Part of the site of the former jail will be used as a pumping station for the Springfield Water Department.

ABOVE: Sheriff Ashe reviewing old York Street Jail record books prior to transferring them to the Springfield Museums for preservation, 1991. The records are now cared for in the archives of the Lyman and Merrie Wood Museum of Springfield History. Republican file photo.

TOP RIGHT: York Street jail complex, 2006. Republican file Photo.

BOTTOM RIGHT: "Jail For Sale" sign on the York Street jail complex. Republican file photo.

OPPOSITE PAGE: Joseph Carvalho III, Director of the Connecticut Valley Historical Museum [today's Lyman and Merrie Wood Museum of Springfield History] (left) and Thomas Costello, President of the Springfield Library and Museums Association (center) touring the Hampden County jail at York Street Feb. 7, 1993 with Guy Wilson, Master of the Royal Armouries at the Tower of London. This was part of the study of the possible use of the former jail as an American branch of the Royal Armouries which would contain among other objects, objects including arms and armor captured from the Irish from the 17th Century to modern times never before displayed in England. The Project was never funded and the Royal Armories moved to Leeds, England. Photo by Michelle Segall/ Republican file photo.

ABOVE: Fence constructed around site to prepare for demolition at the York Street facility, Jan. 21, 2007. Republican file photo.

ABOVE: Demolition of main cell block, York Street Jail, 2008. Republican file photo.

ABOVE: Demolition of the last structures begins, 2008. Republican file photo.

RIGHT: Demolition of remaining segment of the main cell block, 2008. Republican file photo.

OPPOSITE PAGE: Drone photo of former York Street Jail site, Nov. 17, 2020. Photo by Patrick Johnson/The Republican.

OPPOSITE PAGE: Drone photo of a Springfield Water Department pumping station being built on the site of the former York Street jail, Nov. 17, 2020. Photo by Patrick Johnson/The Republican.

CHAPTER SIX

NEW JAIL AND 21ST CENTURY APPROACH TO CORRECTIONS

ABOVE: An inside the walls look at the Hampden County Correctional Center at Stony Brook, Ludlow, Jan. 25, 2017. Photo by (Don Treeger / The Republican.

THE HAMPDEN COUNTY HOUSE OF CORRECTIONS AT STONY BROOK AND THE 21ST CENTURY APPROACH TO CORRECTIONS

- Joseph Carvalho III

With the opening of the new Hampden County House of Corrections in Ludlow, Sheriff Ashe and his team could finally implement the full range of corrections management reforms that were pioneered in his first three terms of office. The Hampden County reform efforts of the sheriff had already received national attention, however, the new facility enabled his reform program to flourish. The recidivism rate continue to stay remarkably low, and the success rate of former inmates returning to the community to lead positive lives was noted far and wide within the Corrections field. In 1996, the Hampden County Sheriff's Department became the first county correctional department in the nation to be awarded four separate accreditations from the American Correctional Association for four different levels of security.

An important part of the sheriff's system of inmate restitution, and preparation for their eventual re-entry into the community was his Community Service Restitution Program. His partnership with Patrick Sullivan, Superintendent of the Springfield park system, was one of his earliest successes. The sheriff credits Sullivan with successfully achieving the cooperation of municipal unions to allow the pro-

gram to be implemented. Inmates performed valuable clean-up work in the parks and particularly at Springfield's "Crown Jewel," Forest Park. The program grew to the point where the sheriff's "restitution" crews became ubiquitous, and institutions reached out to the Sheriff's Department for their services.

By 1999, the Hampden County Community Service Restitution Program was performing more than 75,000 hours of labor throughout Hampden County. Sheriff Ashe stated that, "No one can ever convince me that it is anything but right for inmates to do community service restitution." Captain Thomas Nolan coordinated the program at the Hampden County Minimum Security Center; Sergeant Zygmont Szczawinski coordinated the program at the Western Massachusetts Correctional Alcohol Center; and Rich Devine coordinated the program at the Hampden County Day Reporting Center.

Ashe not only was a proponent of restitution but also of "restorative justice." In September of 2000, the sheriff instituted a new Victim Services Program. Based on the principles of "Restorative Justice," victims would be assisted with confidential conversations; crisis intervention; support and information; safety planning referrals to community resources; mediation; victim/offender conferencing; and short term counselling. Two months later, Ashe began an initiative aimed at making better parents of its incarcerated fathers. The program "Father's Work" developed by Guy P. Prairie, the center's correctional programs director, had among its goals: curbing recidivism, breaking the cycle of fatherless homes, and teaching the impact of fathers on children's development.

That year, The United States Bureau of Justice Statistics recidivism report revealed that the recidivism rate of the Hampden County Correctional Center was 15 percent better than the national average. Sheriff Ashe said, "We finally have proof-positive that our system of challenging the offender with productive activities to pick up the tools and directions to build a law-abiding life has paid off for the citizens and communities of our region with enhanced public safety and the saving of public monies. All the effort we put in to 'correct' rather than 'warehouse' people pays off."

Recognition for Ashe's humane reforms kept coming. In January of 2000, the Hampden County Correctional Facility health clinic led by Dr. Thomas J. Conklin, Director of Health Services, received a national award for "Innovative Community-Based Health Care Program for Inmates." Late that month, Ashe was honored with Holyoke's "Civic Pride Award." In exit remarks at the conclusion of American Correctional Association audits, Auditors, who were experienced practitioners of corrections, said the following:

Major Carlos Jackson of Colorado said: "The Hampden County Sheriff's Department is a model for the corrections industry. I haven't seen better anywhere in the country."

Julie Von Arx of Indiana said: "It is probably the best facility that I've ever been in. I hope the community and the public realize what a gem they have in the Hampden County Sheriff's Department and what a gem they have in Sheriff Ashe."

Gary Gremillon of Louisiana said: "I have never seen anything like this anywhere, in all my years of corrections, and in all my years of

ABOVE: Interior view of the new Hampden County House of Corrections at Stony Brook, Ludlow. Republican file photo.

ABOVE: An inside the walls look at the Hampden County Correctional Center in Ludlow, Jan. 25, 2017. Photo by Don Treeger / The Republican.

American Correctional Association auditing all over the United States. This is, without a doubt, the most professional, the most progressive.

In 2003, Governor Mitt Romney directed that a Governor's Commission on Corrections Reform convene under the leadership of former Attorney General Scott Harshbarger. The purpose of the GCCR would be to conduct a comprehensive review of the Department of Corrections. In July 2004, Harshbarger disseminated the findings of the GCCR's investigation in his report entitled "Strengthening Public Safety, Increasing Accountability, and Instituting Fiscal Responsibility in the Depart-

ment of Corrections." The Massachusetts Governor's Commission "lavished praise on the Hampden County Sheriff's Department for its work with inmates," according to a Springfield Republican editorial.

The Commission's recent prison studies suggested that programs in use in Hampden County could be a model statewide. The report stated that, "The Hampden County Sheriff's Department has created a positive environment for both staff and inmates by paying attention to very basic management duties and by adapting 'best practice' approaches to managing correctional facilities and successful prison reentry. With the bene-

fit of a long-serving Sheriff, Hampden County has introduced approaches to inmate and staff accountability that are mutually reinforcing and that dovetail with high expectations for management personnel. Inmates understand that their status in the institution and their progress toward community release are tied directly to their active participation in programs to prepare for release and to their institutional behavior. Similarly, correctional staff recognize that professional advancement depends upon performance."

Continuing the sheriff's efforts to professionalize his corrections staff, the Hampden County Sheriff's Department conducted its first-ever open competitive examination for correctional officer candidates on Oct. 16, 2004. A first of its kind sheriff's academy graduated its initial class of the Western Massachusetts Regional Reserve Intermittent Police Academy in April of 2005. Twenty-seven men and one woman from the Sheriff's Departments of Hampden, Hampshire, Franklin and Berkshire Counties graduated from the training program that included crowd control, and drug task force work.

During Ashe's tenure, the Hampden County Sheriff's Department has been awarded 27 consecutive scores of 95% or higher by accreditors of the American Correctional Association for its various correctional operations. It also was the first county correctional department in the nation to receive four separate accreditations by the American Correctional Association for four separate levels of security. And most importantly, the recidivism rate of the Hampden County House of Correction is among the lowest, if not the lowest, of any urban county correctional facility in the nation.

ABOVE: This is the textile and upholstery shop at the Hampden County Correctional Center, Jan. 25, 2017.Photo by Don Treeger / The Republican.

NEW JAIL PLANNING INSPIRED NEW SYSTEMS

- By Tom Rovelli

New ideas were needed to continue the success at the new Hampden County House of Corrections. The new systems included:

- Hiring staff with the Sheriff's imprint, new hiring standards, background checks, physical fitness testing, advertising, video aptitude testing, psychological testing, multiple interview panels, study materials.

- Establishment of a career ladder for all staff, both uniformed and non-uniformed. Correctional officers, correctional caseworkers, correctional counselors, residential supervisors, corporals, sergeants, shift supervisors, managers, lieutenants, captains, specialists, directors, maintenance officers, nurses, educational staff, ADS, AS were needed.

- Compensation Systems, performance evaluation, physical fitness standards, annual testing, specialized teams: tactical response team, critical incident response team, CIU, K-9, Apprehension, etc.

- Rotation system for correctional staff based on a numerical matrix to ensure that all staff have equal opportunity for assignments.

- Housing to non-housing and vice versa. All persons are capable to perform all assignments.

- Command inspections, all living and non-living areas receive weekly audits by trained teams of inspectors. There are auditing forms based on hygiene, cell and pod order, sanitation and verbal debrief with unit staff.

- Strategic planning, annual goal and objectives, subcommittees, and reports.

- Inmate and staff handbooks
- Staff training
- Direct supervision offender management philosophy
- Supervisor meetings
- CEUs- formally bi-weekly training
- Unit management philosophy
- Gang management identification system
- Information systems and technology, new jail 1992 Microsoft Network PCs, Trax JMS, customer responsible technology
- Barcode scanning of offender data
- Unit superintendent committee decentralization, resource sharing problem-solving
- Community healthcare model of service
- Intake and booking transition from York Street to open booking stations staffed by non-uniformed clerks and correctional supervisors and officers
- Food service delivery to each living unit, cart system. No centralized dining.
- No central prison yard, individualized pod recreation deck. -New offender orientation units and education program
- Responsibility pod
- Core curriculum for all offenders
- Accountability pod 2000

OPPOSITE TOP: Here, assistant shop instructor Chris Thorington shows a t-shirt that was silk screened at the jail shop at the Hampden County Correctional Center in Ludlow, Jan. 25, 2017.
BOTTOM LEFT: The chapel at the Hampden County Correctional Center, Jan. 25, 2017.
TOP RIGHT: Here, a pre-trial inmate (face blurred to protect his identity) reads in his cell at the Hampden County Correctional Center in Ludlow, Jan. 25, 2017.
RIGHT: The intake area of the Hampden County Correctional Center in Ludlow, Jan. 25, 2017. Photos by Don Treeger / The Republican.

ABOVE: Inside the cell in one of the housing towers the Hampden County Correctional Center in Ludlow. (Photo by Dave Roback / The Republican.

OPPOSITE PAGE TOP LEFT: Lt. Walter L. Currier of the Hampden County Corrections Department brings information from the Text-a-Tip Program onto a computer screen in the central control room at the Hampden County House of Corrections at Stony Brook. Looking on from left: Hampden County Sheriff Michael J. Ashe Jr., Tony Bryant, director of information systems and technology, and John F. Kenney, assistant superintendent for special operations, both with the Hampden County Sheriff's Department and Correction Center, Nov. 23, 2009. Photo by Michael S. Gordon / The Republican.

FAR RIGHT: Sgt Peter Signorelli with Chico at the Hampden County Correctional Center in Ludlow. Photo by Dave Roback / The Republican.

BELOW: Sheriff Ashe and wife Barbara and family with Hampden County Sheriff's Department deputies at the St. Patrick's Day Parade in Holyoke, 2010. Photo courtesy of Sheriff Michael J. Ashe, Jr.

St. Patrick's Parade in Holyoke "2010"

ABOVE: Hampden County Sheriff Michael J. Ashe, right, and sheriff's department Capt. Thomas B. Nolan, head of the community restitution program at the Hampden County Correctional Center, check out the work of inmates along Interstate 91 in Springfield, July 17, 2002. Photo by Dave Roback/The Republican.

RIGHT: Hampden County House of Corrections officers receive the Edward P. Boland Award for outstanding correctional officers. At left is Corporal Sergio M. Mateus and at right is Corporal Mia J. Wollmershauser, May 18, 2007. Photo by Don Treeger/The Republican.

OPPOSITE PAGE

TOP LEFT: At the Hampden County House of Corrections in Ludlow, Capt. Ross Murray tries out the new credit card machine to be used for inmates to get bail money for release, Feb. 21, 1997. Republican file photo.

BOTTOM LEFT: Dr. Thomas Conklin (L) and Sheriff Michael J. Ashe, Jr. (R) at the Hampden County House of Correction in Ludlow, July 18, 2000. Photo by Fred Contrada/The Republican.

TOP RIGHT: Sheriff Michael J. Ashe, left, Connie M. Bauer, head administrative clerk, and corrections officer Mark Young of the Hampden County Sheriff's Dept. hold a $5,000 check donated to the Toy for Joy fund on behalf of the inmates at the Hampden County Correctional Center at Stony Brook in Ludlow, Dec. 7, 2001. Republican file photo.

BOTTOM RIGHT : Hampden County Sheriff Michael J. Ashe, left, and Springfield's Director of Parks, Buildings and Recreation Management Patrick J. Sullivan, discuss improvements at Loon Pond off Pasco Road in Springfield, April 3, 2007. Republican file photo

FAR LEFT: Richard F. Devine of the Hampden County Sheriff's Department laughs with the kids at the Springfield Boys & Girls Club attending the Badges for Baseball Program put on by the Sheriff's Department and funded by the Cal Ripken Jr. Foundation, April 13, 2008. Republican file photo.

LEFT: An inmate at the Hampden County House of Corrections at Stony Brook in Ludlow talking about his experiences to high school youths in the "Behind the Walls " program at the jail, Nov. 17, 1999. Republican file photo.

ABOVE : Dennis M. Sullivan, left, community restitution officer with the Hampden County Sheriff's Dept., left, and three residents of the Hampden County House of Corrections at Stony Brook in Ludlow cut boards from a white pine log using a portable saw mill in Forest Park. Mar. 7, 2007. The boards, made from trees cut down in the park, were taken to the jail and made into furniture for sale. Photo by Michael S. Gordon/ The Republican.

A DREAM COME TRUE:
THE WESTERN MASSACHUSETTS REGIONAL WOMEN'S CORRECTIONAL CENTER

- Wayne E. Phaneuf

In response to the opponents of the siting of a new women's Correctional facility in Chicopee, Sheriff Ashe wrote a letter to the editor of the Springfield Republican in December of 2003 stating: "The new women's facility near the Chicopee/Springfield line was designed to be a facility that seeks to rejoin or join women to the community, not isolate them....Preventing the construction of a new county women's correctional facility in this region will not eliminate incarceration, and as long as women continue to be incarcerated in this country, I will continued to advocate for a separate women's facility which will improve conditions of confinement."

There were days when it looked like the Western Massachusetts Regional Women's Correctional Center would never become a reality. Sept. 13, 2007 wasn't one of those days. With more than 200 people in attendance, Hampden County Sheriff Michael J. Ashe Jr. saw his 14-plus-year dream realized as the new $26.1 million women's jail at 701 Center St. was dedicated.

RIGHT: Patricia A. Murphy, left, Superintendent of the Hampden County Women's Correctional Center, and Sally Johnson Van Wright, assistant superintendent were appointed in September of 2006. Republican file photo.

"There are those who see the construction of a new correctional facility as no cause for celebration," Ashe said during the dedication ceremony on the outdoor track area of the jail. "But it is not incarceration that we celebrate today, any more than at the dedication of a hospital we celebrate physical incapacitation. Rather, we celebrate our communities' efforts to address crime, enhance public safety and reclaim broken lives."

Just over 200 women who were serving time at the Hampden County Correctional Center in Ludlow were transferred to the new jail from the Ludlow jail. The transfer took place in phases and was completed within a month. The jail is a regional partnership between the Hampden, Berkshire, Hampshire and Franklin sheriff's departments, but is operated by Ashe's department. The jail serves female inmates from those four counties who have been sentenced to terms of 2 1/2 years or less.

Treatment has been be a major focus. According to Ashe, 35 to 40 percent of the women have mental health problems, the average education level attained is eighth grade, and 85 percent arrive at jail with substance abuse issues. All of those areas of concern are addressed through special programs designed specifically for the female inmate population. In Ludlow, the female inmates were outnumbered by male inmates 10 to 1.

RIGHT TOP: Construction of the Western Massachusetts Regional Women's Correctional Center in Chicopee. Republican file photo.

RIGHT: Prefabricated concrete cell pods, to be hoisted into place by crane, are delivered Aug. 23, 2006 to the site of the Western Massachusetts Regional Women's Correctional Center under construction on Center Street in Chicopee. Republican file photo.

ABOVE: The entrance to the Western Massachusetts Regional Women's Correctional Center in Chicopee, 2007. Photo by Don Treeger / The Republican.

WESTERN MASSACHUSETTS
REGIONAL WOMEN'S
CORRECTIONAL CENTER

SHERIFF Michael J. Ashe, Jr.

"We begin planning for after-care on day one," according to Patricia A. Murphy, the superintendent of the Chicopee facility. Most of the inmates in the jail are there because of non-violent offenses, such as drugs, prostitution and property crimes. "This isn't a fortress in a woods," Ashe said during the tour at the dedication in 2007. "It's not a warehouse. We're trying to turn their lives around."

The 2007 dedication ceremony was a who's who of politics, public safety, corrections and social services. Berkshire County Sheriff Carmen C. Massimiano, Hampshire County Sheriff Robert J. Garvey and Franklin County Sheriff Frederick B. Macdonald all spoke, along with Mayor Michael D. Bissonnette, state Rep. Joseph D. Wagner, D-Chicopee, state Sen. Stephen J. Buoniconti, D-Springfield, state Commissioner of Division of Capital Asset Management David B. Perini,

OPPOSITE PAGE: Landscape and facilities of the Western Massachusetts Regional Women's Correctional Center in Chicopee.
Photo by Don Treeger / The Republican.

TOP RIGHT: Superintendent Patricia Murphy in the Segregation Unit during a tour of the new Western Massachusetts Regional Women's Correctional Center in Chicopee following the dedication ceremony, Sept. 12, 2007.
Photo by Don Treeger/The Republican.

RIGHT: Superintendent Patricia Murphy (center) , Hampden County Sheriff Michael J. Ashe, Jr. (R) , and Captain Connie R. Burke (L) during a tour of the central control area of the new Western Massachusetts Regional Women's Correctional Center, Sept. 12, 2007. Photo by Don Treeger/The Republican.

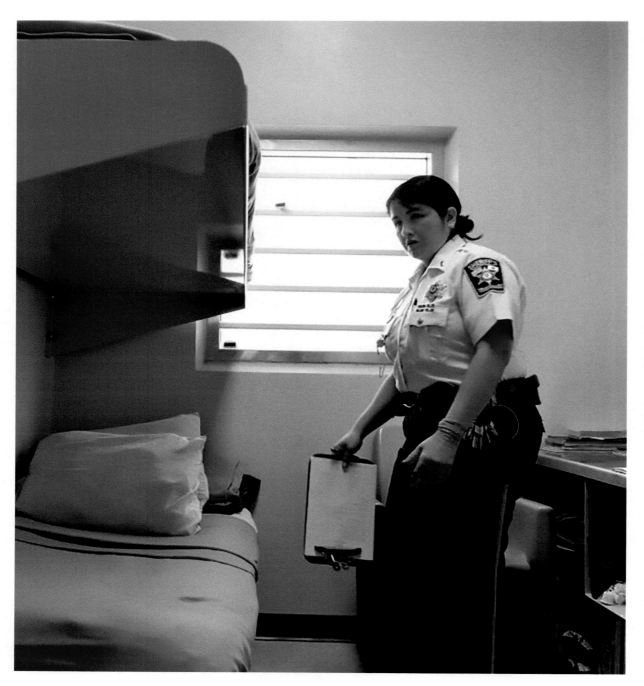

and state Undersecretary of Criminal Justice Mary Elizabeth Heffernan. More than a dozen other state legislators, area mayors and Chicopee city officials were also in attendance.

Again and again, the speakers talked about the struggle to get the jail built, whether it was finding a site or finding the dollars. And they talked about why a regional women's jail was needed.

"The women who are going to be here are not evil women. They're women who cannot manage their lives," Buoniconti said. "I know firmly they'll be in the best hands possible with these four sheriffs."

The new jail marked the first free-standing facility constructed to serve women in Massachusetts since 1877. The architectural firm for the $26.1 million project was Whitney Atwood Norcross Associates, Inc., and the general contractor was Fontaine Bros. Inc.

In 2013, a $14 million addition to the women's jail was completed that added space and helped alleviate overcrowding at the Framingham Women's facility.

OPPOSITE PAGE: Lt. Sandra Daniele conducts an inspection of a cell at the Western Mass. Regional Women's Correctional Center.
Photo by Don Treeger / The Republican

TOP RIGHT: Lt. Sandra Daniele speaks with an inmate during a disciplinary hearing at the Western Massachusetts Regional Women's Correctional Center.
Photo by Don Treeger / The Republican.

RIGHT: Interior view of the housing unit at the Western Massachusetts Regional Women's Correctional Center .
Photo by Don Treeger / The Republican.

ABOVE: Lt. Sandra Daniele performing a security check along the entire perimeter of the Western Mass. Regional Women's Correctional Center. Photo by Don Treeger / The Republican.

WESTERN MASS. REGIONAL WOMEN'S CORRECTIONAL CENTER CHICOPEE, MA

Security Level: Med/Max, Min/ Work Rel.
January 1, 2021 Facility Population: 74

Opened: 2007; Expanded 2014
Average Daily Population (2020): 97

Annual Cost per Inmate (FY20):
$67,993 Operational Capacity: 306

The Western Massachusetts Regional Women's Correctional Center provides pretrial and sentenced care and custody for women primarily from the counties of Hampden, Hampshire, Franklin, Berkshire and Worcester, as well as women participating in the state DOC step-down program, the federal step-down program and probation revocation, county probation diversion, parole, and the US Marshals. The facility also accepts referrals from other counties on a case-by-case basis.

Today, the WCC offers holistic, integrated clinical services including specialized programming for women affected by trauma, mental health and substance use issues, those who have been trafficked or exploited, and services for mothers. WCC offers a continuum of Addiction & Recovery programming that meets the needs of those struggling with Substance Use Disorder and co-occurring diagnosis. Programming is trauma informed

and gender responsive, designed to promote recovery, personal responsibility and pro-social behavior, accomplished through evidence-based interventions; accountability, empowerment and strength based recovery-oriented language. The facility has an integrated team of Licensed Alcohol and Drug Counselors, Correctional Counselors and Mental Health Clinicians that offer psycho-educational groups, education, support and aftercare resources, Medicated Assisted Treatment, and a three-week intensive treatment program that offers skills and techniques that support an individual in understanding her relationship with drugs and alcohol and promotes a recovery culture among participants.

In 2021 following the retirement of Superintendent Patty Murphy, Sheriff Cocchi appointed Colleen Stocks to lead the facility as Assistant Superintendent. Her journey with the Hampden County Sheriff's Department is one that has come full circle. Starting in 1997, she has climbed through the ranks over the years and at various HCSD facilities – finding home at WCC for the past 12 years.

"I am so proud of Colleen and cannot wait to see what she brings to the role of Assistant Superintendent at our women's facility," Sheriff Cocchi said. "She has dedicated the majority of her time here to the betterment of the women in our care and custody, making her the perfect fit for this position."

From her very first position as summer help, to intern, to counselor and much more, Stocks has always had a passion for serving the community.

"I'm excited for this new chapter," said Stocks. "Being able to help build women back up from seemingly low points in their lives is work that I'm extremely proud to be doing. I feel like I'm fully able to bring the Sheriff's vision here and vice versa."

ABOVE: Assistant Superintendent Colleen Stocks

ABOVE: Nick Cocchi, center, deputy chief of security for the Hampden County Sheriff's Department, with Hampden County Sheriff Michael J. Ashe Jr., right, Berkshire County Sheriff Thomas Bowler, left, and Wendi Cocchi (far right) at the Naismith Memorial Basketball Hall of Fame in Springfield after Cocchi announced his candidacy to succeed Sheriff Ashe in two years. June 11, 2014. Photo by Michael S. Gordon/The Republican.

OPPOSITE PAGE: Sheriff Michael J. Ashe, Jr., his management team and the crews of the Community Service Program were honored at a ceremony at the John Shea Technical Training Facility in Forest Park for their work on maintenance projects in parks, public buildings and throughout the City. Sheriff Ashe was presented with the key to the City of Springfield by Mayor Domenic Sarno, Dec. 12, 2016. Photo by Don Treeger / The Republican.

ABOVE: Retired Sheriff Michael J. Ashe, Jr. was honored during a Legacy Tribute for him held on the front lawn of the Hampden County Sheriff's Department in Ludlow. This is Most Reverend Bishop Mitchell Rozanski of the Roman Catholic Diocese of Springfield delivering the invocation, seated from left to right are attorney William Fitzgerald, Governor Charles Baker, Sheriff Michael J. Ashe, Jr., and Lieutenant Governor Karyn Polito, July 10, 2018. Photo by Don Treeger / The Republican.

SHERIFF ASHE HONORED AT WHITE HOUSE

By Patrick Johnson [article published in
The Republican July 1, 2014]

Hampden County Sheriff Michael J. Ashe was honored June 30, 2014 during a White House ceremony that celebrated his 40-year career in criminal justice and recognized him as a "champion of change" in the area of inmate rehabilitation.

Ashe was one of 15 people being recognized under President Barack Obama's "Champions of Change" program in the category of Expanding Reentry Employment Opportunities.

The sheriff was singled out for his work establishing a program at the Hampden County Correctional Center that helps inmates re-adjust to society after their release from incarceration.

As part of his re-entry effort, Sheriff Ashe has utilized some 300 community partnerships to help offenders find 523 jobs in 2013, and more than 10,000 jobs in the past 20 years, having an impact on recidivism and public safety.

Attorney General Eric Holder praised the award recipients, saying their work demonstrates re-entry programs are a critical part of the criminal just agenda.

"Sound reentry policy is much more than an economic and budgetary necessity. It's also a moral imperative. After all, at some point, 95 percent of all incarcerated people will be released," Holder said.

CHAMPIONS OF CHANGE

Ashe was congratulated by U.S. Rep. Richard E. Neal, D-Springfield, Massachusetts Senators Elizabeth Warren and Edward J. Markey, and by Gov. Deval Patrick.

Neal said he was pleased to nominate Ashe, his long-time friend, for the award.

"In my opinion, there is no one in law enforcement more deserving of this special recognition from the White House than Sheriff Ashe. It is a fitting tribute to a remarkable career in public service," Neal said.

"Sheriff Ashe is one of the most passionate and innovative public officials in the country, and this recognition honors his nearly four

decades of exemplary service to the people of Massachusetts," Markey said.

Warren said "Sheriff Ashe has done an outstanding job growing innovative, successful and nationally recognized corrections and reentry programs based on his values of strength, decency, firmness and fairness.

Patrick said "His remarkable record of achievements and his outstanding commitment to the field of criminal justice makes him truly deserving of this honorable recognition."

ABOVE: Unveiling of a "Legacy Tribute" monument in honor of the work of retired Sheriff Michael J. Ashe, Jr. installed at the Hampden County House of Corrections facility at Stony Brook, Ludlow, July 10, 2018. Photo by Don Treeger/The Republican.

CHAPTER SEVEN

THE GUIDING PRINCIPALS

OF HAMPDEN COUNTY CORRECTIONS

GUIDING PRINCIPLES OF BEST CORRECTIONAL POLICY AND PRACTICE
AS DEVELOPED BY THE HAMPDEN COUNTY MODEL 1975 – 2013
BY MICHAEL J. ASHE, JR.

1. Within any correctional facility or operation, there must be an atmosphere and an ethos of respect for the full humanity and potential of any human being within that institution and an effort to maximize that potential. This is the first and overriding principle from which all other principles emanate, and without which no real corrections is possible.

2. Correctional facilities should seek to positively impact those in custody, and not be mere holding agents or human warehouses.

3. Those in custody should put in busy, full and productive days, and should be challenged to pick up the tools and directions to build a law-abiding life.

4. Those in custody should begin their participation in positive and productive activities as soon as possible in their incarceration.

5. All efforts should be made to break down the traditional barriers between correctional security and correctional human services.

6. Productive and positive activities for those in custody should be understood to be investments in the future of the community.

7. Correctional institutions should be communities of lawfulness. There should be "zero tolerance", overt or tacit, for any violence within the institution. Those in custody who assault others in custody should be prose-cuted as if such actions took place in free society. Staff should be diligently trained and monitored in "use of force" that is necessary and non-excessive to maintain safety, security, order and lawfulness.

8. The operational philosophy of positively impacting those in custody and respecting their full humanity must predominate at all levels of security.

9. Offenders should be directed toward understanding their full impact on victims and their community and should make restorative and reparative acts toward their victims and the community-at-large.

10. Offenders should be classified to the least level of security that is consistent with public safety and is merited by their own behavior.

11. There should be a continuum of gradual, supervised and supported community re-entry for offenders.

12. Community partnerships should be cultivated and developed for offender re-entry success. These partnerships should include the criminal justice and law enforcement communities as part of a public safety team.

13. Staff should be held accountable to be positive and productive.

14. All staff should be inspired, encouraged and supervised to "strive for excellence" in their work.

15. A spirit of innovation should permeate the operation. This innovation should be data-informed, evidenced-based, and include process and outcome measures.

16. In-service training should be ongoing and mandatory for all employees.

17. There should be a medical program that links with public health agencies and public health doctors from the home neighborhoods and communities of those in custody and which takes a proactive approach to finding and treating illness and disease in the custodial population.

18. Modern technological advances should be integrated into a correctional operation for optimal efficiency and effectiveness.

19. Any correctional facility, no matter what its locale, should seek to be involved in, and to involve, the local community, to welcome within its fences the positive elements of the community, and to be a positive participant and neighbor in community life. This reaching out should be both toward the community that hosts the facility and the communities from which those in custody come.

20. Balance is the key. A correctional operation should reach for the stars but be rooted in the firm ground of common sense.

PRINCIPLE # 1

Within any correctional facility or operation, there must be an atmosphere and an ethos of respect for the full humanity and potential of any human being within that institution, and an effort to maximize that potential. This is the first and overriding principle from which all other principles emanate, and without which no real corrections is possible.

There are few roles in life that are as massive an exercise in disenfranchisement and discouragement as the role of inmate in a correctional institution.

Likewise, there are few roles in the workforce that receive less approbation across the board than correctional employee.

This principle speaks to giving both groups, inmates and staff, credibility and encouragement for their full personhood, for the positive aspects of their pasts and presents, and for the full possibilities of their futures.

Inmates or staff who do not respect themselves and/or are not respected by others will not be productive or positive with their time incarcerated or their time at work.

A correctional facility can be an environment that engenders and fosters personal growth, if the humanity and potential of all within it are respected.

PRINCIPLE # 2

Correctional Facilities should seek to positively impact those in custody and not be mere holding agents or human warehouses.

If incarceration is allowed to be a "holding pattern", a period of suspended animation, those in custody are more likely to go back to doing what they have always done when they are released, because they will be what they have always been. The only difference may be that they have more anger and more shrewdness as they pursue their criminal career.

It is a simple law of life that nothing changes if nothing changes.

Correctional practitioners are very cognizant of the admonition that they must avoid being perceived as administering a glorified hotel or country club. They must be equally conscious of avoiding the reality of administering a human warehouse that breeds stagnation, frustration and new crime.

Most inmates come to jail or prison with a long history of social maladjustment, carrying a great deal of baggage in the form of histories of substance abuse, deficits in their educational, vocational and ethical development, and disconnectedness to the mores and values of the larger community.

Given the time and resources dedicated to corrections, it is absolute folly in social policy not to seek to address these deficit areas that inmates have brought to their incarceration.

An offender who has begun to treat his addiction; has made up for deficiencies in literacy and education; has begun a habit of showing up on time, ready for a productive day; and has experienced a displacement of values is, sheer common sense tells us, less likely to re-offend.

PRINCIPLE # 3

Those in custody should put in busy, full and productive days, and should be challenged to pick up the tools and directions to build a law-abiding life.

If we expect offenders to become positive and productive members of the larger community when they are released, the momentum of positivity and productivity must begin while they are incarcerated.

There should be a concerted effort to assure that those who are incarcerated put in productive days, just as they will be expected to do if they are to remain crime-free after release, and just as the taxpayers do who pay for their incarceration.

At Hampden County, there is a "40 Hour Work Week" policy for those in custody, whereby they are expected to be involved in productive activities -- either work or life-changing programs -- for at least 40 hours per week. The average inmate, at last count, was involved in these productive activities 47.16 hours per week.

The department doesn't want inmates lying around all day watching cartoons, or drawing dirty pictures on the cell walls, or scheming ways to prey upon each other or beat the system. The department wants them working, or making themselves more ready to work, through vocational, educational and ethical development.

Rather than such an active inmate population being problematic to security, the department has learned that "good programming is good security."

PRINCIPLE # 4

Those in custody should begin their participation in positive and productive activities as soon as possible in their incarceration.

The optimal time to impact someone during their incarceration is at the beginning of their sentence. That is when they are withdrawing from everything and everybody that sustained their wanton lifestyle on the street. That is when the full impact of where they have taken their lives hits home, when they are left high and dry, with no place to escape to and no one to enable their malfeasance. That is when they are thus most open to change, to a displacement of their understandings, perspectives and attitudes.

Traditionally, correctional facilities squander this optimal window for openness to change, instead putting new inmates on waiting lists to become involved in programs that can help them change their lives. While waiting to become involved in these programs, the offender is introduced into the informal system by other inmates,

and the edge for a new direction dulls as he becomes more comfortable in his new role and circumstances. Thus, while waiting to begin a journey down one road that offers hope and change, a new inmate slides down another road that leads back to where he came.

In an attempt to best take advantage of this optimal window of time for the willingness to change, the Hampden County Correctional Center instituted a mandatory "Basic Inmate Intensive Regimen", or "Transitional Program", beginning immediately after the completion of the 7 to 10 day orientation and continuing for four weeks. This program assures that all offenders are involved in basic core programs at the front end of their incarceration. Offenders must meet the expectations of each program to receive additional privileges and lower security consideration.

This Transitional Program can perhaps best be understood as analogous to a basic introductory survey course in college (although one hesitates to compare anything in jail or prison to college, lest he be subject to a knee-jerk backlash), perhaps appearing in a college catalog of courses as "Life Change 101".

The basic core programs offered in this Transitional Program include the following: Substance Abuse Education; Pre-employment Training; Learn to Earn; Violence Prevention; Conflict Resolution; Cognitive Thinking Skills; Victim Impact; Parenting Skills; and Educational Orientation.

The Transitional Program provides a foundation of services for every sentenced offender. This foundation is seen as enabling

offenders to build a successful community re-entry throughout their incarceration and beyond into the community.

After completing the Transitional Program, each inmate is required to participate in mandatory programs outlined in his Individual Service Plan. This Individual Service Plan is the result of a LSI (Level of Service Inventory) screening and psychological assessments completed by counselors during the inmate's participation in the Transitional Program. These programs outlined in his Individual Service Plan are designed to challenge the offender to "pick up the tools and directions to build a law-abiding life" by addressing his areas of social maladjustment.

PRINCIPLE # 5

All efforts should be made to break down the traditional barriers between correctional security and correctional human services.

For the work of "corrections", and not just "warehousing", to take place in a correctional setting, there cannot be a chasm between security and human services staff. They cannot see themselves as being at cross-purposes to each other, or as being in an "either/or" competition for the operational philosophy of an institution.

Good programming is necessary for good security; good security is necessary for good programming. Inmates who are given the opportunity, challenge and responsibility of positive and productive activities in their day are less likely to immerse themselves in negative thinking and actions, or to smoulder in anger which can erupt at any moment toward staff or other inmates. Any edifice of human services effort that is constructed must be built on a foundation of order and lawfulness.

To bridge the all-too-frequent chasm between security and programs in corrections, the Hampden County Sheriff's Department has implemented the following practices:

Most counselors are no longer hired directly into counseling positions. Instead, college and graduate school graduates are hired into correctional officer positions, with the opportunity to work themselves into a counselor position when one opens. Thus, if they do become counselors, they understand first-hand the perspectives and difficulties of security staff. In addition, security staff have worked with them as officers before they became counselors.

The department has created a bridge position between correctional officer and counselor, which we call Correctional Case Worker (CCW), combining duties traditionally performed exclusively by a security person or exclusively by a counselor. The CCW position, still a uniform position, is thus essentially a "hybrid" position. Those in CCW positions can choose to move into a counselor position when one opens; to remain in the CCW role; or to seek promotion to Sergeant, thus moving on from the hybrid position back to the security ranks.

Any individual who is hired directly to a counseling position or to a kitchen or maintenance position goes through the Correctional Officers Basic Training Academy with those hired directly as correctional officers. This togetherness in training creates bonds and connections between officers and other staff that continue during their year

PRINCIPLE # 6

Productive and positive activities for those in custody should be understood to be investments in the future of the community.

Far too often, a sensible, balanced effort at corrections is misrepresented, misunderstood and misinterpreted as some kind of coddling of inmates.

As stated earlier, the Hampden County Correctional Center has a "40 Hour Work Week" policy for those in its custody. Inmates are expected to work within the institution — housekeeping, grounds maintenance, kitchen, laundry etc. --, or to participate in programs that make them more work-ready -- substance abuse education and treatment, GED preparation, vocational training, etc. -- for a minimum of 40 hours every week.

The Hampden County Correctional Center's philosophy is that the true coddling of inmates is when such work and productive activities are not provided, and inmates are left to languish in their cells all day.

To understand why positive and productive activities for inmates should be seen by the community as investments in its future, the Hampden County Sheriff's Department makes an analogy between jails and hospitals. We all wish that the reasons for the existence of a hospital in a community —namely illness, disease, interpersonal violence, and accidents — did not exist, but that does not stop us from wanting the best possible hospital in our community to address these unwanted occurrences, or from respecting the work that the hospital does. Likewise, we all wish that what necessitates a jail or prison — namely crime — did not exist, yet we should also want these institutions to be the best possible to address that crime. We would not suppose that just by putting someone in a hospital bed, without treatment, we would be making our best effort to address illness and trauma. Likewise, we should not suppose that just by putting someone behind institutional fences, without productive corrective activities, we would be making our best effort to address crime. Finally, as regards this analogy, we do not blame hospitals for the illness and trauma that they seek to address. Likewise, we should not blame correctional institutions for the law-breaking and criminality that they seek to address.

As a result of its concerted effort at providing positive and productive activities, the Hampden County Correctional Center has been able to serve its community by fighting recidivism. Despite the fact that offenders are brought to the door of the facility in shackles and chains after long histories of social maladjustment, with a substance abuse problem, educational deficiencies, no appreciable job record and no marketable skills, more than eighty-five percent have not been re-incarcerated for new crimes one year after release and more than two-thirds have not been re-incarcerated for new crimes three years after release. This despite the fact that crimes for which one is sentenced to county jail — drug and property crimes - traditionally have among the highest rates of recidivism.

A great deal is made of how expensive it is to incarcerate an individual. It is even more expensive to society to have an individual in a criminal pattern of activity on its streets. By lessening recidivism, the Hampden County Correctional Center is providing a good return on the investment in positive and productive activities for inmates.

PRINCIPLE # 7

Correctional institutions should be communities of lawfulness. There should be "zero tolerance", overt or tacit, for any violence within the institution. Those in custody who assault others in custody should be prosecuted as if such actions took place in free society. Staff should be diligently trained and monitored in "use of force" that is necessary and non-excessive to maintain safety, security, order and lawfulness.

The Hampden County Correctional Center does not tolerate, overtly or tacitly, the preying of inmates upon other inmates.

Rape is not part of the culture of the institution.

Any inmate suspected of violence toward any other inmate, or towards staff, is prosecuted as if such actions took place in the community.

The wearing of gang colors by inmates, the use of gang signs or signals and participation in gang meetings is forbidden and subject to disciplinary action.

Drugs are not tolerated and are vigorously pursued as contraband within the institution. As proof of this, targeted and random drug testing consistently turns up less than one-half of one percent (.003) positive results. It is the firm belief of Sheriff Ashe that in an institution in which the beginning of recovery from substance abuse is most always an essential element of successful community re-entry, the availability of drugs and alcohol within the institution works against that success. One of the ways that was utilized to achieve this near-total absence of controlled substances within the institution was the implementation of a non-contact visiting policy, with visits taking place with a glass partition between visitors and incarcerates (mothers with children have special contact visiting times with their children). The administration of the Hampden County Sheriff's Department firmly believed that drugs were entering the institution through contact visits, and the dramatic lessening of positive drug test results after the implementation of non-contact visits verified that belief. The administration believes that the privilege of contact visits in lower security is one of the "carrots" for those in its custody, inspiring them to seek to earn lower security status. In a correctional institution in which inmates are serving longer sentenc-

es, such as state prisons, the non-contact visiting policy might be adjusted to reflect this reality of longer separation from loved ones.

This assiduous vigilance against violence, gangs and drugs in the institution is strongly believed to be consistent with preparing individuals to be law-abiding members of society. We cannot expect those incarcerated to grow away from violence, gangs and drugs in an atmosphere filled with these very things.

Staff is trained in the proper use of force, closely monitored for adherence to said policy, and subject to appropriate penalties if said policy is violated.

There should be less lawlessness in a correctional institution than in free society, as the controls are so much greater. A correctional institution should be a place of lawfulness, although it is filled with lawbreakers.

PRINCIPLE # 8

The operational philosophy of positively impacting those in custody and respecting their full humanity must predominate at all levels of security.

Disciplinary Segregation or Maximum-Security units should, as much as is practically possible, provide opportunities for positive and productive activities by inmates.

One of the overriding operational philosophies of the Hampden County Correctional Center is that good things — greater freedom, greater privileges - will happen to an individual who takes care of the business of conducting himself in a positive, productive and law-abiding manner, and less desirable things — less freedom, fewer privileges — will happen to someone who does not. If this "carrot and stick" ethos stops at the door of segregation, and there is only the "stick", the segregation unit becomes a source of stagnation, frustration and new crime.

Common sense tells us that the number of freedoms and privileges on a segregation unit must be necessarily less than in general population. At the same time, if no path is provided for greater freedom on the unit, or for release from the unit contingent on good behavior, an individual has no incentive for good behavior.

In short, segregation units should not be devoid of hope.

In addition, every effort should be made to fight against mental decomposition in an individual due to isolation and sensory deprivation.

Several years ago, the Hampden County Correctional Center instituted changes to its disciplinary segregation unit to assure that there were incentives for positive, productive behavior, and not just disincentives for negative, counter-productive behavior. Educational opportunities are provided for individuals to work on in cells, and individual counseling is offered. Carefully selected groups of individuals who have earned the privilege are allowed group recreation once a week. In addition, changes were instituted to work against possible mental decomposition of inmates

due to the effects of isolation and sensory deprivation, including the utilization of MP3 players as an earned privilege. An article entitled "The Utilization of MP3 Players in Correctional Segregation Units" about the use of MP3 players at the Hampden County Correctional Center appeared in the December 2012/January 2013 issue of Corrections Today magazine.

Anyone wishing to learn more about the above broad-based changes is urged to go to the Hampden County Correctional Center website hcsdmass.org and click on "Department Implements Innovative Improvements To Disciplinary Segregation Unit", or to contact the department directly.

PRINCIPLE # 9

Offenders should be directed toward understanding their full impact on victims and their community and should make restorative and reparative acts toward their victims and the community-at-large.

In addition to the many deficits in education and employment that individuals bring with them to jail and prison, they often bring with them a history of narcissistic, self-pleasuring behavior that takes no account of the effects of their actions on other individuals or on the community as a whole.

Restorative Justice addresses the impact of crime and the actions needed to repair the harm done. This process holds offenders accountable for their behavior, while offering them the opportunity to actively participate in making amends.

As part of the Hampden County Correctional Center Restorative Justice effort, a Victim Impact Program (VIP) was designed, using an existing curriculum developed by the California Youth Authority, the Office for Victims of Crime, and Mothers Against Drunk Driving. The goal of the program is for the offender to gain an understanding of the physical, emotional and spiritual effects that their crimes have had on victims and the impact of crime throughout the community, often referred to as the "ripple effect".

Upon completion of VIP classes, offenders who are classified to lower security have the opportunity to meet with community members to discuss their particular crime and the impact that it has had on others.

Communities are represented by Community Accountability Boards, comprised of volunteer members representing various components of the community (i.e. business, human services, elderly, etc.).

Each board has four to six members that meet with offenders on a monthly basis to develop an "Offender Responsibility Plan". The goal of the plan is to deepen the offender's understanding of the reaction of the community to crime, to learn ways to avoid repeating the same behavior, and to once again reinforce the understanding of the ripple effect.

It is important to note that neither the institutional Victim Impact Program nor the Community Accountability Boards require identification of, or participation by, the actual individual victim of the offender. The Community Boards are representing the victimization of the entire community or neighborhood, including the victim.

The curriculum utilized for the Victim Impact Program is currently available online at the following web address: https//www.ovcttac.gov/victimimpact.gov

PRINCIPLE # 10

Offenders should be classified to the least level of security that is consistent with public safety and is merited by their own behavior.

In some ways, Principle #10 runs counter to many people's knee-jerk beliefs.

The supposition can be that the higher the level of security in which an offender is kept, the greater the community is protected. After laboring for over 38 years on the front lines and frontiers of community corrections, Sheriff Michael J. Ashe, Jr. has concluded that this belief does not result in optimal public safety.

At the Hampden County Correctional Center, the policy and practice are that the least level of security in which an offender is held at the end of his sentence, the less likely he is to return to crime. An offender should be at the least level of security that is consistent with public safety.

The first and foremost reason for this policy and practice is the fact that when an offender gradually re-enters the community on a continuum of lesser levels of security, he is given time to be closely monitored and strongly supported while he involves himself with community recovery groups and / or faith-based groups, finds and begins a job, seeks to involve himself with community resources to continue to correct his educational deficits, seeks housing, repairs his relationship with family and community, etc. This supervised gradualism fights recidivism. The percentage of those in the custody of the Hampden County Correctional Center stepped-down to lower security prior to release rose from 44% in 2001 to 63.1% in 2012; simultaneously, the one-year recidivism rate dropped from 30% to its present 17.4%.

In addition, when individuals are given the incentive of lesser security as their sentence progresses, the positive and productive behavior required for entrance into, and continued participation in, these lesser levels of security becomes a self-selection process for habits of law-abiding behavior. Thus, the incentive of lesser security produces the result of behavior most likely to keep an individual from re-offending.

PRINCIPLE # 11

There should be a continuum of gradual, supervised and supported community re-entry for offenders.

As stated in the previous principle, it is the operating understanding of the Hampden County Sheriff's Department that the least level of security that an offender is on at the time of release, the less likely he is to return to crime.

Proceeding out of this understanding is the implementation of a continuum of gradual, supervised and supported community re-entry.

At the Hampden County Correctional Center, this continuum begins in medium security, behind the fences, and proceeds to the Minimum Security/Pre-Release Center, from which inmates can find and hold a job, attend an off-site substance abuse education and treatment program, and attend community recovery groups and church with staff, as well as participate in community service restitution crews.

Another minimum-security option that may be utilized before or after Minimum Security/Pre-Release is the Western Massachusetts Correctional Alcohol Center. Originally begun for third offense Driving Under The Influence offenders, it now serves those with substance abuse problems who are serving time for offenses other than DUI. In this substance abuse treatment facility, intensive in-house programming is combined with attendance at community recovery groups with "escort" volunteers from those groups. Community restitution work is also an integral part of the program.

The next step after minimum security is the Day Reporting Program, through which those still on sentence are closely monitored and strongly supported as they live at home and follow a closely scripted daily schedule of work and approved community activities. A system of human and technological monitoring assures that schedules are followed. The Hampden County Sheriff's Department established the first such Day Reporting Center for those still on sentence in 1986, and it has since been replicated throughout the country.

The final point in the continuum of lesser security is the After Incarceration Support Systems program by which, despite there being no statutory obligation to do so, the Hampden County Sheriff's Department stays involved with individual offenders in the crucial first months after release. Offenders are invited to attend groups, meet with caseworkers and utilize an array of services, even after they are "off the count" at the correctional facility.

This After Incarceration Support Systems (AISS) program is seen as a bridge between the positive momentum begun in offenders' lives while they are in the various security levels of the Hampden County Correctional Center and successful, positive, productive, law-abiding community re-entry. The decisions made by an offender in the first hours, days, weeks and months of re-entry determine whether he will fall off a cliff into a chasm of old ways.

This program is so successful that a graduation is held each year which honors not only those who have participated in the program during that particular year, but also those graduates of previous years who are still successfully law-abiding in the community and who come back for a "reunion." Who could have imagined that a correctional department would hold an annual reunion of hundreds of successful former inmates who willingly return to celebrate their success?

PRINCIPLE # 12

Community partnerships should be cultivated and developed for offender re-entry success.

The Hampden County Sheriff's Department has established nearly 300 partnerships with public and private non-profit community agencies, organizations and institutions to further its mission of corrections and successful law-abiding re-entry of offenders into the community.

Consistent with, and concurrent with, its belief that a correctional facility should not be an isolated fortress in the woods is the belief that the facility should welcome into its efforts, and align itself with, positive and productive people and programs in the community. By "community" we mean not only the host community of the correctional facility, but also the communities or counties from which its inmates come.

The Hampden County Sheriff's Department believes that it takes a community to successfully reenter an offender.

In Principle 11, we talked of the After-Incarceration Support Systems program serving as a bridge between the positive momentum in an offender's life begun within the facility and positive, productive and law-abiding community living. The open arms of the community take the form of these nearly 300 community partners. By establishing these community partnerships, the Hampden County Sheriff's Department extends the tentacles of its corrective accomplishments into the community.

Obviously the most basic partnerships of a correctional department should be with other criminal justice and law enforcement agencies, and the Hampden County Correctional Center seeks a seamless involvement with these agencies to help ensure and enhance public safety.

In October 2006, Sheriff Ashe implemented a "High Risk Offender Re-entry Program". This program focuses specifically on inmates who have been sentenced on firearm charges, have very violent criminal records, or have been a serious management problem while incarcerated.

One component of the High-Risk Offender Re-entry Program is getting such offenders connected with an After Incarceration Support Systems staff member who specializes in work with this high-risk population. In addition to this utilization of re-entry staff who work closely on the re-entry plan, the department uses external mentors to meet with and encourage offenders to choose a different path after their release.

When a high-risk offender is about to finish his sentence, a specific "Release Notification" is sent to law enforcement agencies, notifying them of very specific information about the individual, including his place or places of residence.

In addition to this Release Notification, the Sheriff's Department holds "Public Safety Exit Meetings" quarterly, to network with other criminal justice and law enforcement agencies regarding the offenders to be released in that quarter.

The soon-to-be released high-risk inmates are brought before the criminal justice agents at these meetings. They are given an opportunity to learn both that those in the criminal justice community wish to support any effort by the offender to build a law-abiding life and that those in criminal justice are ready, willing and able to protect the community from the offender if the offender returns to his old days and ways. Basically, what is conveyed to the re-entering offender is "we're rooting for you, but we'll be aware of you and watching you closely!"

The following week these high-risk offenders are then brought before a second group of individuals representing service providers in the community. These service providers can assist the offender getting connected to specific resources in the community. Areas of service include housing, job development, career placement, mental health, education, vocational instruction, After Incarceration Support Systems, mentoring, faith-based involvement, and family support.

Another tool used to discourage high-risk inmates from re-offending after release is presenting to police roll calls on the day before release.

Without these service provider and criminal justice community partners ready, willing and able to assist community re-entry, the bridge built by After Incarceration Support Systems becomes a bridge to nowhere.

PRINCIPLE # 13

Staff should be held accountable to be positive and productive.

Grade B prison movies are full of corrupt wardens, brutish, sadistic "guards", and improbably innocent inmates.

What this principle speaks to is the vision and the reality of having dynamic, enlightened leadership and a staff that is held accountable to discharge their duties with industry, integrity, teamwork, efficiency, and an overriding sense of professional honor.

Rather than "guards", the department employs modern correctional officers. This is in concurrence with the policy of the American Correctional Association, which considers the word guard to be "offensive and outdated" in referring to the correctional officer position, because, among other reasons, "it implies the job is inherently passive". In the direct supervision/unit management mode of supervision, these officers are professional managers of the locales to which they are posted and the incarcerates within those locales. Modern correctional officers are really "community police" in a community of convicted and accused lawbreakers.

The department seeks to hire and inspire men and women who believe in the philosophy and the possibility of impacting offenders positively, and are committed to leading by example, to being role models, and to working to assure a positive and productive climate in the facility.

In keeping with this expectation of positive and productive professionalism, 51.5% of the Hampden County Correctional Center uniformed staff possess a degree in higher education, including 14 who have Masters Degrees. 53.1% of total staff have degrees, including 87 individuals who have master's degrees and 7 who have Doctorate Degrees.

PRINCIPLE # 14

All staff should be inspired, encouraged and supervised to "strive for excellence" in their work.

Just as the Hampden County Sheriff Department does not believe in only negative reinforcements with the incarcerated population, the Hampden County Sheriff's Department does not believe in only negative reinforcements for its workforce.

It should be communicated to staff that their work is not just "process", that the goal should be the optimal climate throughout the correctional center and the optimal effort to serve public safety by lowering recidivism. The "product" of any correctional institution is a positive, productive, law-abiding community life by those who have been in its custody.

The Department has a good track record of promoting from the ranks, so that staff know that excellence in the uniform and/or non-uniform ranks will result in greater opportunities.

The Department has a system of pins and

medals awarded for good job performance, and these are worn on the breast of the officer's uniform, as in the military.

During National Correctional Officers Week, the Department has designated awards for an outstanding officer, an outstanding supervisory officer, and an outstanding officer with longstanding service. The Department also awards "Professional Excellence Award" certificates on each shift. The three winners of the outstanding officers awards and three randomly selected officers from among the Professional Excellence Award winners are given cash bonuses. The Department also awards a one-year college scholarship to the son or daughter of a correctional officer. The monies for all of these awards do not come from the public budget, but rather from a special "Sunshine Fund".

It is said that only approximately 10% of those who sign a professional baseball contract will ever play in the major leagues. Only a similar percentage of those who start out as blue-shirted correctional officers will achieve the white shirt of a supervisory officer (Sergeant, Lieutenant, Captain, Primary Captain, Major). The Department has instituted the position of Corporal between the position of Officer and Sergeant. Corporals are not supervisors, still wear a blue shirt, and remain in their regular officer rotation, but they get extra pay and two stripes on their arms. It is a way of positively reinforcing the sustained good performance of officers, even though the numbers do not allow promotion to Sergeant.

PRINCIPLE # 15

A spirit of innovation should permeate the operation. This innovation should be data-informed, evidenced-based, and include process and outcome measures.

There can be a tendency to look upon corrections as a static, tired, "grey" sort of endeavor, to be done without enthusiasm or energy. In this scenario, changes and innovations must come from above or outside the department.

Sheriff Ashe believes in an "entrepreneurial attitude" about corrections, where innovation is driven by creative responses to the problems and possibilities of the day, and is data-informed, evidenced-based, and includes process and outcome measures.

The Hampden County Sheriff's Department instituted the nation's first Day Reporting Center, whereby those nearing release can live at home and participate in positive community activities, while being closely monitored and strongly supported in their efforts to re-enter the community.

The department also instituted the nation's first After Incarceration Support Systems program, wherein the department offers an offender the opportunity to utilize its re-entry services after release, although they are no longer in the custody of the department and there is no statutory obligation to assist them.

The department began its Basic Inmate Intensive Regimen or Transitional Program to assure that the window of time at the beginning of a sentence when an offender is most open to change is not squandered.

The department implemented changes in its disciplinary segregation unit which involved positive reinforcements for positive behavior and efforts to prevent mental decompensation resulting from isolation and lack of sensory stimuli.

The department instituted a Public Health Model in Corrections that won an Innovations in American Government Award. The model uses public health doctors and clinics from the neighborhoods from which the inmates come, establishing a continuity of care from the institution into the community. It also takes a pro-active approach to preventing, finding and treating illness.

The department established a restaurant in the community at a local Industrial Park, called the "The Olde Armory Grille", with a workforce made up of offenders re-entering the community from lower security, supervised by department staff.

The department has been in the forefront of prison industries. The chief priority of the Hampden County Correctional Center Prison Industry Program is offering offenders the opportunity to develop the habit of showing up each day for work, on time, and ready for a productive day. Another priority of the institution's Prison Industry Program has been the development of innovative businesses over the years. These businesses include the making of office furniture, wooden household chairs, mattresses, laundry bags, household sheds and inmate uniforms; as well as silk screening, embroidery, and upholstery.

The above are just some examples of the "game-changing" innovation that has resulted from the Hampden County Correctional Center's aforementioned "striving for excellence" with an entrepreneurial attitude.

PRINCIPLE # 16

In-service training should be ongoing and mandatory for all employees.

The Hampden County Correctional Center staff training effort is consistent with the belief that staff should stay connected to training year-round.

In the past, the department had conducted once-a-year blocks of training for staff. When this burst of condensed training was completed, there would be no other broad-based staff interface with training for the rest of the year.

A response to this less than desirable, but perhaps typical, scheduling of training was the conception and inception of the "Bi-weekly Training Regimen".

Coordinated by our Training Department, staff from all areas of expertise and all department facilities "step up" to develop twenty-six bi-weekly trainings during the course of a year, each of one-hour duration. These trainings are available at various times of day during a two-week period, to accommodate all shifts.

Bi-weekly training topics have included the following in the last two years: Drugs and Testing, Use of Force and Tactics, Report

Writing and Analyzing Written Communication, Research, It's Not Just Statistics, Homelessness and How It Impacts Corrections, Stress Management, Special Needs Inmates, Conflict of Interest, Gang Update, Untold Stories of Truancy, Direct Supervision, Pod Leadership, Youth Culture, Process Addictions, Contraband Update, Social Media, In the Line of Duty Situations, Domestic Violence, Bomb Search Techniques, How to Read a BOP, Suicide Prevention, STD's, Advanced/Personal Communication Skills, Direct Supervision, and Sex Offender Treatment.

Beyond this Bi-weekly Training Regimen, all staff are required to do a day-long eight-hour training based on American Correctional Association and Department of Corrections Standards. Topics include Americans with Disabilities Act, Code of Ethics, Conflict of Interest Law, Cultural Diversity, Direct Supervision, Emergency Plans, Fire Prevention, Inmate Rules and Regulations, Interpersonal Relations, Key Control, Medical Topic/Safety and Hygiene, Report Writing, Rights and Responsibilities of Inmates, Security Procedures and Regulations, Sexual Harassment, Sexual Misconduct, Social/Cultural Lifestyle of Inmate Population, Special Needs Inmates, Supervision of Inmates, Use of Force Policy, Tactics and Regulations.

A second full day of training follows, which is mandatory for staff in academy trained positions. This training includes CPR-First Aid required reviews.

In addition to the above trainings, staff can choose from a smorgasbord of training opportunities to fulfill their required

training hours. These trainings include: Roll Call Trainings, which involve a mixture of live presentations and thirty minute taped trainings provided to all correctional officer staff during roll calls, Counselor Training, Leadership Training, Supervisor Training Meetings, Workshops, On-The-Job Rotation Training, Uniform Supervisor Cross-training, POD Net Training, and off-site trainings.

Security, maintenance, food service, counseling and health services staff are expected to train for forty hours each year. Administrative and clerical staff are expected to train for sixteen to twenty-four hours each year, depending on the position.

In addition to all of the above, in order to acclimate new security staff to a correctional environment, new staff are assigned an experienced staff person in a mentor/mentee relationship.

The training department includes a Wellness program, with staff involved in an intensive and extensive effort to achieve the best possible fitness and wellness of both staff and inmates. The benefits of the fitness and wellness of both staff and inmates extend not only to the individuals themselves, but also to the department as a whole and to the taxpayers who fund both the medical care of indigent inmates and staff sick and compensation benefits.

PRINCIPLE # 17

There should be a medical program that links with public health agencies and public health doctors from the home neighborhoods and communities of those in custody and which takes a pro-active approach to finding and treating illness and disease in the custodial population.

About 75% of those in the custody of the Hampden County Sheriff's Department come from four neighborhoods within the county. These neighborhoods are inner-city neighborhoods. Each of them has a public community health center.

Traditionally in corrections, institutions or departments contracted with private doctors.

The Hampden County Sheriff's Department decided that since most of those in its custody came from what it called the "same zip codes", it would seek out a partnership with the public health centers from those neighborhoods, through which dedicated public health professionals would come into its facility and begin relationships with patients from their neighborhoods; relationships that continued after release.

The Department believed that jails were effectively "reservoirs of illness", including many public health diseases that are communicable such as HIV/AIDS, hepatitis, sexually transmitted diseases, tuberculosis, etc.

What was meant by "reservoirs of illness" is that most of its inmates are not in any health care system before they come to the correctional facility. Thus, their illnesses are often undetected and untreated. During their jail time, incarcerates are in a "holding pattern" during which their illnesses can be diagnosed and treated, and treatment can continue after release.

AS A RESULT OF THIS PROGRAM:

Offenders' serious and often unmet health care needs are addressed, and ongoing treatment is maintained.

Offenders establish relationships with health centers and with health care providers at the health sites. These health care providers are often from the local community and represent the culture and best values of the neighborhood. More than 88% of HIV/AIDS inmates, for instance, keep their initial medical appointment at a designated community health center.

The educational element of the program helps make inmates aware of how to reduce the spread of communicable disease and manage their own chronic diseases, such as diabetes.

Poor young people who are largely uninsured and under-educated about health issues, individuals who have existed outside the health care system, are connected to that vital element of society.

Public Health improves because of immediate care of offenders after release. Education, early detection and treatment of infectious disease prevents spread and costly complications.

There is significant downstream savings in community health care costs. Early detection and effective early treatment save costs in the future.

When a person is healthy and receiving proper and adequate care, he is more "socialized", more connected to the positive elements of the community, and truly less likely to be living a criminal lifestyle. To put it simply, someone who is keeping a medical appointment at 9:00 AM to take care of their health with competent, caring health center staff is less likely to be someone climbing in a window at three o'clock in the morning to rob someone.

There is a drastic decrease in the use of emergency rooms as de facto primary care providers, with resultant huge cost savings.

Some patients no longer wait for symptoms to become severe before seeking care; treatment becomes less costly.

This program was awarded the Innovations in American Government Award, an awards program of the Ford Foundation, administered by the John F. Kennedy School of Government at Harvard University, in partnership with the Council for Excellence in Government.

PRINCIPLE # 18

Modern technological advances should be integrated into a correctional operation for optimal efficiency and effectiveness.

As with other fields, modern technology opens worlds of opportunity in corrections.

The Hampden County Sheriff's Department's vision for its Management Information System (MIS) is quite simple in its approach.

The Department does not merely capture data. The Department acts on the belief that you must know from the onset what you will be doing with the captured data, if anything. The Department seeks to understand how vital the information can be to any area of operations or any user.

MIS staff understand the process flows of all Sheriff's Department missions and are thus able to determine where to begin with data capture, and to whom to pass that captured data without duplication of effort.

Gathered data is analyzed thoroughly and shared. The data can be scrutinized to ferret out trends which can help make the best decisions in planning. With the existence of solid data, reports can be written to fit the needs of staff.

MIS can reduce many person-hours in all departments by doing efficiency sweeps.

The Hampden County Sheriff's Department is invested in barcoding strategies. It has incorporated wristbands and ID cards for respective security levels. Barcoding is very simple, very inexpensive, and pays high dividends when it comes to the control and capturing of data. A simple scan of the barcode, which represents the inmate person ID, is the catalyst into the multitudes of data captured on the respective inmate.

Officers posted to the visiting areas scan

2D barcodes off the back of a visitor's driver's license to automatically load data into the visiting database.

The Hampden County Sheriff's Department was approached on a daily basis by police departments from throughout the county looking for vital data about specific inmates, released or active, within its system. A simple, interactive website with the department's backend data was set up for these external agencies to do investigative work. What started out as a one county project, (JEDI - Justice Exchange Delivery Infrastructure) became a federate project of the four Western Massachusetts Sheriffs (WMSIN — Western Massachusetts Sheriffs' Information Network), allowing correctional and law enforcement personnel to access information from all four counties. The project grew yet again, when all 14 sheriffs of the commonwealth and the Department of Corrections founded a statewide system that mirrored the Western Massachusetts product (MIDNET — Massachusetts Inmate Data Network), which can be accessed by police departments, District Attorneys, the Registry of Motor Vehicles, the Probation Department, and other appropriate agencies from throughout the commonwealth.

In the Hampden County Re-entry Project, Sheriff's Department data is presented to service providers in the community. This data helps the provider understand the background and needs of the offender before his/her release. The offender is referred to a particular agency, and this message is relayed to an inbox at the service provider's level, stating that an individual in custody is scheduled for release and has

been referred. The provider, within their inbox, can click on the particular referred offender and receive all non-classified, non-confidential assessment data.

The MIS Director says: "We are tool makers in the rawest sense. What we pride ourselves in is making the sharpest, most precise and easiest to use tools. Our toolbox is not cluttered with rusty, antique tools, but shiny well-honed utensils, at the ready for any task, big or small."

PRINCIPLE # 19

Any correctional facility, no matter what its locale, should seek to be involved in, and to involve, the local community, to welcome within its fences the positive elements of the community, and to be a positive participant and neighbor in community life. This reaching out should be both toward the community that hosts the facility and the communities from which those in custody come.

The desired product of a correctional facility is public safety. That safety is accomplished not only by incapacitating criminals, but also by returning to the community individuals who have the desire and the assistance to live positive, productive, law-abiding lives.

Jails and prisons, to be successful, cannot be isolated fortresses in the woods. They must be part of a community team.

Most inmates come to jail lacking any real sense of neighborhood cohesion or any connectedness to the mores and values, the means and ends, of the larger community. Part of any successful corrective effort, behind the fences or in community re-entry, must involve an attempt to facilitate in the offender a sense of connectedness with the law-abiding, positive and productive people and ways of their neighborhood and of the larger community.

Community corrections involves a correctional department both inviting into its facilities the positive people and organizations of the larger community and attempting to "plug in" offenders to these positive elements to utilize as part of community re-entry.

The Hampden County Correctional Center's volunteer directory now contains 370 names of community volunteers who come into the facility. These volunteers represent a total of 77 different groups. In the year 2012, 50 college students completed internships at the Hampden County Correctional Center.

To be a good neighbor, the Hampden County Correctional Center oversees the performance of 80,000 hours each year of volunteer community service restitution by minimum security offenders who are out in the communities of Hampden County every weekday cleaning litter, weeds and bushes from streets and highways; assisting Departments of Public Works and Park Departments; working to maintain elderly housing complexes; getting children's summer camps ready in the spring; helping clean up illegal dumping eyesores; helping with food drives; maintaining community gardens and cemeteries, etc. Sheriff Ashe

considers this program a "double winner", because offenders are given the opportunity to build "sweat equity" in their successful community re-entry by "giving to" rather than "taking from" the community, while, at the same time, communities get projects accomplished that would otherwise go undone.

PRINCIPLE # 20

Balance is the key. A correctional operation should reach for the stars but be rooted in the firm ground of common sense.

In dedicating a newly built facility, Sheriff Ashe said the following:

"We gather today in a new facility that reflects the balanced, realistic, progressive philosophy of corrections of this department. They tell me that there is a comedian who tells of going through life with a prayer book in one hand and a .45 revolver in the other hand. That is a humorous representation of our approach. We are vigilant and aware that our mission is to administer a safe, secure, orderly facility where staff and inmates are free from violence. But we also provide the tools and directions to build a law-abiding life to those who wish to do so. I'm not interested in administering a country club or a hotel. I'm also not interested in administering a cesspool that breeds frustration, stagnation and new crime. Our departmental motto of correctional supervision has been, and shall remain, 'strength reinforced with decency, firmness dignified with fairness.'

This new facility enhances our capacity for both strength and humanity."

The Hampden County Sheriff's Department operates in the belief that the real coddling of inmates takes place when they are not challenged with a demanding regimen of productive activities that can help them change their lives.

The Hampden County Sheriff's Department also operates in the belief that any such corrective effort must be built on a solid foundation of safety, security, order and lawfulness.

CHAPTER EIGHT

THE LEGACY CONTINUES:
SHERIFF COCCHI EVOLVES CORRECTIONS AND COMMUNITY CARE

THE LEGACY CONTINUES

- Wayne E. Phaneuf

When six-term Hampden County Sheriff Michael J. Ashe Jr. dropped a bombshell in January of 2014 that he wasn't going to run in 2016 he gave those interested in the job two years to make their case to the electorate.

The sheriff said he'd like his successor to be selected "on the basis of ability." As the months went by candidates began to emerge. By the time the 2016 election arrived there were six potential candidates who would be on the ballot. Among them was deputy chief of security at the Hampden County Jail, Nicholas Cocchi who launched his campaign at the Naismith Memorial Basketball Hall of Fame in downtown Springfield on June 11, 2014. A crowd of 1,200 supporters attended the announcement. When all the cheering subsided, Cocchi, a 21-year veteran at the sheriff's department, told the crowd he has the training, experience and values to continue Ashe's legacy as the county's next sheriff. If elected, Cocchi promised to follow in his bosses footsteps and place "public service before self, before politics."

In October of 2015, Sheriff Ashe issued about 1,200 invitations to his personal supporters, asking them to attend a fall fundraiser for Cocchi, a Democrat from Ludlow. Ashe told his supporters in the personalized notes that he "thinks the world" of Cocchi, whom he referred to as a "good man of great professional accomplishment."

On Sept. 4, 2016, *The Republican* endorsed Nick Cocchi in the Democratic preliminary election for Hampden County sheriff. In its editorial, *The Republican* stated that, Ashe's legacy "was an impressive list of local, regional and national law enforcement officials who say the Ashe tenure will go down as a pioneering and groundbreaking record of public service and accomplishment, particularly in identifying rehabilitation as a crucial element to the penal justice system," And that, "If Cocchi is indeed the 'establishment candidate,' as has been portrayed during this campaign, he represents an establishment that has served the needs of the county well, attracted acclaim from many quarters and does not require a disruption."

Nick Cocchi was elected Sheriff of Hampden County on Nov. 8, 2016. The victory came just over a month after Cocchi won a three-way Democratic primary. In his victory speech newly elected Sheriff Cocchi lauded Michael Ashe as his mentor after 23 years with the department. "You just have to take him in, watch what he does, listen to what he says. ... He's never going to put you down the wrong path," Cocchi said. "What you have done for the county of Hampden, what you have done for the offender population ... can never be repaid."

Michael Ashe accepted his share of handshakes as well. He said he felt "terrific" about passing the torch to Cocchi. "To be honest, Nick's the one. We're dealing with the least loved in society. You really have to have a passion for it. That's key, and Nick has that," Michael Ashe said. "We need people who want to motivate and inspire inmates, not just guard them."

ABOVE: Election pamphlet "Cocchi for Sheriff" with endorsement from retiring Sheriff Michael J. Ashe, Jr. Photo courtesy retired Sheriff Michael J. Ashe, Jr.

OPPOSITE PAGE: Nick Cocchi, deputy chief of security for the Hampden County Sheriff's Department, ascends to the podium to announce his candidacy for Hampden County Sheriff Wednesday at the Naismith Memorial Basketball Hall of Fame, June 11, 2014. (Michael S. Gordon/The Republican)

TOP: Hampden County District Attorney Anthony Gulluni (left) endorsed Hampden County Sheriff candidate Nick Cocchi during an announcement on the steps of the Hampden County Hall of Justice.
(Don Treeger / The Republican)

LEFT: State Senator Eric Lesser, left, chats with Hampden County Sheriff candidate Nick Cocchi outside the Hampden County House of Corrections in Ludlow. Lesser backed Cocchi's campaign for Hampden County Sheriff, Aug. 30, 2016. Photo by Dave Roback / The Republican.

ABOVE: East Longmeadow celebrates the July 4th holiday with their annual parade through town. Here is Nick Cocchi, candidate for Hampden County Sheriff with his wife Wendi. (Dave Roback / The Republican)

ABOVE: G. Michael Dobbs, center, managing editor of Reminder Publications, introducing the candidates for Hampden County Sheriff during a televised pre-primary debate in Springfield, July 26, 2016.
Photo by Frederick Gore/The Republican.

ELECTION 2016

New sheriffs in town: Cocchi, Cahillane win

Follow in footsteps
of long-serving
predecessors

By Stephanie Barry and
Jordan Grice

Now that the voting is over,
Nick Cocchi and Patrick
Cahillane have big shoes to
fill.

Cocchi, elected Hampden
County sheriff yesterday, and
Cahillane, winning the same
post for Hampshire County,
are succeeding longtime
fixtures in the Western Massachusetts law enforcement
community.

Cocchi takes over for his former boss, Michael J. Ashe Jr.,
who held the position for 42
years before announcing his
retirement. Cahillane, likewise, follows his boss, Robert
J. Garvey, who had held the
post since 1984.

Both men are Democrats.

For Cocchi, 'deja vu'

The victory came just over a
month after Cocchi, an assistant superintendent at the jail,
won a three-way Democratic
primary. He met a similarly
loud and jubilant crowd of
supporters as he did six weeks
ago at the Lusitano Club in his
hometown.

"This is a little deja vu from
a month-and-a-half ago but it
feels a little better today," he
told the crowd after a bulk of
the results had come in and it
was indisputable that Cocchi
had become the next sheriff.

With just 34 percent of votes
in, Cocchi had 40- to 50-point
leads over his two opponents.

Cocchi bested independent
candidate James Gill, a deputy
superintendent at the jail, and
Republican candidate John
Comerford in every precinct
in the 23 cities and towns
across Hampden County.

Comerford made an impressive second-place showing
despite doing nearly zero
campaigning and no fundraising, obviously winning GOP
devotees.

Cocchi replaces Ashe, who
was already on the phone with
Cocchi before the candidate
and his team left their "war
room" at a nearby office suite
in Ludlow, collecting reports
from more than 160 voting
precincts across the county in
rapid-fire fashion.

Chris Gelonese managed
the process, designed by
campaign adviser Jon D'Angelo, a key member of U.S. Sen.
Elizabeth Warren's team from
Western Massachusetts who
was campaigning for Hillary
Clinton in New Hampshire
yesterday.

"4A Westfield — go," ordered Gelonese, a member of
the executive committee for

Nick Cocchi celebrates winning the race for Hampden County Sheriff with supporters at the Lusitano Club in Ludlow last night.
For more photos, visit www.masslive.com. (DON TREEGER / THE REPUBLICAN)

HAMPDEN COUNTY SHERIFF
with 97 percent of precincts reporting

121,150	31,056	26,239
NICK COCCHI (D) ✓	JOHN M. COMERFORD (R)	JAMES GILL

**Cocchi bested
independent
candidate James
Gill, a deputy
superintendent
at the jail, and
Republican
candidate John
Comerford in every
precinct in the 23
cities and towns
across Hampden
County.**

Comerford 240," was the
swift response.

"I have the booming
metropolis of Wales," joked
Theresa Finnegan, another
member at the table. "Cocchi 446; Gill 113; Comerford
364."

Gelonese logged numbers
into an intricate spreadsheet
projected on a wall, with
total tallies registering at the
bottom.

It became clear just minutes
after the polls closed that
Cocchi was sweeping the
precincts.

"Yeah, we're kicking their
asses," Gelonese said about

the group readied to head out
to the Lusitano Club — but
not before Cocchi received a
somewhat worried call from
Ashe on his cellphone.

"Hey, kid, kid ... what's going on? Everything OK?" Ashe
could be heard asking in his
distinctive voice.

"We're on our way, sheriff, how'd we do?" Cocchi
responded for the sake of the
crowd, wearing a broad grin.

The seat is among the most
coveted in the region, as it
comes with significant political power and visibility forged
by Ashe — not to mention a
$75 million budget and a staff
of over 1,000 plus a profound
position in social service.

Case in point: Cocchi beat
two seasoned politicians who
also sought the seat in the
Democratic primary: former
four-term Springfield mayor and current Governor's
Councilor Michael J. Albano
and Springfield City Councilor Tom Ashe. The Democratic
primary was nothing short of
a dogfight. Cocchi capitalized
on Michael Ashe's popularity and support and built a
campaign war chest hovering
around $500,000.

Patrick Cahillane, a native of Ireland, was victorious in his bid
Hampshire County sheriff.

> **"The people
> want a sheriff's
> department that is
> answerable to the
> people."**
>
> Patrick Cahillane

the Lusitano Club, Cocchi was
joined on stage by his wife,
Wendy, and three sons. He
thanked his family and supporters, urging them to pause
for a throwback karaoke moment to sing along to "Winning it All" by the Outfield.

"When I say family, this
whole room is my family,"
Cocchi said.

He also lauded Michael
Ashe as his mentor after 23
years with the department.

"You just have to take him
in, watch what he does, listen

Michael Ashe accepted his
share of handshakes as well.
He said he felt "terrific" about
passing the torch to Cocchi.

"To be honest, Nick's the
one. We're dealing with the
least loved in society. You
really have to have a passion
for it. That's key, and Nick
has that," Michael Ashe said.

"We need people who want to
motivate and inspire inmates,
not just guard them."

Cocchi launched his campaign in 2014 with much
fanfare at a gathering at the
Naismith Memorial Basketball Hall of Fame and campaigned consistently over the
ensuing two years.

Cahillane humbled

In Northampton, the crowd

HAMPSHIRE COUNTY SHERIFF

53,987	15,965
PATRICK CAHILLANE (D) ✓	DAVID ISAKSON (R)

with 91% of precincts reporting

at Union Station Banquets
was abuzz with the news that
Cahillane was victorious in his
bid Hampshire County sheriff.

Cahillane, a native of Ireland, defeated Republican David Isakson, of South Hadley,
a Hadley police officer and
owner of Ebenezer's Bar and
Grill in Westfield and South
Hadley.

Since Cahillane announced
his candidacy in February
2015, he said the campaigning
process has been "one of the
most humbling experiences of
my life."

The Northampton resident
said his efforts to communicate with the community
about the work the sheriff's
department does and his aims
for the future received positive feedback.

"The people want a sheriff's
department that is answerable
to the people," he said.

Cahillane added that
transparency with the people
he met during his campaign
was an underlying message
that he feels he got across to
voters.

Earlier in the fall, the
Northampton resident was
pitted in a three-way Democratic primary where he
clinched the spot over Kavern
Lewis, of Amherst, and Melissa Perry of Northampton.

Cahillane boasted 30 years
of experience in criminal justice. He began as a correctional officer in 1977 in Northampton, while rising through the
ranks in the Sheriff's Department under Garvey, holding
positions from shift supervisor to deputy superintendent
and eventually special sheriff.

Throughout his campaign
Cahillane maintained a platform of improving the criminal justice system through
pre- and post-incarceration
programs that can provide incoming and outgoing inmates
with aid in rehabilitation.

Cahillane plans to build
upon mental health and
substance abuse programs
for inmates impacted by the
opiod crisis, add more pre-release and re-entry housing
programs, and improve jail facilities and employee training.

*Stephanie Barry can be
reached at sbarry@repub.com.
Jordan Grice can be reached at
jgrice@repub.com*

ABOVE: Nick Cocchi celebrating his win in the Hampden County sheriff's race primary at
the Lusitano Club in Ludlow, Sept. 8, 2016. Photo by Dave Roback / The Republican.

179

ABOVE: Nicholas Cocchi takes the oath of office of Sheriff of Hampden County in ceremonies at the facility in Ludlow. At right swearing Cocchi in is Lt. Gov Karyn Polito and Donald E. Ashe, Hampden County Register of Deeds. Next to Cocchi is his wife Wendi Cocchi. Photo by Dave Roback/The Republican.

MESSAGE FROM HAMPDEN COUNTY SHERIFF NICHOLAS COCCHI

The COVID-19 pandemic presented challenges not seen in a century and our very way of life has changed as a result. We once shook hands but now we more frequently bump elbows or gesture from across the room. We once shared smiles but those expressions have been tucked away behind a medical mask for over two years.

One thing that hasn't changed, however, is our commitment to serving the justice-involved individuals in our care and the public. As the role of the Sheriff's office has evolved from care while in custody to prevention before incarceration, I have asked many of my staff to take on additional duties and responsibilities. As they've stepped up, we've made a positive impact on the people of Hampden County and beyond.

Section 35 referrals from judges to our Stonybrook Stabilization and Treatment Center program have steadily increased as our reputation for effective and compassionate substance use disorder treatment has spread. Since we opened our doors in 2018, we've helped more than 2,300 people get a new chance at life without addiction, and we've done that right here in Hampden County - close to where the afflicted individuals live. We will keep fighting to be able to save lives in the Commonwealth, because addiction and the opioid crisis doesn't take days off.

On the public safety front, we are offering a regional lock-up for the 23 towns and cities around the county. As the police departments make an arrest, there is no place safer than one of our facilities to bring someone to be held until court. We have proper medical and mental health staff, as well as our trained correctional officers and employees who ensure their safe arrival for their next court appearance.

We are also doing several things to engage young people and to build a bridge ahead of their critical years when many of their decisions have the potential to impact the rest of their lives. We are out in the schools reading, visiting, explaining what we do, and taking time to mentor students. We have a successful basketball program in both Holyoke and Springfield, which teaches skills that transcend from the sport into the real world. We have a successful anti-truancy program that uses a variety of innovative clinical interventions to persuade students to return to school on any given day. In short, our outreach efforts are impactful and always expanding.

Our Youth Leadership Academy summer camp is a hit, serving around 75 kids in the greater Springfield area over the course of 6 weeks. Now in its third year, the primary focus is on children with incarcerated parents or who live in economically challenged neighborhoods in the Springfield area. This camp is a way of giving back to the community and hopefully will build a positive relationship with law enforcement at a young age. My goal is for this to continue to grow each year to have a positive impact on even more young people across Hampden County.

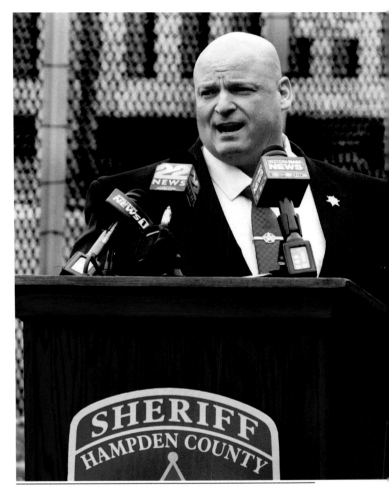

ABOVE: Hampden County Sheriff Nicholas Cocchi

I am honored to be the Sheriff of Hampden County and I'm so proud of the men and women who work here at the department. I'm thankful for being able to continue to lead a department that promotes a legacy of service above self and helps people in their darkest times find hope and a chance for a brighter future.

SHERIFF NICK COCCHI'S 15 PRINCIPLES OF CORRECTIONS

1. The correctional agency must maintain an atmosphere of dignity and respect for all. Every individual, staff or offender is encouraged to maximize their human potential.

2. The correctional agency strives to positively impact those in custody, not be a human warehouse.

3. Those in custody are challenged to address the risk factors that led to incarceration through participation in evidence-based, trauma-informed programs. These factors are identified by a validated risk assessment tool.

4. Preparation for a positive and productive reentry into the community begins on the first day of incarceration. Reentry services are the foundation for the future and protect the investment of taxpayer dollars.

5. The correctional agency promotes a collaborative relationship between security and human service staff.

6. Potential staff are recruited and selected based on education, ability to communicate and passion for public safety and service. The pursuit of excellence begins with prioritizing training and placement of personnel in positions where everybody wins.

7. Training reflects the most current information, trends and laws relative to the profession of inmate care and custody. Training is ongoing and consistent to promote excellence and proficiency.

8. Individuals are housed in an environment that is clean, safe and enforces clear standards of conduct. Any use of force necessary to maintain or restore order is balanced, reasonable and appropriate to the circumstances.

9. Offenders are guided toward an awareness of the full impact of their actions on victims and the community. Opportunities are provided for community service and restorative justice is encouraged.

10. There is a continuum of gradual step-down to lower levels of security. Offenders are classified to the lowest level of security appropriate to the safety of the public, correctional staff and the offender.

11. Health care for the population is based on community standards and establishes linkages with providers in the communities to which they will return. When possible, providers are dually based at the correctional facility and in the community.

12. Management Information Systems are integrated into all aspects of operations for optimal efficiency and effectiveness. This allows the capture of data that can be analyzed and utilized to help staff "work smarter, not harder".

13. The correctional agency cultivates partnerships with community agencies, both public and private, to enhance offender reentry. A strong system of human services combined with supervision and communication among criminal justice agencies leads to stronger, healthier, safer communities.

14. The correctional agency is a good neighbor in its host community and is a positive participant in all the communities it serves.

15. The correctional agency fosters a spirit of ingenuity and innovation in all its operations.

AN EVIDENCE-BASED APPROACH TO CORRECTIONS, DRIVEN BY PHILOSOPHY AND DATA

The Hampden County Sheriff's Department is a leader in the evolving paradigm of corrections and reform. Under the leadership of Sheriff Nicholas Cocchi, we provide a continuum of care designed to empower offenders to reclaim their liberty through informed and responsible choices and promote successful reentry into the community as law-abiding socially and civically responsible citizens.

The Department enhances public safety through the corrections process by providing offenders proper classification, security, treatment, and programs to accomplish positive lifestyle changes and minimize and/or eradicate negative social traits and criminogenic behaviors.

The successes of the Hampden County Sheriff's Department come thanks to the staff and the approach taken by the administration. The 15 Principles of Corrections, which steer the policies of and approach taken by the department, define the culture of the agency.

With the collaboration of the Information Systems and Technology and Research Departments, the team is able to use data to steer our techniques toward best practices, to improve outcomes for the offenders, improve the morale of the staff and boast one of the lowest recidivism rates in the nation.

IS&T works to understand what information is crucial to every department and user, and work with the Research team to drill down to clean metrics. This has resulted in a system of electronic data collection and research that allows us to monitor all aspects of population management and intervention, for all individuals served, from initial assessment to reentry into the community. Outside the department, HCSD collaborates with counterparts from numerous agencies as the Commonwealth moves forward in its efforts to use research data to inform evidenced-based policies and practices throughout the broader field of corrections.

Analysis of recidivism guides research at HCSD, with inquiries either feeding into or growing out of the recidivism study. Ongoing recidivism tracking follows each sentenced offender from the beginning of incarceration for a period of three years post release. Beginning with the 2174 offenders released in 2000, the study now covers nearly 40,000 individuals released over a 20-year period. Recidivism measures at one-year and three-year post release intervals capture both technical violations and new crimes. With a large sample size over an extensive time period, data from the study reveal trends in offender characteristics and behavior that are useful in making security, classification, and programming decisions.

HCSD allocates resources to enhance each offender's potential for successful reintegration into society. Data also provides information as to how other agencies such as parole, probation, and the courts affect the population and support the need for collaboration with both public and private partners to respond to emerging issues. HCSD strives to be a good neighbor and a positive participant in all communities it serves. Our data capacity can be a valuable resource, helping to promote effective approaches, to cultivate partnerships, and to support allocation of community resources.

ACCREDITATIONS AND AWARDS

The Hampden County Sheriff's Department's programs, dedication and aggressive reentry philosophy has brought repeated national recognition for innovative inmate initiatives ranging from connecting inmates to the public health system to near perfect scores on national accreditation audits.

The department has a deserved national reputation for its innovation in facility and community programs. Our approach to corrections and community reentry are considered a model of safe, secure, orderly, lawful, humane, and productive corrections, where inmates are challenged to pick up the tools and directions to build a law-abiding life in an atmosphere free from violence. The HCSD is one of the few county correctional centers with a professional Ph.D. level researcher on staff, analyzing operations.

The HCSD has received four 'Grade A' scores from the auditors of the American Correctional Association, and been described by the ACA as a "model facility for the industry." Looking toward FY 2022, an ACA audit is underway with additional high marks expected.

Additional inspections and audits by the Department of Public Health, Department of Public Safety, the Federal Bureau of Prisons, Prison Rape Elimination Act (independently contracted though the Department of Justice), the National Commission on Correctional Health Care, Bureau of Substance Addiction Services, as well as the MA Department of Corrections are always ongoing.

Also of note, the Hampden County Sheriff's Department received the President's Champions of Change for Reentry Award in June 2014 at the White House under President Barack Obama. The department was one of 16 awardees nationally recognized for its model of supported community reentry for offenders to successfully reenter society as productive, law-abiding citizens.

EDUCATIONAL LEVELS OF
FULL-TIME SHERIFF'S DEPT. EMPLOYEES (FY 2020)

	Uniform Staff	Non-Uniform Staff	Total Staff (n=976)
Ph.D./J.D./D.O.C	1	11	12
Master's Degree	11	94	105
Batchelor's Degree	180	139	319
Associate's Degree	92	64	156
MAS (Military)	46	11	57
Total Degrees	330	319	649
Total Non-Degrees	185	142	327

HCSD TRAINING & STAFF DEVELOPMENT DEPARTMENT

The Hampden County Sheriff's Department Training and Staff Development team is comprised of six full-time training staff, four full-time wellness staff and one staff assigned to leadership development and mentoring programs. The staff is a high energy, fast paced working group. They provide continuous training to the HCSD staff and to community-based programs upon request.

The training curriculum is developed in adherence to the Department of Corrections (DOC), the American Correctional Association (ACA), National Commission of Correctional Health Care (NCCHC) and the Massachusetts Sheriff's Association (MSA).

An overview of annual training is as follows: 16 hour in-service (CPR, First Responder, Defensive Tactics, Verbal De-escalation, Use of Force Report Writing, Emergency Plans, and Mindfulness Training), Continuing Education Trainings, POD Net (online training), and Firearms. In addition, the Supervisory staff attends 10 hours of training specifically designed to enhance their knowledge base.

Other trainings that occur within the Training Department are New Staff Orientation, cadet training program, summer staff program, and the Western Massachusetts County Correctional Officers Academy.

BEHAVORIAL HEALTH

SUBSTANCE USE DISORDER SERVICES

A primary concern across the nation and particularly in the Commonwealth is the treatment of drug dependent individuals, an effort recently exacerbated by the increase in opiate use. In 2001 the Sheriff's Department identified changes in the trends around opioid use and began training staff and implementing offender programming specific to what would become a heroin epidemic. Since then, the Hampden County Sheriff's Department has been aggressive in our efforts to positively impact the opioid crisis. We are committed to providing Substance Use Disorder services throughout the entire department. We are on the cutting edge of modern corrections in our approach to address treatment of the addicted and have expanded our capabilities substantially to provide the most comprehensive care possible during this crisis.

Within the Main Institution is a transitional detoxification unit where inmates are closely monitored for up to 28 days and where we begin to lay the foundation for long-term recovery. They then transition to our Substance Use Unit specifically dedicated to providing an ongoing treatment program as well as providing services to the other housing units on the compound.

The Women's Correctional Center (WCC) offers a continuum of addiction and recovery programming that meets the needs of those struggling with substance use disorder and co-occurring diagnosis. Programming is

trauma-informed and gender responsive, designed to promote recovery, personal responsibility and pro-social behavior, accomplished through evidence-based interventions, accountability, empowerment and strength-based recovery-oriented language. The facility has an integrated team of licensed alcohol and drug counselors (LADC), correctional counselors and mental health clinicians that offer psycho-educational groups, support and aftercare resources, medication-assisted treatment and a three-week treatment program that offers skills and techniques that support the individual in understanding her relationship with drugs and alcohol.

The Western Mass Recovery and Wellness Center is the Hampden County Sheriff's Department's community based, trauma informed, co-educational specialized Substance Use Disorder treatment center. The program structure at the center provides educational services, special needs groups, group therapy, individual counseling and case management. Partnerships with community service providers assure that participants have the opportunity to not only receive treatment services but also to take a personally active role in starting on their path to recovery.

Post-release, we offer our Foundation House (halfway house) program to men and women who have successfully completed our substance use disorder treatment program, but perhaps aren't ready to go directly to an independent living situation. Additionally we partner with several community agencies which offer halfway and sober house living options as men and women transition back to society with a soft handoff to the community.

Recovery from Substance Use Disorder and/or Mental Health Disorders involves a process of change by improving health and wellness, living a self-directed life, and striving to reach full potential.

Individual classes focus on such things as the disease of addiction, ongoing treatment options, relapse prevention, family unification and risk reduction. With diverse residential treatment staff, counselors, caseworkers, medical & clinical staff, it allows for a multi-disciplinary, client centered approach, thereby carrying out the mission of the Stonybrook Stabilization & Treatment Center. While at SSTC, clients are medically monitored as they progress through the medical detoxification process. When the medical detoxification phase is completed, they begin participating in a well-designed, holistic program towards recovery. The individual classes focus on such things as the disease of addiction, ongoing treatment options, relapse prevention, family roles and risk reduction. Clients are encouraged to fully engage in the SSTC program in order to receive substance use education that will assist in their community reentry and wellbeing.

Discharge from the SSTC program is determined on a case by case basis with certain criteria such as a client's program attendance and participation, housing plan, intended aftercare plan as well as client behavior. As each client is assigned a counselor who will assist with their aftercare planning, it is client specific and includes a structured treatment plan after discharge.

The average stay is 55 days. That is more than double the average stay in treatment in Massachusetts, and the time spent is a central

STONYBROOK STABILIZATION & TREATMENT CENTER

(Section 35 Civil Commitments)

Prior to the department opening a substance use disorder treatment program in 2018 for men involuntarily committed for treatment, there were zero options for Section 35 treatment in this half of the Commonwealth.

Our mission is to help individuals affected by Substance Use Disorder to stabilize and gain access to treatment in the community where they live. Our primary goal is to maintain a clean, safe and secure environment wherein addiction treatment programming is provided that promotes the recovery of addicted clients. We are committed to help our clients take the steps to move toward an improved quality of life. SSTC recognizes there are many different pathways to recovery, and each individual determines their own way.

component of the program's successes. About 43% of those who were sectioned had previously been incarcerated with our department. And around 17 percent of those sectioned have a criminal hold at the time of intake. And while around 20 percent of clients self-report being homeless at intake, our thorough discharge planning results in only around seven percent of clients being discharged to local shelters.

Since opening in May 2018, our SSTC program has treated over 2,100 men with a recommitment rate around ten percent. Those who are "sectioned" are deemed to be dangers to themselves or others, and unwilling to seek treatment voluntarily. All committed men start their journey to recovery in acute treatment where they detox under around-the-clock medical supervision before transitioning to our living unit, where their pathway to sobriety is complimented by various programs and supports, which continue through their eventual reentry into the community.

PUBLIC HEALTH MODEL

Incarcerated individuals experience disproportionately higher rates of infectious and chronic diseases, substance use, mental illness and trauma than the general population. Inmates are also overwhelmingly poorer, less educated and more likely to be persons of color than the general population. Since the majority of inmates are eventually released back to their communities, interventions to address their health and mental health problems present opportunities to improve public health and safety.

The Hampden County Sheriff's Department's Public Health Model for Correctional Health

Care values wellness, treatment of disease, prevention of illness, and access to care during and after incarceration. Health care is based on community standards and establishes close linkages with providers in the communities to which inmates return. Providers are dually-based at the correctional facility and in the community which allows for substantial collaboration and communication between corrections and health care professionals.

The public health model benefits inmates whose health problems have often gone unaddressed in the community. For many, it is the first time they have received adequate health care from a caring group of providers. The commitment to continue their care is evidenced by the high rate of inmates who keep their medical appointments after release.

MEDICATION ASSISTED TREATMENT PROGRAM

The Medication Assisted Treatment (MAT) program further enhances the Hampden County Correctional Center's award-winning public health model of correctional health care.

As one of seven Sheriff's Departments across the Commonwealth participating in the MAT pilot program, our Department offers evidence-based, FDA approved medications including buprenorphine (Suboxone), methadone and naltrexone (Vivitrol) for treatment of opioid use and alcohol use disorder. Education, including overdose prevention, is included for each MAT participant. HCSD has partnered

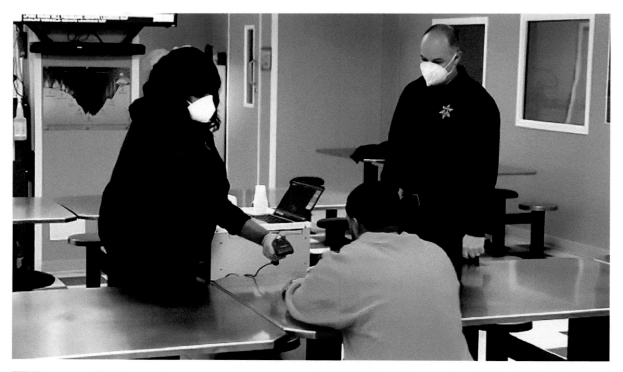

with CODAC, a licensed opioid treatment provider to provide MAT, weekly psycho-educational classes and monthly clinical meeting. Behavioral Health Network maintains the discharge planning for the client in conjunction with HCSD medical staff, and HCSD program staff. Community placements are based on home location and client comfort and previous relationship with their neighborhood community service providers.

In 2020 the Hampden County Sheriff's Department and CODAC provided MAT services to 1036 individuals (257 women, 779 men). 65% were on buprenorphine and 35% on methadone. Providing pre-release treatment and post-release services to our offenders provides them the best chance at treating this disease, long term.

MENTAL HEALTH SERVICES

Mental health services at the Hampden County Sheriff's Department is comprised of two different programs; a regional inpatient Evaluation and Stabilization Unit (ESU) servicing male patients from Hampden, Hampshire, Franklin, Berkshire and Worcester County and outpatient mental health services provided to men and women in the living units. Mental health clinicians assigned to living units work closely with correctional staff in recognizing, understanding and managing mental health needs of offenders. Services include comprehensive diagnostic evaluations, emergency risk assessments, crisis intervention, ongoing supportive treatment, medication monitoring and aftercare referrals.

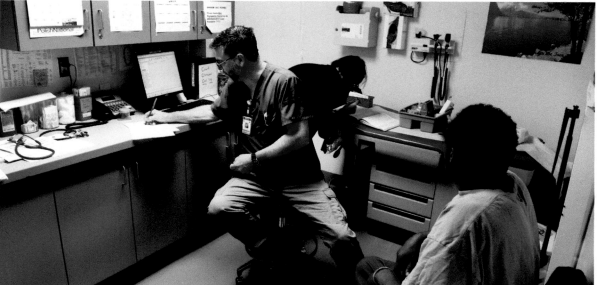

The ESU is a maximum security unit that is closely monitored by mental health staff in collaboration with security staff. Reasons for admission to the ESU include suicidal ideations, threats of harm to others, psychotic symptoms, bizarre behavior, inability to function in general population due to mental illness and return from any DMH or psychiatric hospitalization. ESU counselors conduct daily groups and supervise daily Therapeutic Education Counseling (TEC). Patients meet with a treatment team and a plan is developed that is regularly reviewed and updated with the goal of possible return to general housing. While the WCC does not have a separate ESU, similar services are provided to women in the Emergency Stabilization Program.

In 2019, the ESU moved to a larger unit within the Ludlow facility, which added two additional beds, and incorporated a 29-bed Mental Health Unit (MHU). The MHU is a living unit for inmates with chronic and persistent mental illness who have difficulty functioning in general population.

The MHU allows for a step-down for patients leaving the ESU, and offers space for individuals requiring a respite from general population, which can prevent decompensation.

With over 40% of the inmate population served having documented mental health issues, the Hampden County Sheriff's Department Mental Health Services utilizes a team approach to stabilize and maintain some of our most difficult cases in population with chronic mental health and behavioral issues, reducing the need for 18A commitments to state psychiatric hospitals.

REDUCING RECIDIVISM & INCREASING OPPORTUNITIES

EDUCATION

The Hampden County Sheriff's Department has a long-standing history of implementing Adult Basic Education (ABE) programs that are both demand-driven and innovative. At the start of an offender's time with the Hampden County Sheriff's Department, potential students are identified and assessed with the goal of improving the students' educational functioning level. Remedial and Adult Secondary Education classes are offered in math, reading/writing, history, with opportunities to grow into higher education.

Our current ABE program design includes content-based instruction offered five days a week to those who have been identified as lacking a secondary school diploma or equivalency. Our program serves students who receive a GLE of 3.0 or higher on the Test of Adult Basic

Education by then placing them in leveled classes that meet, on average, six to seven hours per week. The enrolled students are offered supplemental academic instruction between two to six hours per week. In addition to their ABE classes, students also meet with the Career and Education Advisor, who assists the student in filling out the Career and Education Plan, explores potential job openings in the student's area of interest, and provides guidance for next steps for education and employment upon release. And since 1992, approximately 5,000 men and women have obtained high school equivalency degrees.

The Western Massachusetts Regional Women's Correctional Center has offered incarcerated women a Bridge to College program and credit-bearing college classes through UMass Amherst. Bridge to College helps prepare the women to attend college upon their release by providing remedial lessons on topics ranging from language and math, to women's studies and work readiness. Since 1994, more than 1,000 offenders (men and women) have enrolled in college courses at Springfield Technical Community College. Since 2012, more than 80 students have graduated from the Bridge to College program to attend one of the areas' community colleges.

Our Integrated Education and Training Culinary Arts and Career Development programs are diverse and well attended. In collaboration with Holyoke Community College, culinary programs offered through the department prepare offenders to become ServSafe certified and teach basic food handling and knife skills to prepare them for jobs in the community.

JOB TRAINING & EMPLOYMENT

The HCSD has developed an extensive employment model to focus on job readiness, placement and retention through a gradual, supervised, and supportive four-phase program. In Phase One, offenders create an employment portfolio that includes a replacement Social Security card, birth certificate, awards or certificates earned, job application and resume. They also enroll in education and vocational programs. Phase Two covers interview techniques, computer search and networking skills and mock interviews. Phase Three includes assessment and job matching and job search. Phase Four stresses job retention through targeted triage to support both employer and employee.

The HCSD offers a wide range of vocational and skills training in culinary, construction, painting, landscaping, welding, custodial maintenance, graphics and repair and re-upholstery of office furniture. We have actual factories within the walls of both the Main Institution and Western Mass Women's Correctional Center, where we provide real world job opportunities for offenders while producing goods and services that save the institution and community hundreds of thousands of dollars. Certificate programs are offered in OSHA 10 (279 to-date), ServSafe (155 to-date), Precision Machining and Blueprint Reading. The department also operates the Olde Armory Grille Restaurant, a café in Springfield, which offers offenders real life work experience. The HCSD has averaged 400 job placements per year for the past 15 years, with over 10,000 former offenders placed since 1989. In 2018, we placed 274 people into jobs.

The Arborist Program is a multi-faceted horticultural program designed to introduce resident participants to all aspects of tree care, which is a growing, and well-paying trade. The participants (up to six at a time) develop competencies in tree management and removal; learn proper work site safety habits, chainsaw use and maintenance, use of splitting tools, rigging techniques, knot skills and heavy equipment operation.

These skills and certifications equip the participant to be competitive in an industry that currently has a high demand for employees. Furthermore, the participants engage in tree and limb removal in the community as part of their educational experience.

SEX OFFENDER TREATMENT

The HCSD contracts with the Counseling and Psychotherapy Centers, Inc. (CPC) to provide weekly groups for sex offenders. Casework staffers refer any inmates sentenced with a current sex offense or Sex Offender Registry Board (SORB) level or pretrial detainees with a SORB level to the program. The program is recorded under a generic name to ensure the safety and confidentiality of incarcerated sex offenders.

The treatment program is designed for clients who have engaged in sexually abusive and/or inappropriate behaviors who must participate in a specialized program to reduce the chance of a repeat offense. CPC programming, including weekly support groups at AISS, is guided by four principles of sex offense specific treatment.

The acronym RULE stands for:

Responsibility for the impact of offender behavior on victims, self and others

Understanding how offender's experiences and decisions in life have led him to this point

Learning new patterns of appropriate behavior

Experience practicing new skills in relating to others, dealing with stress and finding new experiences that enhance self-esteem.

IDENTIFYING AND HELPING INCARCERATED VETERANS

The Hampden County Sheriff's Department in coordination with the U.S. Department of Veterans Affairs (VA), accesses a secure website that enables the department to identify pretrial and sentenced offenders who have served in the United States military. This identification allows for individuals identified as a Veteran to participate in programs and to meet agencies specific to the veteran population. These individuals are also reviewed and referred to the Western Massachusetts Veteran's Treatment Court if they meet the eligibility criteria for participation. This is a treatment-focused specialty court for eligible defendants who have served in the United States Armed Forces.

es any ambivalence surrounding change. Beginning in 2020, MBSR strategies have been incorporated in annual staff training as an integral part of the wellness component.

For offenders, MBSR is introduced by pre and post-testing evidence based cognitions, beliefs and behaviors that create habitual patterns that support a criminal lifestyle. We also provide Stress, Anger and Violence Reduction (SAVR) programming to inmates at the men's medium security facility several times daily.

SAVR is essentially the same as MBSR, with a focus on anger and violence reduction. Early results reveal a significant reduction in anger-based incidents in the living units, and many offenders attend daily sessions voluntarily.

HUMAN TRAFFICKING & SEXUAL EXPLOITATION

The issues of human trafficking and sexual exploitation continue to be a priority for the department. Since 2015 the Women's Correctional Center, the Western MA Recovery and Wellness Center and All Inclusive Support Services have provided treatment services for survivors of sexual exploitation. The Living in Freedom Together (LIFT) program from Worcester provides counseling, classes and reentry services for our regional survivors. The YWCA of Greater Springfield has also provided services. A Violence Against Women Act (VAWA) grant continues to help support these initiatives as well as supporting ongoing education opportunities for staff.

The HCSD also conducts a Veterans Program that meets every Tuesday in our Programs Building. Here, all Veteran agencies are invited to attend and meet the veterans in our custody to provide information and services. Some of the agencies that attend or provide services regularly are the Department of Veteran's Affairs Veteran Justice Outreach Coordinator, the Town of Ludlow's Veteran Service Officer, Soldier-On, the Vet Center and the National Association for Black Veterans (NABVETS).

MINDFULNESS BASED STRESS REDUCTION

The HCSD is working to introduce mindfulness-based concepts and strategies to support both staff and offenders. The objectives of MBSR are to enhance self-control and reduce unconscious reactions through increased focus and attention regulation, to promote values of ethical and engaged citizenship through mindfulness, and to provide an environment that promotes and challeng-

Sheriff's Department staff serves on the federal Homeland Security task force and the U.S. Attorney's Human Trafficking Committee and collaborates with the State Police and the state-wide work of LIFT. Locally we participate in the YWCA's Strategic Prevention Framework Team, a local drop in center for exploited women.

As with a number of initiatives within the Department, some of our community involvement has been curtailed this past year because of COVID. We look ahead with renewed hope and determination to responding in new ways to the needs of this vulnerable population.

VICTIM AND FAMILY SERVICES UNIT

The Hampden County Victim and Family Services Unit provides information, assistance and support to victims of crime as well as the families and loved ones of those in our custody. As a good community partner, services extend to meet community needs beyond those being held in our facilities. The Victim Bill of Rights mandates that all victims and family members of deceased, incompetent, or minor victims have the right "upon request to advance notice when an offender is moved from a secure to a less secure facility, has received temporary, provisional, or final release from custody, or escapes." In order to be notified of release or obtain information about an offender from post-conviction agencies, victims must apply for CORI certification. We are able to assist an individual with that process.

Services offered by this unit include, but are not limited to:

- Crisis Intervention
- Support & Information
- Safety Planning
- Referrals to Community Resources for all members of the family
- Victim/Offender Conferencing
- Assistance to better understand the Corrections process
- Notification of Release or transfer of those in our custody (CORI Certification)
- Information about your rights as a victim
- Family Transition meetings between those in our custody and their loved ones prior to release

The HCSD has partnered with various agencies in the community, one of which is the STOP Domestic Violence Team. The STOP team was created by the Hampden County District Attorney's Task Force on Domestic Violence to enhance victim's safety, track high risk offenders, hold offenders accountable and prevent further abuse. The team meets monthly to discuss, to review, and share information. The HCSD's role is to follow STOP team offender policy and procedure at the facilities, bring information on suggested candidates to monthly team meetings and provide a list of offender's end of sentence and parole eligibility dates to the team each month.

RESTORATIVE JUSTICE

Restorative Justice addresses the impact of crime on not just the victims, but our communities. This process invites active participation by giving voice to those involved in, and affected by the crime. Restorative Justice works toward healing what has been broken by addressing harm, both tangible and intangible, taking into account the needs of all affected. The offender and the community work together in a process that fosters accountability and seeks to reintegrate where there has been division, acknowledging and understanding that crime may be a symptom of these conditions. The Restorative Justice process creates a sense of safety and empowerment for the whole community.

There is currently a State Restorative Justice Advisory Board whose purpose is to get Restorative Justice practices in the criminal justice system. This board has been meeting since 2019. The Massachusetts Sheriffs' Association has a seat on this board in which Sheriff Cocchi was chosen as the representative. The law that formed this board gives credence to the work that has been occurring at the Hampden County Sheriff's Department for over two decades.

The first Restorative Justice initiative within the HCSD began in the late 1990's with the inception of the Community Accountability Board (CAB) program. Upon completing victim awareness classes, offenders that are classified to lower security have the opportunity to meet with community members to discuss their crime and its impact on others. Goals of the program are to have the offender work to restore damage done and make amends to victims and the community, learn about the impact of crime and learn ways to avoid reoffending. Boards are comprised of community volunteers who are screened and have completed a background check. They receive training on principles of restorative justice, CORI law, confidentiality, conflict of interest and sexual misconduct policy. Ideally, volunteers have ties to the community where the board takes place.

The second initiative, which has been in place for fifteen years, is our availability to offer Victim/Offender dialogs. Victim offender dialogues involve a meeting between the victim of a crime and the offender facilitated by a trained mediator or facilitator. With the assistance of the facilitator, the victim and offender begin the process of mutual understanding, and to construct their own approach to achieving justice in the face of their particular crime.

We are currently working on an initiative to use Restorative Circle practices for both community building and behavior management in our facilities. Staff are in the process of attending trainings to become proficient in these techniques.

DEPARTMENT OF CORRECTIONS STEP-DOWN PROGRAM

The Hampden County Sheriff's Department is a participant in the DOC step-down program. DOC inmates who are returning to Hampden County communities can transfer to Hampden County to prepare for reentry. Since the inception of the current HCSD/DOC Reentry Partnership in October 2010 through 2020, 757 offenders have transferred (92 women, 665 men) and 724 have been

released (89 women, 635 men). In calendar year 2020, the Hampden County Sheriff's Department had 37 DOC intakes, and 92 releases. 75% were released from lower security, 48 were paroled and 29% had no post-release supervision.

Due to the nature of charges and the individual's length of sentences, this is a population requiring intensive services while in custody and post-release. The HCSD is committed to working with these inmates to become productive members of the community upon release. Our success rate is exceptional. The one-year recidivism rate for DOC inmates who released in 2019 from the Hampden County Sheriff's Department is just 1.2% and the three-year re-incarceration rate

is only 10.3%. Since the program began in 2010 only 15 participants have been returned to DOC.

STRENGTHENING AND REUNITING FAMILIES

The department supports several initiatives on the local level designed to keep family bonds strong, reunite families where appropriate, and meet Department of Children & Families standards for reunification. These efforts include parenting classes, family visitation, specialized mother-child visitation, a mother-child Christmas Party, and partnering with organizations across the Commonwealth aimed at helping with joint placement upon release. The department also funds a dedicated bus line to the Main Institution, the Stonybrook Express, to provide families of offenders daily access to the correctional center for visitations.

OTHER PROGRAMS INCLUDE:

- Men's Leadership is an intensive, interactive and introspective ten-week program designed to address men's daily issues with hope, encouragement and perseverance. The goal is to become a positive influence on their families, communities, and society. Topics include leadership, character, integrity, accountability, trust, humility, pride anger, courage, fear, conflict resolution and fatherhood.

- Fathers In Trust is a program designed to assist residents in parenting from an incarcerated perspective. Topics include nurturing skills, effective listening, age appropriate behaviors, logical consequences for inappropriate behaviors and positive vs. negative reinforcement. Importance is also placed on reunification after incarceration.

- The Nurturing Fathers Program is facilitated by Enlace de Familias in Holyoke. The Nurturing Fathers Program is a 13-week evidence-based program for developing attitudes and skills for male nurturance. The group of 10-to-20 fathers meets weekly for 2-1/2 hours. We aim to train the residents of Holyoke, especially in the lowest income neighborhoods, to be the center and guiding force of the transformation of school reform and other policies that have an impact on the men and their families.

- The Mother Child Program offers parenting classes at both medium and minimum security for moms with children of all ages, pre and post-natal classes, health services and support services including resources for families, a breast milk pumping program, specialized visits and reunification services in conjunction with DCF.

Reunification meetings are offered to family members prior to an offender's discharge via mediation, conflict resolution and family facilitation models conducted by trained clinical staff from the Sheriff's Department.

CHESS HOUSING PROGRAM

CHESS is an acronym for Community Housing that is Earned, Safe and Supportive. A key element of the Sheriff's Department All

Inclusive Support Services (AISS), CHESS is an innovative program that provides stable, safe housing and extensive supportive services including individuals formerly incarcerated in the Hampden County House of Correction. Each phase of the program has multiple eligibility criteria which participants must meet, including income, criminal behavior, recovery, mental health, stages of change and compliance with an Individual Service Plan. The goal of CHESS is to prevent homelessness, increase public safety and fiscal responsibility.

CHESS has three phases. Phase 1 is preparation. The potential participant must be actively involved in AISS services and demonstrate

they have developed the skills to live outside a structured program. In Phase 2 Supportive Housing, participants are placed in scattered site units where they receive a high level of case management including random urine screenings and Breathalyzer testing, housing inspections and monthly Individual Service Plan reviews. This intensive phase is designed to help participants enhance and apply life skills needed for independent living. In Phase 3, participants have demonstrated residential stability and may apply for a project-based mobile voucher through the Springfield Housing Authority.

ALL INCLUSIVE SUPPORT SERVICES

(formerly After Incarceration Support Systems)

Launched in 1996, the AISS program aimed to help justice-involved individuals to stabilize upon release and become productive community members. In October 2019, AISS revealed a new name and logo, signaling welcome to any community members who can benefit from our services, whether there is history of incarceration or not. Many individuals seek our support after a treatment episode, while in a homeless shelter, or simply when they decide they are ready to seek help in making

Square One, Healthcare for the Homeless through Mercy Behavioral Health Care, Supplemental Nutrition Assistance Program (SNAP) through Food Bank of Western Massachusetts, Women's Writing Group through Voices From Inside, Men of Color Health Alliance and Assurance Wireless.

On average, 38 new members register for service weekly, with a total of more than 1,500 new members per year. We offer "lifetime membership," supporting participants through short or long-term connections and ultimately a pathway to give back to others through Mentoring.

CRIME PREVENTION/ COMMUNITY OUTREACH & IMPACT

COMMUNITY RESTITUTION PROGRAM

The Community Restitution Program has been in existence at the Hampden County Sheriff's Department since 1993. Since its inception, over 35,000 participants in the program have provided over 1.6 million hours of service to the community.

The Community Restitution Program is a vocational program that not only provides a service to the community but also helps build work ethics among our offender population. The program is a cost savings to the cities and towns in Hampden County as well as non-profit organizations. The daily work the Sheriff's Department provides to the Spring-

a change. We turn away no one whom we can help.

Designed as a one-stop connection point for a range of community stabilization issues, AISS provides services and opportunity in three related and interdependent areas of need: support, housing, and employment. By co-creating a Wellness Action Plan or Rapid Service Engagement strategy, AISS mobilizes the community connections that support our members.

AISS staff can be found each weekday connecting with those in HCSD's custody— at the Main Institution, Women's Correctional Center, Recovery and Wellness Center (including Pre-Release men), Day Reporting Program, and Stonybrook Stabilization and

Treatment Center (SUD civil commitment). Simultaneously, staff members work with voluntary as well as probation / parole-supervised clients in the community to navigate challenges in home communities. Caring staff work with members to reduce risk, sustain recovery, and build better futures. AISS and more than 300 agencies assist clients to access employment, housing, court proceedings, and needed services such as Registry of Motor Vehicles, Department of Revenue, Department of Transitional Assistance, and Department of Children and Family Services.

On-site community provider services include clinical support through Behavioral Health Network, Fathers In Trust (FIT) Men's Parenting Group through Children's Study Home, Women's Parenting Group through

field Parks Department, Springfield Housing Authority, MA D.O.T., Holyoke DPW and Holyoke Housing Authority is very valuable to our commitment to the community and local municipalities. Each resident assigned to the program is provided with knowledge, training and guidance to work in the community on a specific crew. These crews consist of construction, painting, landscaping and forestry type of work. In fiscal year 2020, 17 community service crews from the Western Massachusetts Recovery & Wellness Center and the Women's Correctional Center worked over 33,000 hours. During the COVID-19 pandemic, staff and residents provided continuous services to the cities of Springfield, Holyoke and the MA Department of Transportation through the Community Restitution Program.

SCHOOL TRUANCY PROGRAM

Since 2009, the Hampden County Sheriff's Department has collaborated with the City of Springfield on a truancy initiative that has contributed to a higher graduation rate and a lower dropout rate.

Unlike some truancy initiatives which involve heavy handed policing techniques, this partnership utilizes well-recognized cognitive-behavioral intervention, student engagement and simple conversation to help truant students understand that attendance increases their chances of success in school as well as life and that absence from school contributes to a lack of educational progress and unnecessary challenges on their overall path to adulthood.

Teams consisting of a uniformed Deputy Sheriff and a Springfield School Department

attendance officer patrol the streets for truant students in a marked cruiser, but also conduct proactive outreach within the schools and provide at-home intervention to families who request assistance.

A district's graduation and dropout rates are tied to several variables, but Springfield officials credit the HCSD truancy initiative for contributing to the overall positive trend in the statistics, with better outcomes for hundreds of students each year.

Increase in Graduation Rates
Springfield Graduation Rate: 2009- 54.5%
Springfield Graduation Rate: 2019- 73.8%

Decrease in Dropout Rates
Springfield Dropout Rate: 2009- 9.6%
Springfield Dropout Rate: 2019- 4.4%

2017-2018 School Year truancy initiative statistics
Total number of Home Visits: 545
Total number of Student Contacts: 1052
Total number of Community Visits: 987

NEIGHBORHOOD WATCH

Since 2007, officers from the Sheriff's Department have helped organize and lead neighborhood watch groups throughout Springfield and Holyoke, holding monthly meetings in the neighborhoods. The goals of the initiative include creating greater public safety by empowering neighbors to get involved in the process of resolving and preventing crime within their communities.

Neighborhood Watch is a tool to bring neighbors into the work of improving the quality of life and crime issues in a given neighborhood. Neighborhood Watch creates opportunities for concerned citizens to partner with law enforcement officers in identifying neighborhood issues while implementing ways of improving them.

The program includes 16 neighborhoods in Springfield and Holyoke, with hundreds of active community participants. Citizens are trained on various techniques such as observation skills, target hardening and reporting suspicious activity. HCSD has also provided the community with various anonymous reporting numbers, including Text-A-Tip. We are able to mobilize hundreds of community residents working towards making our communities, healthier, safer and more economically viable through information sharing and youth and family referrals.

THE HOLYOKE SAFE NEIGHBORHOOD INITIATIVE

The Holyoke Safe Neighborhood Initiative (HSNI) is a comprehensive collaboration in terms of developing grassroots relationships, getting folks in the community connected to services and building healthy, long lasting relationships. One of our goals is to identify youth and families that need services and support. We provide connections to these support agencies that will enhance their livelihood. As a way to provide positive engagement for youth and families, we host community-wide activities including family fun nights, sport leagues and back to school events, and other events specific to each neighborhood including walks, meetings, and cookouts. By strengthening our community through these programs, each person becomes healthier and happier.

We have a focus of engaging youth and being intentional around mentorship, role modeling and structured character development. Through our basketball league, we intertwine character development curricula into each of our 12-week summer and winter programs.

In addition to youth outreach, HSNI focuses on helping single mothers get connected with much needed services, assists community residents in the completion of certificate programs, enrolling in GED and Hi-Set Classes, register for college and supports others in landing jobs. The program's goal is to build community, one person at a time.

On a community level, we work in six neighborhoods in Holyoke; Wards 1-6. Through our community program, our vision is that by strengthening the community, each person becomes healthier and happier. We do this by engaging neighborhood stakeholders and residents through monthly networking meetings. The meetings are action driven with a focus on identifying the quality of life and crime issues in each neighborhood. With a Hampden County Sheriff's Department coordinator in each of the neighborhoods, we are able to actively participate and make positive changes to the community. Another important aspect of the neighborhood work is to raise up community leaders, both adults and young people that can be leaders in our neighborhoods, as well as immobilizing them in their neighborhoods.

AS A RESULT OF THE HOLYOKE SAFE NEIGHBORHOOD INITIATIVE, OVER THE PAST 9 YEARS WE HAVE HAD:

15,000+ residents engaged through 200 plus hours of Family Fun Nights

3,785+ volunteer hours serving our community

13,000+ community residents impacted through 9 Annual Back to School Events

HAMPDEN COUNTY ADDICTION TASK FORCE (HCAT)

The Hampden County Addiction Task Force (HCAT) is a collaboration of community resources, law enforcement (local and state), health care institutions, service providers, schools and community coalitions, individ-

uals, and families whose goal is to focus on a county-wide approach to address drug addiction, overdose and prevention. One of the most exciting and current initiatives of the group is the creation of the HCAT Coordinator position which will oversee the new Rapid Response and Connection Program.

A $900,000 grant, from the U.S. Department of Justice Comprehensive Opioid, Stimulant and Substance Abuse Program (COSSAP), will help fund the position and the creation of the team, which HCAT hopes to deploy before the end of 2021.

Thanks to the grant, within 24-72 hours of an overdose in Hampden County, HCAT's Rapid Response Team will arrive at a home,

assess the needs and offer an evidence-based approach with treatment options and wrap-around services for those struggling with addiction and their families. While the COVID-19 pandemic complicated life for everybody, statistics show the impact was felt even more for people struggling with substance use disorder. With reporting of addiction-related issues, including relapse and sometimes fatal overdoses, on the rise, Hampden County Sheriff Nick Cocchi feels the creation of the team will bridge a critical gap in services at a time when it is needed the most.

In addition to funding the HCAT coordinator position and enabling the Rapid Response Team, the grant will help the roll-out of a county-wide database to document overdose incidents, high-risk individuals, and subsequent follow-up in real time.

Overall, HCAT is aiming to provide a data-driven, integrated response to the residents who are the most vulnerable and at-risk for opioid & substance use-related incidents while improving community safety and overall well-being. This comes at a time when in the last three years, there has been a 112% increase in opioid-related deaths in Hampden County alone.

HAMPDEN COUNTY REGIONAL REENTRY TASK FORCE

The Hampden County Sheriff's Department has provided consistent leadership in addressing the issues related to offender reentry at the national, state and local level. The work of numerous committees addressing reentry issues, many in existence since the mid-1990's, were brought together under the aegis of the Hampden County Regional Reentry Task Force in 2010. The role of the Regional Reentry Task Force is to provide the continuity necessary for the seamless reintegration of formerly incarcerated individuals into our local communities. Each member agency, public and private, is called upon to recognize how its mission and services can contribute to helping former inmates be successful and remain crime free. Task Force members are committed to working together, sharing ideas, information and resources to achieve the common goal of stronger, safer, healthier communities.

The Task Force, which includes reentry

assistants from Berkshire, Worcester, Hampshire and Franklin Counties, meets quarterly to hear reports of working groups, discuss local and statewide issues, identify specific barriers to reentry and explore solutions. Current committees include DOC Reentry, Public Safety, Behavioral Health, Employment, Housing, Education, Community Supervision and Human Trafficking. Member agencies include the Sheriff's Department, Mass DOC, Probation, Parole Board, Hampden County District Attorney, US Attorney, Office of the Mass Attorney General, City of Springfield, Mass Department of Mental Health, Career Centers, ROCA, Behavioral Health Network, Mercy Hospital, Springfield Housing Authority, Friends of the Homeless, Holyoke Community College, Children's Study Home (Family Services), and YWCA.

DIVERSION PROGRAMS

The Hampden County Sheriff's Department has partnered with criminal justice agencies to offer diversionary programming to many first time or low level offenders that have committed nonviolent felonies or misdemeanors. These programs are designed to help offenders avoid criminal convictions and/or loss of freedom by participating in and successfully completing diversion programming. Through this programming, offenders are given the opportunity to receive treatment as well as contribute to the community.

Chief probation officers from Holyoke, Chicopee, Palmer, Springfield and Westfield District Courts may refer individuals who have shown a need for substance use treatment, detoxification or both. Participants may

be held up to 45 days on a non-criminal violation while in the program. Referrals are also accepted from the Springfield Drug Court. Parole officers can also refer parolees who are at risk of a violation of parole due to relapse. Parolees must agree to a voluntary 30-day commitment to the program. In 2020 there were 61 referrals to the diversion program, 31 from Probation, 1 from Drug Court and 29 from Parole. 56 participants successfully completed.

PARTNERSHIP WITH FRIENDS OF THE HOMELESS

Answering a request from the community to assist the county's most vulnerable citizens, the Sheriff's Department has partnered with Friends of the Homeless to add capacity for 30 additional beds throughout the critical winter months.

The Hampden County Sheriff's Department has officers at the shelter on Worthington Street in Springfield covering the 4 p.m. to 12 a.m. shift, and the 12 a.m. to 8 p.m. shift, seven days a week from December through March. The partnership allowed the shelter to accommodate an additional 30 people in need of emergency shelter and services during the coldest time of the year in New England.

Friends of the Homeless in Springfield serves more than 1,000 guests annually. In addition to providing an emergency shelter and three meals a day to anyone in need, the facility's case workers help every guest with a variety of offerings ranging from finding work and permanent housing to connecting with behavioral and addiction-related services.

YOUTH LEADERSHIP ACADEMY SUMMER CAMP

In its inaugural year, Sheriff Nick Cocchi's Youth Leadership Academy summer camp served nearly 50 young people ranging in age from 7 to 12 over the course of 6 weeks. With a focus on children with at least one parent who is incarcerated, the camp aims to deliver a positive experience that the young people might not otherwise experience.

The camp is held at the Elias Brookings School in Springfield. Children are able to take part in daily activities ranging from arts and crafts to mindfulness and reflexive yoga, as well as video production. Breakfast and lunch are provided for all campers unless children choose to bring their own meals.

A range of guests including the Springfield Fire Department, the Buffalo Soldiers Motorcycle Club, and the Sheriff's Department K-9 team, visit campers. In addition to cultural and educational enrichment activities, the children engage in activities including volleyball, gardening and a slip-and-slide on hot days.

Once a week, field trips take them to places such as the Lupa Zoo in Ludlow, Look Memorial Park in Northampton, the Naismith Memorial Basketball Hall of Fame and Six Flags New England in Agawam.

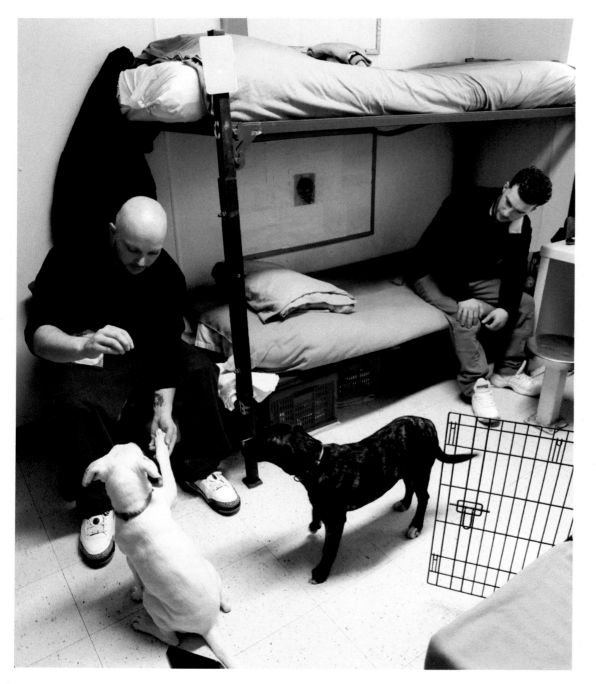

HCSD K-9 INITIATIVES
FREEDOM PUPS PROGRAM

In Sept. of 2017, Sheriff Nick Cocchi created a program to integrate rescued dogs with the minimum security inmate population. In partnership with Second Chance Animal Services in East Brookfield, the Freedom Pups Program pairs rescued dogs with inmate handlers who work with the dogs to teach basic obedience training in an effort to make them more adoptable to the public.

"This is a unique opportunity to provide our residents with the chance to improve their lives by affording them interactive experiences with canines," states Sheriff Cocchi. "The benefits for our residents and the dogs will be exceptional. Having these dogs here will help to foster empathy, relieve stress and learn responsibility for our residents." For the dogs, this will provide needed training that ultimately will make them more adoptable and give them a greater opportunity to be socialized with close personal contact.

Second Chance Animal Services provides all food, bedding and medical care for the animals at no cost to the jail. All dogs are medically screened and cleared, fully up to date on all vaccines and spayed or neutered. Each dog participating in the program is at the House of Corrections Pre-Release Center for 8-12 weeks. "This program is instrumental in helping to prepare animals for adoption that need a little extra help with socialization or training and helps to open up space at the shelter for more pets in need", states Second Chance Development Manager Lindsay Doray.

EMOTIONAL SUPPORT DIVISION

We recently welcomed four new therapy dogs as part of our latest department initiative, The Emotional Support Division. This division was developed by Sheriff Nick Cocchi and Trainer Nina Valentino with a goal of creating a team that can improve the lives of the people they come into contact with. The Emotional Support Division aims to not only have a positive impact on the staff and the people in our care and custody, but the people we serve in the community. At the center of this effort, you will find our therapy dog teams.

Sheriff Cocchi has always been an animal advocate. But over the past few years, he has begun to grow more interest in the use of therapy dogs and ways to incorporate them into what we do here at the Hampden County Sheriff's Department. Finding a way to provide as many people as possible access to these dogs was very important to him.

The dogs and handlers of the Emotional Support Division touch the lives of many people and the hope is that it will continue to inspire other departments to follow.

The division works closely with schools, senior centers and hospitals to positively impact the general public when the teams are not busy working to uplift our staff, the incarcerated individuals and the Section 35 clients in our care.

K-9 SECURITY DOGS

Our K-9 Security Team is comprised of highly-trained dogs of various breeds that are

trained in building search, apprehension and rescue operations. They also work as illicit drug detection dogs inside the jail and in the community.

Their handlers and the dogs work as a team together to keep our compound and community safe. In late 2019, the department added "Scout" Hazen Ouimet, a Bloodhound puppy who will be trained in search and rescue operations across the region.

With the addition of Scout, the Department has expanded its offerings to the community to provide K-9s for a variety of situations all focused on enhancing public safety and uplifting the public.

appearance and re-classed to the House of Correction, and 16 were admitted to the Stonybrook Stabilization and Treatment Center on a Section 35 civil commitment.

SPRINGFIELD FOREST PARK PATROLS

From March to November, two Deputy Sheriffs patrol Forest Park in Hampden County Sheriff's Department marked cruisers for two shifts daily, reporting to Springfield Police Commissioner Clapprood. This program was developed at the request of Springfield Mayor Domenic Sarno, who asked for assistance in patrolling Hampden County's largest urban park during the busy summer months.

The Sheriff's Department does not charge the city any fee for the patrols, who work alongside city police and continue to respond to calls for service at the park. The Deputy Sheriffs have full arrest and citation powers for disturbance of the peace and certain park regulations.

Built into the shifts is a two-hour overlap of the deputies, which occurs at an important time when there is a shift change at the Springfield Police Department and students end their school day. This enhances public safety and the experience of park goers and in future years, the partnership may expand to other city parks.

CIVILIAN OUTREACH ACADEMY

Anyone interested in a behind-the-walls look at the Hampden County Correctional Center and a window into the work of the Sheriff's Department need not look further than Sheriff Cocchi's Civilian Outreach Academy.

REGIONAL LOCK-UP

In January 2017, as a way to increase public safety and reduce costs to local municipalities, the Hampden County Sheriff's Department implemented a regional lock-up facility. A regional lock-up allows more police officers to patrol the streets while allowing correctional officers to provide care, custody and transportation to court for individuals during the pre-arraignment process.

Our facility provides 24-hour nursing care which allows us to triage medical situations and stabilize patients rather than utilizing additional resources for outside hospital transports.

In 2020, the Hampden County Sheriff's Department completed 3,275 intakes (537 females, 2,737 males, 1 transperson) on behalf of 18 cities and towns across the county as well as the Massachusetts State Police and the Massachusetts Gaming Commission.

51% of regional lock-up admissions were released on or before their first court appearance. 47% returned after their court appearance and were re-classed to pretrial status. Six individuals were sentenced at their first court

The department's civilian academy is designed for citizens looking to learn about topics ranging from the opioid epidemic and how to administer Narcan to understanding what a day in the life of a Corrections Officer is really like.

The academy, which is held free of charge, is a six-week program that includes practical training in CPR, what you need to know about drug addiction, gang awareness and security, as well as K-9 demonstrations, a tour of the jail and a "Day in the Life of a Corrections Officer." To be considered, interested individuals must be at least 18 years old and submit to a CORI background screening.

MARINE PATROL UNIT

With the aim of enhancing public safety throughout the many waterways around Western Massachusetts, Hampden County Sheriff Nick Cocchi launched the department's Marine Patrol Unit in 2021.

Comprised of two boats and ten specially trained staff members, the MPU works alongside their local law enforcement counterparts in the region on searches for missing swimmers, rescue/recovery operations and safety patrols on the Connecticut River and Congamond Lakes.

"The goal of the Hampden County Marine Patrol Unit is to build upon what some local and state law enforcement agencies already do on the water in the region. We are here to enhance public safety by proactively having a presence on the waterways with the intention of keeping people in compliance with the rules of the water," said Sheriff Nick Cocchi.

"This unit, like everything that our department does, is designed to meet a need in the community and make Western Massachusetts a safer place to live, work and play."

The Marine Patrol Unit takes a proactive approach to ensuring the safety of people who are out enjoying activities including water skiing, rafting, swimming, boating and fishing on Hampden County waterways. The Sheriff's Marine Patrol Unit joined the Connecticut River Task Force, and works alongside Chicopee and Southwick police on patrols in their respective municipalities.

The officers on the Marine Patrol Unit all received specialized training relative to the equipment they have at their disposal, the vessels they are operating and water safety in general. Both boats are also equipped with Narcan in case the team needs to reverse an opioid overdose. To qualify for membership on the team, all members of the Sheriff's Marine Patrol Unit must participate in annual ongoing education trainings, maintain an exemplary record of conduct and pass an annual physical fitness exam which includes a swimming test.

TRIAD PROGRAM FOR SENIORS

Hampden County TRIAD, started by Sheriff Cocchi in 2021, is a safety initiative that focuses on empowering, educating and improving the lives, safety, security, and peace of mind of the senior community in Western Massachusetts. The goals of TRIAD are to reduce criminal activity that targets the senior community; provide education and services that will build confidence and improve the quality of life for seniors in our community; enhance trust and safety with law enforcement in the senior community by ensuring access to services and alleviate fear of victimization among seniors.

ABOVE: Corporals Liz Carpenter and Jenn Holley are seen demonstrating Project Lifesaver, a tracking system for people with cognitive conditions who are at risk of wandering.

TRIAD PROJECTS INCLUDE:

- **Project Lifesaver** – A tracking system for individuals with cognitive conditions who are at risk of wandering.

- **Hampden County Life Files** – A magnetic sleeve with an information card listing all medications a person uses and any special health conditions they may have, which is posted on the refrigerator.

- **"Are You Ok?"**– A daily telephone reassurance program to check on the well-being of seniors who live alone.

- **Is Your Number Up?** – A house number initiative that assists Police, Fire and EMS in their efforts to respond quickly to 9-1-1 calls.

- **Speaker Series**– Local law enforcement members meet with senior groups to discuss issues such as identity theft, domestic violence & scams targeting seniors.

- **Y.E.S** – Youth Empowering Seniors is an education initiative to assist older adults in learning how to use technology.

- **Senior Home Safety Inspection** – Certified inspector completes 240-point safety and accessibility assessment in and around home.

ARE YOU OK? HAMPDEN SHERIFF NICK COCCHI LAUNCHES WELLNESS PROGRAM FOR SENIORS

By Cynthia G. Simison, The Republican

Are you OK?

The expression of concern for the wellbeing of others may have gone viral this week to a worldwide audience when The New York Times published Meghan Markle's op-ed in which she shared news of her and Prince Harry's loss of a child to miscarriage during the summer. In it, she also shared her concern for others struggling through the challenges of the global pandemic.

For weeks and months, Sheriff Nick Cocchi, like the duchess of Sussex, had been growing increasingly concerned about so many people he doesn't know all across his domain in Hampden County. Senior citizens and the disabled who live alone and who are in need of a human connection have been on his radar.

More than 540,000 people over the age of 50 live alone in Massachusetts, according to AARP. They are of higher risk of social isolation during this COVID-19 pandemic, AARP says, and experts say social isolation over prolonged periods can be as harmful to one's health as smoking 15 cigarettes a day and is linked to a greater likelihood of early death, accelerated cognitive decline, stroke and depression in senior citizens.

When AARP of Massachusetts launched

a campaign in October with a hashtag #ReachOutMa to urge older residents to "stay connected," Cocchi took notice. It proved the perfect time, he says, for his latest initiative: Are You OK?

Are You OK? is a program to help give senior citizens living alone a daily lifeline to connect them with others. It's not a new concept as it's been used by other sheriffs in Massachusetts, according to Cocchi, but it is one he hopes will not only help those it serves but also deliver peace of mind to their loved ones.

Cocchi says he knows how fortunate he is. His aging parents and in-laws, as well as his disabled brother, live independently and have weathered the storm that is COVID-19. Cocchi also knows there's a generation of people who've earned the attention he wants to give them.

"Whenever I have visited our senior centers, I tell them that I feel my generation has failed the generation before us," Cocchi says. "They are responsible for the good ethics and morals of my generation and our kids, and I don't think we are doing the same for them. This is my opportunity to give back to the generation who brought us up."

The program's concept is a simple one. Every day at about the same time, the Sheriff's Department will place a telephone call to the seniors who are registered. If no one answers, they'll call again, and, then, if there is still no response, local first responders will be notified and asked to dispatch an officer for a wellness check, Cocchi says.

"This is a way to make family members feel their loved ones aren't by themselves, when

they are by themselves," Cocchi explains. "It brings a lot of gratitude from family members, sons and daughters, knowing someone checking in on them. We (also) hope if someone is in crisis that we can save a life. And, god forbid, if something were to happen during the night, we don't have a case of days on days going by without someone noticing."

Are You OK? will join the lineup of services offered through Cocchi's TRIAD program, a three-way partnership among his office, area police departments and councils on aging across Hampden County's 23 communities.

Early next year, Cocchi expects to launch another program, called Project Lifesaver, which, with the use of state-of-the-art tracking devices, will help people with autism and cognitive difficulties.

"We've been working on this pre-COVID," explains Cocchi. "I want to enhance and do much more work with our senior centers." The pandemic threw a curve ball into the process, limiting the places where his department could publicize the programs and register participants.

So engaged in the programs that Cocchi is planning, some members of his team say it's already changed their own lives. Take Jennifer Holley, a caseworker and canine officer with just over 21 years of service.

She had been looking at retirement soon, but now those thoughts are off the table. Holley will be a team leader for Project Lifesaver, having completed the training necessary and been tasked by Cocchi with another correctional officer, Liz Carpenter, to organize the electronic search-and-rescue program.

"It's probably the most amazing program I've been involved in," Holley says. "I could have retired at 20 years. Now, I have no retirement date in the future knowing I'm a part of this. It has 100 percent success rate."

Unlike Are You OK?, which is totally free, Project Lifesaver carries some costs. The bracelets cost $300, and the batteries and bands, which need to be replaced every 60 days or less, cost $10. Every dollar collected, though, will go directly into the Project Lifesaver fund thanks to the nonprofit that Cocchi established. (It's the same nonprofit that earlier this year helped fund Cocchi's First Responder Recovery Home, a place for first responders diagnosed with COVID-19 to recover.)

Will Project Lifesaver be cost prohibitive for those who may be on limited incomes? Not a problem, according to the sheriff. "I try never to say never," Cocchi says. His office is looking to sponsor the service for families in need. In fact, his team held an in-house pie fundraiser for Project Fundraiser in the run-up to Thanksgiving.

"It is amazing, absolutely amazing," says Holley. "I don't know why the world doesn't know about it." Nationwide, according to the statistics from the program thus far, close to 2,000 lives have been saved and it's logged a 100% success rate in finding missing adults and children who have wandered due to Alzheimer's, autism, dementia and other disorders. Ninety-nine percent of those searches were completed within 30 minutes.

Says Cocchi, "I'm committed as it grows to grow with it. I'm doing this to save lives and help people with the care their loved ones need. If it gets to 100, 200, 300 people, I have

met a major need in the community."

His focus right now, though, will be the launch of Are You OK? Cocchi's team is ready to welcome the first subscribers to the service. "If you're interested, call us," he says. "We want this to be a personal connection, not to an answering machine. We'll begin with a 'Good morning, are you OK,' and the connection can go from there."

In talking about Are You OK?, Cocchi references one of his neighbors, a 79-year-old man, who's been in good health and lives alone but who has no family living locally. "He was in the hospital for three days. He tried calling

me to bring him to the hospital. It ended up he had his appendix out, but no one knew he needed help," Cocchi says.

If you or someone you know might benefit, call 413-858-0080 to learn more about the wellness program.

"This is a great way to save lives, but to me, it's about respect," the sheriff explains. "No one should be in peril and not be able to reach out."

CHAPTER NINE

HCSD NAVIGATES THE COVID-19 PANDEMIC

HCSD NAVIGATES THE COVID-19 PANDEMIC

By Robert Rizzuto,
Hampden County Sheriff's Department

The COVID-19 Pandemic presented challenges not seen in a generation, and the impact of managing a respiratory virus was unbelievably difficult in congregate care settings like a correctional institution.

It was early March 2020, and Sheriff Nick Cocchi was mindful of the news as the virus, which was first detected in Wuhan, China, began to make its way around the United States. The annual Holyoke St. Patrick's Parade was the first big Western Massachusetts event to get axed due to the pandemic, and at that point the virus, which had already forced countries like Italy into a lockdown, felt real.

Sheriff Cocchi assembled his medical and administrative teams and began to strategize about how they would prepare for and handle the virus, which inevitably was going to make its way to Western Massachusetts and the institutions managed by the department in Hampden County. With tangible plans in hand, the Sheriff called a press conference to let the public know his department was taking the threat seriously and to reassure the families of the incarcerated that their loved ones would be safe through the upcoming storm.

Well ahead of CDC guidance that recommended mask wearing as a means to prevent the spread of the virus, Sheriff Cocchi instituted a mandatory mask policy for all staff and the incarcerated individuals in the department's care.

Before these precautions were commonplace, he made all staff pass through a medical screening station and instituted new disinfection standards department-wide. Decontamination included new stringent standards for housing units and transportation vehicles as well as staff, who were encouraged to use hand sanitizer and underwent decontamination of their footwear upon entering and exiting every facility.

The early intervention is credited with limiting exposure in the facilities at a time when other congregate care settings were reeling from significant outbreaks behind their walls. By summer of 2021, the department had not recorded a single death due to COVID-19, although more than 300 inmates and over 200 staff members had contracted virus throughout the pandemic.

Due to the pandemic, the department changed virtually every facet of how it operates, including pausing in-person visits for over a year and refining and expanding the capacity for video visits and video appearances in court. In-person visiting was finally reopened on a limited basis in May 2021. The daily medical screenings to ensure everyone was healthy and symptom-free continued for all staff until the staff vaccination rate had climbed to nearly 70%, at which point screenings were focused only on unvaccinated staff.

While concentrating on maintaining a safe environment for staff and inmates alike, Sheriff Cocchi and his administration understood that this virus could cause catastrophic consequences reaching far beyond our walls. The department aimed to assist where needed and that included advocating for and helping operate local COVID-19 vaccine clinics in Western Massachusetts.

In an editorial, The Republican newspaper of Springfield said, "During our struggle with coronavirus, Cocchi and the Sheriff's Department have been proactive to help provide solutions for our communities. Surrounding areas would do well to consider using these actions as an example. As the federal government has proven inconsistent in providing resources, state and local officials must act creatively to protect front-line responders and the public. Cocchi's agency is working to fill those gaps."

What follows is a snapshot of pandemic-related activities that the Hampden County Sheriff's Department accomplished in the midst of the most challenging situation mankind has seen in over 100 years.

PPE PRODUCTION

The Hampden County Sheriff's Department's York Street Industries Program shifted production at the beginning of the pandemic to craft life-saving personal protective equipment to address a critical nationwide shortage. According to the World Health Organization, the shortage was caused by spiking demand, panic buying, hoarding, the misuse of materials, which led to medical professionals reusing contaminated masks and gowns and a lack of availability for citizens trying to protect themselves.

Unlike disposable PPE, the items created by York Street Industries were manufactured with the durability to be washed to medical disinfectant standards and reused.

With inmate volunteers feeling pride from being part of the solution to a global problem,

production was running in two shifts for a total of 16 hours a day at both the Main Institution in Ludlow and the Western Massachusetts Regional Women's Correctional Center in Chicopee.

Additionally, Sheriff Cocchi teamed up with the Western Massachusetts 3D-Printing Collaborative, a team of high school students led by Sontino Allentuck, a junior at Longmeadow High School. The group produced face shields, which the department assembled and distributed to anyone in need throughout the pandemic.

THE PPE EFFORT, WHICH EARNED RECOGNITION ON THE NATIONAL LEVEL FROM U.S. CONGRESSMAN RICHARD E. NEAL, D-SPRINGFIELD, YIELDED THE FOLLOWING RESULTS:

- Produced over 67,000 masks that were distributed to organizations large and small all over Massachusetts & New England.

- Produced masks for every single inmate in county or state custody across the Commonwealth of Massachusetts.

- Produced nearly 1,000 medical gowns for hospitals across the region.

- Assembled and distributed medical-grade face shields to hospitals, dental practices, salons, and other area businesses.

- Collected and distributed hundreds of cases of hand sanitizer for first responders across Massachusetts.

COVID-RELATED TRANSPORTS

The Sheriff's transportation team was extremely busy during the COVID-19 Pandemic, helping drive people to and from the designated isolation hotels across Massachusetts.

These hotels were specifically operating to serve our neighbors who were recovering from COVID-19. However, when the state asked for volunteer agencies to help take infected people to and from these hotels, there were no hands up, with the exception of Sheriff Cocchi. Guided by the advice of the department's medical team, our teams safely helped transport private citizens and first responders sick with and recovering from COVID-19 throughout the state, as far as the Berkshires and Cape Cod.

The staff at the Hampden County Sheriff's Office transported around 775 patients to isolation hotels and 702 back home for a total of almost 144,000 miles traveled for such operations during the pandemic.

FIRST RESPONDER RECOVERY HOME

As the pandemic unfolded and Sheriff Cocchi saw the shifting needs, an area where he saw an unmet must was a place for frontline workers infected with COVID-19 to safely go to recover. That idea spawned the Hampden County Sheriff's Department First Responder Recovery Home. The department's Pre-release Center was transformed to a safe haven for frontline workers, including doctors, nurses, EMTs, police, firefighters, corrections professionals, retail and grocery store workers who were diagnosed with COVID-19, but couldn't safely go home to recover without jeopardizing the health of a vulnerable family member.

With a full-time staff onsite, the facility also provided all the amenities of home, including gourmet meals, streaming smart TVs, wireless Internet as well as a doctor and nurses, thanks to our many generous community supporters. As the pandemic evolved and the numbers dropped in the summer and early fall of 2020, the First Responder Recovery Home was closed but heralded as an innovation and success, with an editorial in The Republican calling the recovery home "a smart, innovative and compassionate way to assist those who risk their lives on a daily basis to fulfill their commitment to service, public protection and safety."

HELPING STAFF MEMA'S WESTERN MASS. COMMAND CENTER

When the Massachusetts Emergency Management Agency (MEMA) activated its Western Region Center in Agawam, the department provided full-time employees to help man the post.

Working alongside MEMA staff and planners, the department helped coordinate the commonwealth's regional response to the COVID-19 Pandemic, including the distribution of life-saving PPE to agencies across this half of the state.

Sheriff Cocchi's team start its Forest Park patrols early to help with an influx of visitors.

As the crowds flooded into the city's flagship recreational space, members of the department were on hand to ensure people were following the rules and felt safe. Additionally, the team stayed on patrol for an additional month to assist in the park through the end of fall 2020, before returning once again in early 2021 for the third season of the partnership.

"We're very fond of this partnership," Sheriff Cocchi said at the press conference announcing a return to the park in 2021. "We're here for the hospitality. We're going to get out of our cars, walk around and make sure everyone is having a good time and that they feel safe."

The department now has two deputy sheriffs working from 8 a.m. to 4 p.m., and 2 p.m. to 10 p.m. each day, March 1 through November 31. The deputy sheriffs can be seen daily, positively impacting the park visitors, and they have arrest and citation powers as well as the jurisdiction to enforce park regulations.

EXTENDED AND EXPANDED PATROLS IN SPRINGFIELD'S FOREST PARK

As the pandemic started to take hold in Massachusetts, most residents were forced to stay in their homes, only leaving the house for necessary supply runs as well as medical appointments and emergencies. An exception was getting outdoors, since the virus has less chance of spreading when people are at least 6 feet from each other, especially outside. So as the parks became places of refuge for people looking to simply get out of the house, Springfield Mayor Domenic Sarno requested

HONORING THE VICTIMS OF THE HOLYOKE SOLDIERS' HOME

As the pandemic evolved, some congregate care facilities fared better than others. Unfortunately, one of the facilities that suffered a significant loss of life and drew national attention as a result, was the Holyoke Soldiers' Home here in Western Massachusetts.

The elderly veterans in the home were already in the high-risk category for COVID-19 complications, but a variety of factors, including a decision to combine two dementia units filled with both sick and seemingly well veterans in late March 2020, led to the death of 77 veterans in a matter of months.

To ensure the 77 veterans who died as a result of the COVID-19 outbreak at the Holyoke Soldiers' Home were laid to rest with dignity, the department's honor guard escorted each procession of vehicles to the cemetery.

The effort was of the utmost importance to Sheriff Cocchi who called it "the right thing to do" and "a matter of proper respect to show there are important people being laid to rest." The initiative was a partnership with members of the Massachusetts Air National Guard 104th Fighter Wing's Fatality Search and Recovery Team, and spanned several months.

COMMUNITY SERVICE STAFF REPLACE INMATES

During the pandemic, we mostly avoided transfers into and between facilities, although our Community Service teams were missing the incarcerated individuals in our care for several months due to the pandemic, our staff was still out in the community every day helping with projects large and small.

They also stepped up to fill in for our community partners, who were struggling to provide employees to cover critical services while people were out sick. The Community Service team took on a variety of projects throughout the 23 cities and towns that make up Hampden County.

CONSULTATION TO OTHER LAW ENFORCEMENT AGENCIES ON BEST PRACTICES

Most correctional institutions have no full-time medical staff, let alone several doctors, nurses, behavioral health specialists and an award-winning program. With that in mind, Sheriff Cocchi connected our medical team, who was working to prevent COVID-19 from running through our facilities, with other law enforcement agencies and correctional institutions across New England to offer advice, best practices, and help them develop plans to keep people safe.

video visits, we help strengthen the bridge to families, which is shown to positively impact not only the recidivism rate, but how well a person's relationship with their loved ones progresses upon release," Sheriff Cocchi said at the time. "If we're not able to offer normal visitation to keep everybody safe, this is a no-brainer and just the right thing to do."

As many pandemic restrictions were lifted across the state, Sheriff Cocchi chose to keep the free calling time and video visits in place to keep the inmate population connected to loved ones in the community.

The proliferation of science-based information from our award-winning doctors and nurses prevented and limited the spread of the virus, diminishing the rate of infection and in a global sense, saving lives.

MAINTAINING FAMILY CONNECTIONS AND EXPANDING VIDEO VISITS AND COURT APPEARANCES

As of mid-March 2020, all inmate visits were paused until the vaccination rate climbed to more than 50% in Massachusetts in June 2021. As a means to maintain outside communication and a connection with family and friends, Sheriff Cocchi authorized two hours of free phone calls each week for our offender population. Our inmates also received three stamped envelopes per week to send letters to their loved ones at no cost.

Additionally, Sheriff Cocchi directed staff to establish video visiting and expand the use of such technology to maintain court appearances without exposing inmates and staff to more outside contact. The video technology maintained crucial court appearances and due process, and has allowed families to celebrate holidays and birthdays with loved ones, all while strengthening the bridge to the community that is crucial to a person's success upon release from custody.

"By offering free phone time and no-cost

MANAGING REGIONAL SAFE-KEEPS FOR POLICE DEPARTMENTS IN HAMPDEN COUNTY

In order to support the department's public safety partners, Sheriff Cocchi decided to continue accepting people accused of a crime with changes to the intake procedures designed to keep everybody safe.

All Regional safe-keeps at the Main Institution in Ludlow and at the Western Mass. Regional Women's Correctional Center in Chicopee were housed in separate medical quarantine units in order to isolate this temporary population for the protection of our staff and the general population. Additionally, all incoming detainees and inmates are now offered and encouraged to receive the COVID-19 vaccine with an appointment at the next available clinic.

COMMUNITY COVID-19 TESTING

As the pandemic ebbed and flowed, the Hampden County Sheriff's Department was constantly modifying its plans to assist the community where the need was at that moment. When testing was a central priority and difficult to obtain, the department helped organize a community testing site on its grounds in Ludlow for first responders and those who work or live in the town.

In just five hours, over 600 people came to be tested, and received their results before Christmas 2020. The testing, done in partnership with American Medical Response EMS, allowed citizens to make responsible decisions about their holiday plans, and not jeopardize the health of loved ones.

COVID-19 VACCINE ROLLOUT BEHIND THE WALLS

In December 2020, the department's health care workers were vaccinated, in accordance with the timeline established by the Baker-Polito Administration and the Department of Public Health in consultation with the Massachusetts Vaccine Advisory Group.

During the week of Jan. 18, 2021 correctional facilities kicked off their vaccination plans for congregate care settings. Members of the incarcerated population and correctional officers fell within the first phase of the rollout, where inmates and correctional staff were vaccinated concurrently.

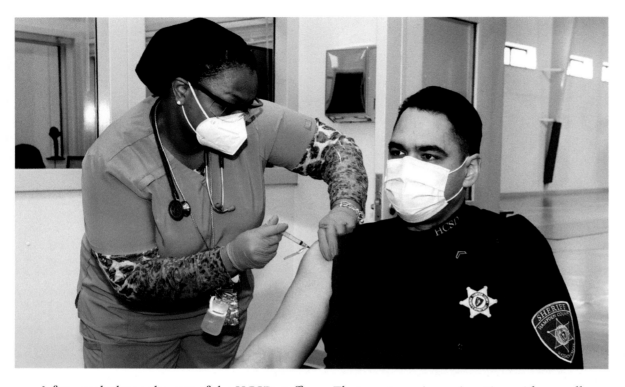

A few weeks later, the rest of the HCSD staff became eligible. The vaccination campaign, which still continues today, is one that involves constant education and outreach. As of publication, the department has administered the vaccine to hundreds of inmates and as part of the intake process, every person who comes into the custody of the department is offered a vaccine.

To dispel myths among the inmate population, with the guidance of Dr. Alysse Wurcel, a specialist in infectious disease with Tufts Medical Center, Hampden County launched an "Ask Me Anything" campaign, where medical professionals were dispatched into the living units to answer literally anything COVID-related someone may want to know.

That program, in conjunction with overall staff education, helped the department inoculate staff and inmates at a rate that surpassed its counterparts across the Commonwealth, especially among staff, with more than 70 percent being documented as fully vaccinated.

COVID-19 VACCINE REGISTRATION

When the COVID-19 vaccine became available to the public in early 2021, the demand outweighed the supply, forcing a game of cat-and-mouse with residents and available appointments at state vaccine sites. Complicating initial registration efforts was the fact that appointments could only be made via an

online portal, causing issues for the elderly and others with limited access to, or knowledge of technology.

To bridge those divides, the staff at the HCSD All Inclusive Support Services center in Springfield stepped up. Around 25 staffers ran a hotline from February until May 2021, fielding more than 1,500 calls; answering a variety of questions and helping more than 500 people get registered to receive a vaccine.

COMMUNITY COVID-19 VACCINE ADMINISTRATION

Once the COVID-19 vaccine became available to the general public, the HCSD rose to the occasion and offered support with two vaccination sites.

At the Eastern States Exposition in West Springfield, Sheriff Cocchi pledged staff to assist with registration at the West of the River Regional Collaborative Vaccine Site. Through a partnership with municipalities including West Springfield, Agawam, Westfield, Southwick, Granville and Tolland, the site had a capacity to administer up to 1,250 vaccine doses per day. By the time that vaccine clinic closed due to diminished demand, it had helped more than 10,000 people get inoculated against the virus.

In Chicopee, the department helped with a vaccination site at the Castle of Knights on Memorial Drive. Holyoke Community College nursing students worked alongside medical personnel with the Sheriff's Office to help administer the vaccine.

221

That site, which the Sheriff's Office helped operate in collaboration with the cities of Chicopee and Holyoke and the towns of South Hadley and Granby, administered more than 1,700 shots of the COVID-19 vaccine before the center closed in May 2021.

APPREHENSION TEAM ROUNDS UP COVID-19 RELEASES WITH ACTIVE WARRANTS

Following a lawsuit filed to compel mass releases from jails across Massachusetts in light of the COVID-19 Pandemic, the state Supreme Judicial Court on April 3, 2020 ordered the Massachusetts Trial Courts to review certain individuals for presumptive release from custody.

It was supposed to be only non-violent offenders considered for release but in reality, those released had charges including Aggravated Rape of a Child, Paying for Sex with a Child Under 14, Failure to Register as a Sex Offender, Assault with Intent to Murder, Assault & Battery on a Family/Household Member, Assault & Battery on a Child with Injury and Assault & Battery on a Police Officer.

Sheriff Nick Cocchi consistently voiced his opposition to early releases in Hampden County, citing the lack of time to establish dependable release plans, an unprecedented difficulty in establishing bridges to community-based services for substance use disorder and the level of seriousness of the crimes

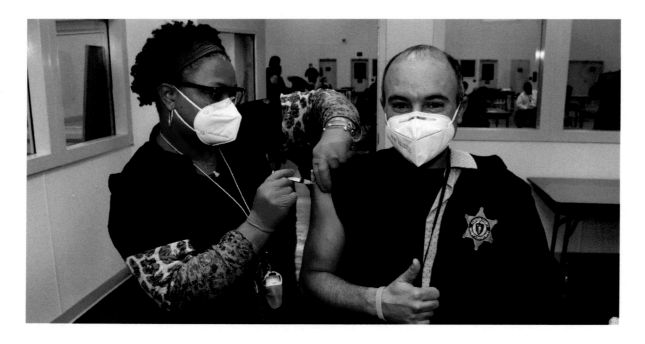

ABOVE: Stephanie Burgess, Infection Control Nurse with the Hampden County Sheriff's Department, administers a Moderna COVID-19 vaccine to Senior Public Information Officer Robert Rizzuto during one of the department's initial vaccine clinics in Jan. 2021. (HCSD Photo by Mark M. Murray)

some of the people being released are accused of committing.

For those who committed new crimes in Hampden County after being released by the courts relative to the SJC order, including a man who cut off his GPS monitoring device and was later arrested for carjacking and armed robbery, the HCSD Apprehension Team was dispatched to round them up.

Over the course of several months, they re-arrested more than 20 individuals, bringing them to justice and making the community safer in the process.

FINDING A NEW NORMAL IN THE PANDEMIC

As the spring turned to summer, and Massachusetts held the best vaccination rate in the nation, some things started to normalize. Behind the walls, visitation restarted in a limited capacity and overall restrictions eased among the vaccinated.

As concerning and highly contagious COVID variants circulated in society, Sheriff Cocchi reported that more than 70% of full-time staff had opted to receive the Moderna vaccine, as offered by the department via Department of Public Health protocols. Of the correctional staff, which includes correctional officers, correctional caseworkers, and counselors, the number was around 65% and growing each week, as more people chose to get the vaccine.

"The vaccine is one of the most important tools we have in the fight against a virus that not only upended our operations but our very way of life for more than a year," said Sheriff Cocchi. "I trust the science and I've already received the second shot of the Moderna vaccine. For me, being vaccinated ensures I am protecting my family, the staff, the inmates in our care and the general public which we serve. And although the vaccine is voluntary, we strongly encourage everyone take it."

While the FDA had issued emergency use authorizations for the Pfizer, Moderna and Johnson & Johnson vaccines in the U.S., correctional facilities in Massachusetts had thus far been receiving vaccines from Moderna, which is headquartered in Cambridge with a production facility in Norwood. But the Johnson & Johnson vaccine's simpler storage and handling protocols, along with the fact that it is a one-shot vaccine, prompted the sheriff's office to seek it, primarily to streamline inoculating the inmate population.

Regarding safety of the vaccine, of the more than 750 Moderna vaccine shots given out to HCSD staff, contractors, part-time and volunteers, only one person who happened to have a pre-existing medical condition reported having a potentially serious side effect. And in that case, the allergic reaction was handled promptly by the employee, who is now inoculated against the virus.

SHERIFF COCCHI'S MOVE TO OFFER COMFORT TO CORONAVIRUS FIRST RESPONDERS UPLIFTING

By The Republican Editorials

Nick Cocchi and the Hampden County Sheriff's Department's efforts will provide some comfort for first responders that have tested positive for COVID-19. The 84-room First Responder Recovery Home, located at the Pre-Release Center, is available to doctors, nurses, police, firefighters, emergency medical technicians, corrections professionals and U.S. military.

Cocchi has enlisted a Ludlow physician, Dr. Shaukat Matin, to help coordinate medical services. The facility will provide three designated meals and a pantry with snacks, juices and pastries.

As of Tuesday, the facility received pledges of $36,000 toward its operation.

"This is a place to show respect, compassion and gratitude to our first responders. It's our job as a community to give them a place to recover," Cocchi said.

RIGHT TOP: Hampden County Sheriff Nick Cocchi talks with Ludlow MD Shaukat Matin and officer Ollari about kitchen and cafeteria of the First Responder Recovery Home. (Hoang 'Leon' Nguyen / The Republican)

RIGHT: The library at the First Responder Recovery Home. (Hoang 'Leon' Nguyen / The Republican)

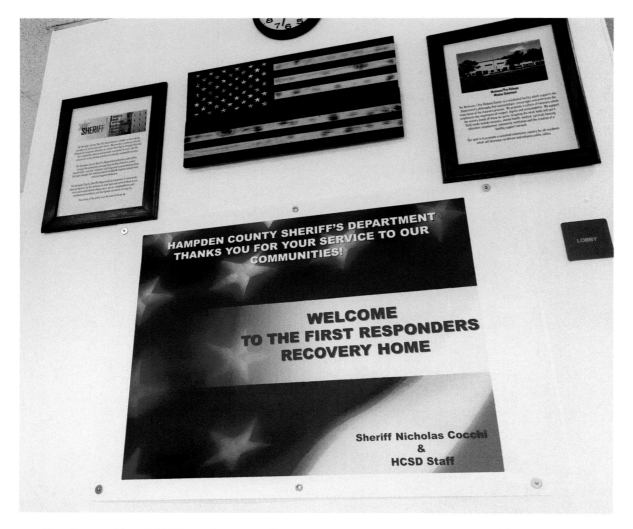

gowns, meeting CDC specifications, for their personal use. After the inmates produced enough protective equipment to meet internal need, Cocchi then looked to the external need of doctors, nurses and first responders. Cocchi said they are making 500 masks and 35 gowns per day. This effort is critical, as masks and other protective equipment have been in short supply and states have been scrambling to keep up as demand increases daily.

During our struggle with coronavirus, Cocchi and the sheriff's department have been proactive to help provide solutions for our communities. Surrounding areas would do well to consider using these actions as an example. As the federal government has proven inconsistent in providing resources, state and local officials must act creatively to protect front-line responders and the public. Cocchi's agency is working to fill those gaps. As public health officials warn COVID-19 infections are expected to rise quickly, immediate action is critical. And the sheriff's department is working in creative and effective ways to offer support.

For those with a COVID-19 diagnosis this facility will ease the burden of returning home, where many live with small children or elderly parents that may have compromised immune systems.

The recovery home is a smart, innovative and compassionate way to assist those who risk their lives on a daily basis to fulfill their commitment to service, public protection and safety.

In a similar move to address community need, ahead of a recent advisory from the Centers for Disease Control and Prevention and a call for Springfield residents to wear masks while in public, Cocchi initiated a program for inmates to construct masks and

CHAPTER TEN

STONYBROOK STABILIZATION & TREATMENT CENTER

ADDRESSING A CRISIS HEAD-ON:
SHERIFF COCCHI MORE THAN DOUBLES TREATMENT BEDS IN WESTERN MASSACHUSETTS

BY CAROLYN ROBBINS

Just before the holidays in 2017, a cry for help from a young mother in Chicopee, battling alcohol addiction turned into a death sentence because there was no place in Hampden County to get treatment when she needed it the most.

The 39-year-old mother of three was in crisis when she appeared before a judge in Chicopee District Court, brought there under the state's civil commitment statute, referred to as Section 35. Under the law, a petitioner – in this case the woman's family can file for a Section 35 civil commitment on someone's behalf. In doing so, they can be held involuntarily for treatment of substance use disorder if they pose a danger to themselves or others, due to their addiction.

As is required by law, the court remanded her to the custody of the Hampden County Sheriff's Department for transportation to a facility in the eastern part of the state, the primary place in the commonwealth where treatment under Section 35 for women is available. By the time the Hampden County Sheriff's Department arrived to transport her to the facility, she had spent almost a full day in court lockup.

On the way to a Department of Mental

Health treatment facility in Taunton, the woman, already in the throes of detox, experienced a medical emergency and although HCSD staff revived her once on the side of the road, she was pronounced dead on arrival to a hospital.

The tragic incident was a gut punch to newly elected Sheriff Nicholas Cocchi, who over his 20 years with the department knew all too well the terrible toll alcohol and opioid abuse takes on individuals and their families.

He has a vivid memory about when he got the call about the incident. It was on Dec. 1, 2017 while out for a holiday dinner with outgoing Sheriff Michael J. Ashe Jr. to discuss his new job.

The next day, when talking with the woman's parents, Cocchi learned of her struggles with

alcohol and other medical issues and he vowed to the family that he would do everything in his power to prevent another tragic incident from happening again.

A plan to establish a Western Massachusetts-based addiction treatment center had already been identified as a top priority for Cocchi and the woman's death only heightened his sense of urgency.

Before Cocchi took office, the opioid epidemic had already been declared a national public health emergency, impacting families across the socio-economic spectrum.

Overdose rates were skyrocketing in Western Massachusetts, especially in Greater Springfield. But the small number of treatment beds in the region were booked with a months-long

when someone reaches out for help, greater success is achieved when you move quickly and address the issue while the will is there to do so.

After persistent and passionate legislative lobbying, Cocchi's vision to open a professionally staffed state-of-the art treatment center in Ludlow seemed in reach.

There were some stumbling blocks along the way, however. There was significant opposition from those who argued that the notion of a Sheriff's Department being involved in providing substance use disorder treatment was punitive and demeaning.

"I'm proud to say it's one of the best programs in the commonwealth. We offer an average of 50-plus days of treatment compared to a 21-day state average in other facilities," he said. "The program offers a pause to destructive behavior and gives family's hope that their loved one will at least make it to tomorrow and at best, come back to them with the tools to maintain sobriety and long-term recovery.

"Our fight was long and loud, but we didn't give up," said Cocchi. "We weren't going to take 'no' for an answer."

In May 2018, the Stonybrook Stabilization and Treatment Center opened with the goal of providing around 80 inpatient beds where treatment would include everything from medically managed withdrawal to dual diagnosis treatment and counseling.

The program initially opened in the department's Main Institution in Ludlow and the Western Massachusetts Recovery and Wellness Center in Springfield, and was set up as a step-down model.

waiting list for anyone who was brave enough to seek help.

After some research, he found that a current law on the books prevented him from setting up a local treatment program for women, but it did allow him to establish one for men.

So Cocchi set out to open a treatment center for men that would provide a seven-day period for the medically managed withdrawal of clients -- followed by weeks of holistic treatment for both the psychological and physical medical conditions that accompany substance abuse disorder.

The unfortunate reality is that many people who are addicted to opioids and alcohol may not have months to wait for help, Cocchi said. And with the nature of addiction in general,

Since those humble beginnings, the program has grown in the waning days of the COVID-19 Pandemic, offering just over 130 beds at the Ludlow campus in a building that was previously the pre-release center.

Although the treatment center was initially created to serve people residing in Western Massachusetts and Worcester, it has expanded its scope. Based on the department's reputation and the program's success, it now accepts clients from other parts of the state and prides itself on never turning away someone in need.

Under a plan negotiated by Cocchi, the Stonybrook Stabilization and Treatment Center (SSTC) operates under a partnership with the Department of Corrections. Stonybrook provides an evidence-based approach to tackling addiction that has proven successful.

Unlike Stonybrook, some privately run treatment centers only provide a 14-day inpatient stay – the minimum period which health insurance is mandated to cover in Massachusetts. At Stonybrook, without insurance limitations, a client's stay could be as long as 54 days or more, including the detox period. Studies of the data show that the longer the stay, the better the chances a person will be able to maintain sobriety and work into long-term recovery.

With the opening of Stonybrook, as a facility run by a Sheriff's Department, the programs story has gained national attention and praise from local medical professionals including Baystate Health CEO Dr. Mark Keroack, who called it "the kind of innovative, effective program that the opioid crisis now demands," noting that fewer than 10 percent of clients who have gone through the program have been recommitted – a statewide low.

The Stonybrook program has been featured in medical trade publications and in national media, including the TV show, "The Doctors" and was featured in a PBS Newshour report by Hari Sreenivasan, who toured the facility with Cocchi as his guide in November 2019.

In both appearances, Cocchi answered critics, arguing, that the data proved the program was effective and desperately needed by a community ravaged by the ills associated with substance abuse.

Even though Stonybrook is a completely separate building located at a different address from the Hampden County Correctional Center and there are no correctional officers working there, opponents argue that it's "still a jail."

Bonnie Tenneriello, an attorney for Prisoners' Legal Services, is a vocal critic of the program which has filed a lawsuit targeting the Department of Corrections and the Hampden County Sheriff's Department, arguing that "a jail is a jail" and that it is the wrong environment to place people struggling with addiction.

"Nobody who is sectioned for substance use disorder should be incarcerated," Tenneriello said in an interview with MassInc. about the lawsuit.

Not one to mince words when discussing his treatment concept, Cocchi answered critics of the program during an interview with PBS Newshour:

"When people point at us and say it shouldn't happen here, well, where else is it going to happen? There was not one bed for these types of men in Western Massachusetts. We opened this program a year ago, and now they tell me

but you shouldn't be doing it? Take my 120 beds away? Then what? How many funerals are we going to? How many family members have got to bury a loved one? I'm not going to be on that side of the coin," he said.

"I'm not going to let someone die behind a dumpster because they are cold and afraid. We're giving them some hope and a place to go because it's the right thing to do."

The suit by the Prisoners' Legal Services to close the Stonybrook treatment facility down is still pending at the time of publication.

In the meantime, the work at Stonybrook goes on as the need for its services is great, according to Nick Melikian, Assistant Superintendent of the center.

Stonybrook's emphasis is on treatment, not correction, he said, explaining the difference between the SSTC and the jail.

"There are no badges worn or locked doors," Melikian said.

Local judges visited the treatment center when it first opened and agree that the system developed by Sheriff Cocchi had a better chance at helping the people struggling with addiction; kick their habits than many of the alternatives. After that visit, civil commitments from the court skyrocketed, according to Sheriff Cocchi.

As of publication, the program has served more than 2,200 men, with around 20 new commitments each week.

"This is the Sheriff's baby," Melikian said, while mentioning that Cocchi was adamant from the start that no one would be turned

away.

When clients arrive at Stonybrook, they are given a Covid test and are offered a shower, clean clothes and a meal.

The next step is a period of medically managed withdrawal, which is perhaps the toughest time period for both the patients and the people who care for them.

Thomas Foye, a substance abuse educator and counselor at SSTC, said there is no such thing as a typical client, citing his own battle with addiction.

A former law enforcement officer in the town of Ludlow, Foye wound up behind bars, after becoming addicted to pain killers to treat a medical condition.

"We work to help the client find the truth and surrender to get help and move forward with their lives," Foye said, adding that clients have different thresholds of denial at the beginning.

"There is a process of de-escalation where we help them find their own way to get to recovery," he said. "We help them understand cravings and help them develop coping mechanisms to control them.

Foye understands that he has credibility as a "man in recovery."

Referring to the work he does at Stonybrook as the most rewarding of his life, Foye said, "it was my destiny."

Melissa Bellingham, SSTC unit manager, said when the center opened with a staff of just 20 people, including four counselors, they were engaged in transferring clients from a treatment facility in Plymouth and other operational issues.

In the first week, the program had enrolled 48 clients. The next week, the caseload climbed into the 60s.

The facility offers eight to ten programs a day, including AA meetings, group therapy sessions, recreational activities with specialized focuses such as mindful meditation and a drum circle – offering clients other tools to tap into on their road to recovery.

Stephen O'Neil, who recently retired after serving as the Public Information Officer for the Hampden County Sheriff's Department, leads the meditation and drum circle programs, which is typically the first program of the day for the clients at SSTC.

"Research shows the efficacy of the programs," said O'Neil, adding that data shows that meditation helps lay the groundwork for building self-awareness and confidence after the trauma many clients had faced.

The drum circle provides both entertainment and therapeutic release- a duality achieved by many of the programs at Stonybrook. "It's a way of getting in touch with themselves with no distractions and it's good for the soul," O'Neil said.

EPILOGUE

As this book is being published, we are closing in on two years of living in "the new normal" with the COVID-19 Pandemic bringing shifting and highly contagious variants. But just as the virus itself changes over time, the Hampden County Sheriff's Department remains nimble enough to match it, and hopefully keep it at bay.

While the challenges of COVID-19 continue, the department remains unwavering in its commitment to enlightened corrections and community engagement.

We are safely getting out into the community every day and working to enhance the relationship between law enforcement and citizens by demonstrating our desire to be positive change agents. We are working behind the walls of our institutions to offer the people in our custody the opportunities that life previous to incarceration may have been lacking. In short- this department exists to make the world a better place by banking on

the exponential effect that helping one person can have on a family, a neighborhood and a community.

This approach, crafted by Sheriff Michael J. Ashe Jr. and refined by Sheriff Nick Cocchi, has had two profound effects, with the first being an international reputation for how to effectively and compassionately run correctional facilities. The second, in terms of the correctional side of the department, is reflected in boasting some of the lowest recidivism rates anywhere in the United States.

For example, statistics show that over a three year period about 34 percent of those incarcerated in Hampden County had returned to jail. Nationally, the rate was around 67 percent, according to 2016 statistics.

Locally, the low rate of people returning to jail following incarceration is a testament to the staff at the department and the guiding principle that a successful reentry to the

community begins on day one of incarceration. We had the first after-care program for inmates in the nation and today, we have the most innovative, offering wrap-around services of all kinds to ensure people who want to be successful have every opportunity to be so.

Sheriff Cocchi has expanded the department's reach into the towns and cities of Hampden County through task force partnerships with other law enforcement agencies and through initiatives like the TRIAD Program for senior citizens and the creation of the Emotional Support Division of therapy dogs. Those programs are among the dozens all meant to bridge a gap between a need in the community and what exists to fulfill it.

In Sheriff Cocchi's view, the department's staff is to embody the mantra of service above self, and to ensure that wherever assistance is needed, the Hampden County Sheriff's Office steps in to do its part.

SHERIFF MICHAEL J. ASHE, JR.

Retired Sheriff Michael J. Ashe, Jr. is a native of Springfield, Massachusetts.

He holds a bachelor's degree from St. Anselm's College and a Master's degree in Social Work from Boston College.

He worked for the Division of Child Guardianship, including serving as a supervisor in a program for battered children in Western Massachusetts, and then he and his wife Barbara served as the first house parents of Downey Side homes for youth. Downey Side was founded to provide long-term care to children in need of stability in their home situations.
Michael Ashe was elected Sheriff in 1974. He was re-elected every six years since without opposition before retiring in 2016.

Former Sheriff Michael Ashe's motto of correctional supervision is "Strength reinforced with decency; firmness dignified with fairness." Sheriff Ashe strongly believes that the offender who desires to build a law-abiding life should be challenged with the opportunity to pick up the tools and directions to do so, and that this should take place in a safe, secure, orderly, demanding, lawful and humane environment, where staff and inmates are free from violence.

Facilities under Sheriff Ashe's administration received 27 consecutive audits of 95% or higher by the American Correctional Association. Sheriff Ashe was a believer in "community corrections." Toward that end, he helped establish 300 community partnerships with non-profit and public agencies throughout the region to assist in the correction and community re-entry effort.

SHERIFF NICK COCCHI

Nick Cocchi is a lifelong resident of Ludlow. He earned his Bachelors of Science Degree in Government from Western New England University and his Master's in Business Administration from Elms College.

Nick is the recipient of several of the Sheriff's Department awards including; Employee of the Month, The Distinguished Service Award and the prestigious Dodson Award. He is married to his high school sweetheart Wendi and father to their three sons, Owen, Max, and Sam. Nick began his career as a seasonal, part-time correctional officer with the Hampden County Sheriff's Office, working his way up the ladder to eventually be elected by the voters of Hamden County to serve as Sheriff.

Since taking office in 2017, Sheriff Cocchi has expanded the department's level of community engagement, including taking on the opioid epidemic head-on. He started a medication assisted treatment program to help people battling addiction and he opened a substance use disorder treatment facility to help people involuntarily committed by the courts under the state's Section 35 law.

Behind the walls of the facilities he oversees, Sheriff Cocchi has expanded career training and job placement efforts to include the high- paying forestry profession as well as advanced manufacturing. And with an eye toward the future, Sheriff Cocchi is always looking at ways his team can help address unmet needs in the community, and partner with the various groups that make the 23 cities and towns in Hampden County a great place to live, work and play.

JAY CARON COMMUNITY IMPACT FOUNDATION

The Jay Caron Community Impact Foundation honors the memory and legacy of local businessman and philanthropist Jay Caron, who passed away in Oct. 2020 following a medical complication relative to contracting COVID-19.

Caron was the president and CEO of the family business, Bee-Line Corp., in Springfield. He was a founder and board member of NUVO Bank & Trust and also served as an advisor to the Hampden County Sheriff's Department.

Caron was also the founder of East Longmeadow's youth lacrosse program and later was inducted into the Western Mass. Lacrosse Hall of Fame.

The Jay Caron Community Impact Foundation's mission is to support, provide and promote efforts that encourage creative strategies to improve economic growth, academic and personal development, social and civic welfare and urban beautification within the 23 cities and towns of Hampden County.

"My friend Jay worked tirelessly behind the scenes to make Western Massachusetts a better place. And since his passing, the impact foundation, now named after him, has been continuing the work in his honor," said Hampden County Sheriff Nick Cocchi, the president of the Jay Caron Community Impact Foundation. "Whether it's donating gifts to the less fortunate at Christmas time, or helping organize and publicize local food giveaways, we are always looking at creative ways to continue the organization's mission and make this an even better place to live, work and play."

Jay Caron Community
Impact Foundation

HAMPDEN COUNTY
HONORARY DEPUTY SHERIFFS ASSOCIATION

Since most community members only experience corrections activities through TV and movies, the Hampden County Honorary Deputy Sheriffs Association was created to provide genuine opportunities for civilians to get the real story and become Hampden County Sheriff's Department ambassadors.

The mission of the Hampden County Deputy Sheriffs Association, Inc. is to assist and support various community-based support services, including but not limited to charitable, community service and educational based organizations and programs. These services must operate within the Commonwealth of Massachusetts and be utilized for the promotion of public safety and the Office of the Sheriff.

Members are encouraged to participate by volunteering their time and skills, as well as financial resources to maintain and support the Deputy Sheriffs Association mission.

OUT OF THE DARKNESS BOOK SPONSORS

Bronze Sponsor

Mercy Medical Center

Community Sponsorships

Astro Chemicals Inc

Behavioral Health Network, Inc.

C & W Realty Enterprises, LLC

CODAC Behavioral Healthcare

Congressman Richard E. Neal

Holyoke Medical Center

Mayor Domenic J. Sarno

Vince Group Inc/Anthony Ravosa

The Republican and MassLive.com

MERCY MEDICAL CENTER

Since 1899

The Sisters of Providence—courageous and pioneering women—came to Western Massachusetts from Canada 140 years ago to care for the poor, the orphans and the immigrants working in the Holyoke mills. Over the years, the Sisters established a compassionate, transformative presence, providing health care, food, and shelter for the homeless and needy, in addition to social services and care of the elderly and disabled.

At Mercy Medical Center, we are committed to preserving and strengthening their legacy of care and service. We are part of an extraordinary Mission; a Mission that allows us to make a positive difference in the world around us and a profound difference in the lives of those who need our healing touch.

Mercy Medical Center is fully accredited and recognized with an "A" safety grade from The Leapfrog Group, an independent national organization committed to health care quality and safety. Mercy Medical Center includes our Rehabilitation Hospital and Brightside for Families and Children and our hallmark programs include the Sister Caritas Cancer Center, Center for Breast Health and Gynecologic Oncology, Family Life Center for Maternity, Emergency Department, a state-of-the-art Intensive Care Unit, and the most advanced Magnetic Resonance Imaging (MRI) services.

Mercy Medical Center is part of Trinity Health Of New England, an integrated health care delivery system formed in 2015. Trinity Health Of New England is a member of Trinity Health located in Livonia, MI, one of the largest multi-institutional Catholic health care delivery systems in the nation.

Ever mindful of the inspiration we derive from the Sisters of Providence, we continue to move forward by focusing on our Mission to serve as a "transforming, healing presence" and our commitment to care for the most vulnerable in our community.

Top photo: Mercy Hospital, 1899;
Bottom photo: Mercy Medical Center today.

A Legacy of the
Sisters of Providence

ASTRO CHEMICALS INC.

Since 1970

Astro Chemicals, Inc. was founded in 1970 by Leo Diamond and Bill Cunningham and is a 3rd generation family-owned business located in Springfield, MA. Since its incorporation, Astro has grown into a premier chemical and adhesive distributor in the Northeast, providing superior customer service and a safe, courteous workplace that promotes continuous improvement. Astro stocks 1000 different molecules and can provide next–day delivery on its own fleet of trucks. Our knowledgeable team can help organizations meet any technical or logistical challenges. Astro provides products for water treatment, pharmaceuticals, paints, coatings, laboratories, cleaning compounds and many other industries.

Astro Chemicals, Inc. is proud to be a sponsor of the Hampden County Sheriff's Department's Out of the Darkness book, that celebrates the achievements of our correctional and law enforcement agencies in Western Mass. Positive changes, innovations, and contributions to the community are keystones of our culture in Western Mass and the successful implementation of the HCSD's practices continue to uphold these values. We thank Sherriff Cocchi and the law enforcement officers that labor in all the Western Mass cities and correctional facilities for their service, especially during the COVID-19 pandemic.

For more information about Astro Chemicals, Inc. products and services please visit https://astrochemicals.com/ or call 800-223-0776.

The Astro Chemicals Inc. warehouse, located in Springfield, MA.

Astro stocks products from over 100 different domestic and foreign chemical manufacturers.

astro
CHEMICALS, INC.

126 Memorial Drive, Springfield, MA

BEHAVIORAL HEALTH NETWORK, INC.

Since 1938

Behavioral Health Network, Inc. (BHN) is a regional provider of comprehensive behavioral health services for adults, children, and families. BHN began as the Child Guidance Clinic in 1938 and has grown into the largest behavioral health service provider in Western Massachusetts. BHN serves those with life challenges due to mental illness, substance abuse, or intellectual and developmental disabilities. Across all BHN programs, staff and caregivers offer support, guidance and tools that help individuals make positive, life-altering changes.

BHN serves approximately 32,000 individuals annually and employs over 2,400 individuals. Services and programming are rendered at 40 locations across the four-county area and include:

- Addiction & Recovery
- Community-Based Services for Children and Families
- Counseling & Wellness
- Crisis Intervention & Stabilization
- Domestic Violence
- Forensic Services
- Integrated Healthcare
- Intellectual & Developmental Services
- Residential, Individual and Family Supports

BHN is proud to partner with Hampden County Sheriff's Department as they promote positive change in corrections and law enforcement.
BHN assists with the re-entry process by providing community-based wrap around services to help men and women sustain long-term recovery and avoid recidivism. These services are initiated behind the wall and carry forward into the community through discharge planning. Coordination of community Medication Assisted Treatment (MAT), referrals to recovery coaching, and the transitional addiction support team, are just a few of the ways that BHN serves this population.

Visit bhninc.org to learn more about BHN's service offering.
To schedule services call, 413-BHN-WORK (413-246-9675)
24-Hour Crisis Line: 413-733-6661

bhn
Behavioral Health Network

417 Liberty Street, Springfield, Massachusetts 01104

C & W REALTY ENTERPRISES, LLC

Sheriff Michael J. Ashe and Sheriff Nicholas Cocchi

C & W Realty salutes Mike Ashe and Nick Cocchi for their life-long efforts to reform Hampden County's Correctional system. Sheriff Ashe and his successor Sheriff Cocchi have rebuilt a system that has resulted in the transformation of the entire correctional system of the county. From the design and construction of two state-of-the-art correctional facilities for men and for women, to the many special programs design to rehabilitate inmates and significantly reduced re-cidivism. Their work has inspired other correctional systems around the State and nation to adopt aspects of their reforms. It was an honor for C & W Realty to have worked with the Sheriff's Department in providing spaces at Howard Street and 311 State Street for their alcohol and substance abuse rehabilitation programs.

C & W Realty Enterprises, LLC

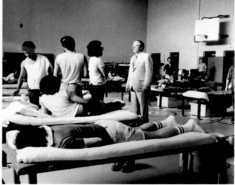

Sheriff Ashe speaking with inmates

WMass Correctional Addiction Center

Ashe takes over National Guard Armory

Demolition of York Street Jail

WMass Women's Correctional Center

Hampden County House of Corrections at Stony Brook

CODAC Behavioral Healthcare

Service for Over 51 Years

CODAC Behavioral Healthcare is Rhode Island's oldest and largest non-profit provider of outpatient services for Opioid Use Disorder (OUD). CODAC has been a leader in adopting and creating programming that reflect emergent needs in opioid treatment and recovery. COVID-19 has changed every facet of life and recent CDC data suggest it worsened the already over-whelming opioid epidemic. While addiction-related issues have spiked during the pandemic, the Hampden County Sheriff's Medication Assisted Treatment (MAT) program has helped hundreds of men and women battling substance use disorder.

CODAC has proudly partnered with Sheriff Nicholas Cocchi to implement the first MAT program at Hampden County House of Corrections which has been highly effective in assisting inmates to receive treatment while reducing fatalities upon release. Through this partnership, the Hampden County MAT program pairs counseling, behavioral therapy and access to all three FDA-approved addiction medications for treatment of substance use disorder.

More than 80% of incarcerated individuals report battling with some level of substance use disorder. Since the MAT program's inception on Sept. 1, 2019, it has provided a critical bridge to treatment for more than 1,400 men and women who came into the custody of the sheriff's office.

Linda Hurley, President/CEO of CODAC, stated, "We are proud to be working with the Hampden County Sheriff's Department on this important initiative that helps move the needle forward in treating all those struggling with addiction as patients, just like those facing diabetes or cancer, and offer them the most comprehensive, evidence-based therapeutic approaches available, such as MAT. The progress we are making in Hampden County underscores that the program we pioneered in Rhode Island is both scalable and feasible elsewhere, and we are always available to help patients in other states."

1052 Park Avenue, Cranston, RI, 02910

CODAC's Linda Hurley, CEO works fervently to expand Medication Assisted Treatment (MAT) services into underserved areas. Establishment of federal and community-based partnerships have become instrumental in the battle against Substance Use Disorder (SUD) including the current opioid use epidemic.

CONGRESSMAN RICHARD E. NEAL

In Office Since 1988

Sheriff Ashe has spent his life embodying the fundamental principle that all who are willing to work for a second chance ought to receive one. His signature philosophy of "strength reinforced with decency; firmness dignified in fairness" led to countless lives being changed for the better, while resulting in one of the lowest reincarceration rates in the United States.

Anyone who has gotten to know Sheriff Ashe will affirm that he had never been in the business of incarceration, rather his focus was on corrections. His doctrine on correctional supervision was guided by the simple principle that inmates should be held accountable and be positive and productive. The Sheriff long understood that if he were to adequately rehabilitate his inmates, he would need to put together a competent coalition of staff and volunteers who could command the situation, while exemplifying the upmost professionalism.

Throughout his career, Sheriff Ashe's tireless work has made our community a safer, more just, caring place. During his tenure, Sheriff Ashe witnessed over 4,600 inmates graduate his educational programs, earning a GED or a high school equivalent diploma. Sheriff Ashe oversaw the inmates in his facilities contribute over 1 million hours of community service to Hampden County communities.

Sheriff Nick Cocchi has continued Sheriff Ashe's legacy and policies and added new practices that have kept the Hampden County Correctional System a model for the nation. These men have made the Commonwealth proud while illustrating that the United States is indeed a nation of second chances. I am proud to call them both dear friends.

Congressman Richard E. Neal
First Congressional District of Massachusetts
Chair, House Committee on Ways and Means

HOLYOKE MEDICAL CENTER

Since 1893

From its beginnings in 1893, Holyoke Medical Center has always responded to the healthcare needs of the greater Holyoke community. The hospital has continuously expanded to accommodate an ever-growing population of patients, offering state-of-the-art technological services, as well as routine exams and treatments. It has remained dedicated to attracting exceptional, highly skilled physicians, nurses, and healthcare providers to serve patients with the highest quality of care, compassion and individualized attention that they deserve.

A nationally accredited hospital, Holyoke Medical Center received the Top Hospital Award from the Leapfrog Group for excellence in quality of care and patient safety in 2020, 2016, and 2014. This full-service hospital provides a complete line of inpatient and outpatient medical and surgical services, including an award-winning Stroke Service, which has been consistently recognized in the state by the Massachusetts Department of Public Health and the American Heart Association/American Stroke Association.

Our Mission at Holyoke Medical Center is to improve the health of all people in our community. We do that with honesty, respect and dignity for our patients, visitors and staff. We do that through expert and compassionate care, education and knowledge sharing, community partnerships, fostering innovation and growth and by inspiring hope in all we touch. We do that by being good stewards of our resources and providing efficient and cost effective care to all.

Holyoke Medical Center is a member of Valley Health Systems, which also includes the affiliates Holyoke Medical Group, Holyoke Visiting Nurse Association & Hospice Life Care, and River Valley Counseling Center.

Holyoke Medical Center

575 Beech Street, Holyoke, MA 01040
HolyokeHealth.com

MAYOR DOMENIC J. SARNO

Simply put, Sheriff Ashe, aka 'Rock', and Sheriff Cocchi and Team, you have saved and guided so many of lives towards redemption and a positive path in life – Thank You!

Good health and continued success. God Bless.

Respectfully, Mayor Domenic J. Sarno

P.S. Thank you for your friendship and continued support.

THE VINCE GROUP, INC.

Since 1996

Founded in 1996 by Tony Ravosa, The Vince Group is a boutique consulting firm providing public affairs, government relations, strategic marketing, business development, issues advocacy, and project origination advisory services to a diverse group of clients with varying interests. Among them: real estate development, renewable energy (solar, wind, battery storage), electric transmission and power grid resiliency, affordable and workforce housing, information technology, telecommunications, emergency preparedness and disaster recovery, architectural design, site civil and environmental engineering, and cannabis. Mr. Ravosa formerly served as a member of the Springfield City Council (1989-1995) and as Government Affairs Liaison for the Maritime Department of the Massachusetts Port Authority (Massport) and the Port of Boston.

While primarily focused on issues and projects here in New England, The Vince Group enjoys an established network of reputable associates strategically situated throughout the Northeast and beyond. The services provided by the firm on behalf of its clients is multi-faceted. We assist those we represent in maneuvering through bureaucratic red tape, while acting as their primary conduit to state and local government agencies and regulatory bodies. We utilize our extensive business and political contacts to augment our clients' efforts to achieve their aims and objectives. Our primary goal always is to enhance every client's opportunity for success. From the point of introduction through project permitting and approval, the Vince Group is a formidable ally committed to driving the process forward, reducing cumbersome and costly delays, and achieving a successful end result for our clients.

THE VINCE GROUP

140 Glastonbury Blvd #26, Glastonbury, CT 06033

Sheriff Michael J. Ashe, Lt. Governor Karyn Polito, and Tony Ravosa

Tony Ravosa and Sheriff Nick Cocchi

THE REPUBLICAN AND MASSLIVE.COM

Since 1824

The Republican has been telling the stories of the people who live and work in Western Massachusetts since the newspaper was founded by Samuel Bowles in 1824. The rich history of this region can be found on the pages of the paper, printed day after day.

There is perhaps no recorded history of the region as detailed as that told by the journalists whose stories and photos have appeared in the pages of The Republican and MassLive.com.

From the earliest days of the colonial settlement of Springfield, the community set about creating rules and regulations on how individuals should conduct themselves and their businesses in a "well-ordered" society. The community also required someone to oversee the corrections system, the county's sheriff. Since the 17th Century, the county sheriff has played a vital role in maintaining the peace, and safety of our community.

We are particularly proud of Hampden County's record of corrections reform, its humane treatment of those incarcerated, its positive work in our community, and its remarkable record of reducing recidivism. We commend the good work of retired Sheriff Michael J. Ashe, and today's Sheriff, Nick Cocchi for their leadership, innovation, and the blueprint they have provided to the nation for successful corrections management and reform

For almost 200 years, The Republican has been telling the stories and recording the history of one of the oldest and most important regions in America. This book would not have been possible without the vital information gleaned from the pages of one of this nation's oldest newspapers.

The Republican. | **MASS LIVE**

1860 Main Street, Springfield, MA 01103

INDEX

Y

Z